SPECTACULAR
SUFFERING

UNNATURAL ACTS

Theorizing the Performative

SUE-ELLEN CASE

PHILIP BRETT

SUSAN LEIGH FOSTER

The partitioning of performance into obligatory appearances and strict disallowances is a complex social code assumed to be "natural" until recent notions of performativity unmasked its operations. Performance partitions, strictly enforced within traditional conceptions of the arts, foreground the gestures of the dancer, but ignore those of the orchestra player, assign significance to the elocution of the actor, but not to the utterances of the audience. The critical notion of performativity both reveals these partitions as unnatural and opens the way for the consideration of all cultural intercourse as performance. It also exposes the compulsory nature of some orders of performance. The oppressive requirements of systems that organize gender and sexual practices mark who may wear the dress and who may perform the kiss. Further, the fashion of the dress and the colorizing of the skin that dons it are disciplined by systems of class and "race." These cultural performances are critical sites for study.

The series Unnatural Acts encourages further interrogations of all varieties of performance both in the traditional sense of the term and from the broader perspective provided by performativity.

SPECTACULAR SUFFERING

THEATRE,

FASCISM, AND

THE HOLOCAUST

VIVIAN M. PATRAKA

INDIANA UNIVERSITY PRESS

BLOOMINGTON • INDIANAPOLIS

This book is a publication of

Indiana University Press
601 North Morton Street
Bloomington, IN 47404-3797 USA

www.indiana.edu/~iupress

Telephone orders 800-842-6796
Fax orders 812-855-7931
Orders by e-mail iuporder@indiana.edu

The paper used in this publication meets the minimum requirements of
American National Standard for Information Sciences—Permanence of
Paper for Printed Library Materials, ANSI Z39.48-1984.

Manufactured in the United States of America

Library of Congress Cataloging-in-Publication Data

Patraka, Vivian.
    Spectacular suffering : theatre, fascism, and the Holocaust /
Vivian M. Patraka.
      p. cm. — (Unnatural acts)
    Includes bibliographical references and index.
    ISBN 0-253-33532-9 (cl : alk. paper). — ISBN 0-253-21292-8 (pa :
alk. paper)
    1. Holocaust, Jewish (1939–1945), in literature. 2. Holocaust,
Jewish (1939–1945)—Influence. 3. Holocaust, Jewish (1939–
1945)—Drama. I. Title. II. Series.
PN56.H55P37 1999
809'.93358—dc21   98-43476

1 2 3 4 5 04 03 02 01 00 99

*For those who are gone
and those who remember them.*

CONTENTS

ACKNOWLEDGMENTS

Over the course of preparing this manuscript, I benefitted from two summer residencies sponsored by the Kentucky Foundation for Women in 1989 and 1990. My earliest ideas were shaped by my NEH summer seminar on "Fascism as a Generic Phenomenon" at Yale University in 1985. Another NEH summer seminar—"Performance Theory, Modern Drama and Postmodern Theatre" in 1991 at the University of Wisconsin, Milwaukee—helped shape the larger contours of the book.

I thank my own institution, Bowling Green State University, for providing me with critical resources. I thank the Graduate College for three summer grants—a "major grant" in 1990 for "Staging the Body in Pain," a Summer Research Associateship for "Representations of Fascism in Drama" in 1988, and another in 1987 for "New Questions on Contemporary Drama, Fascism, and the Holocaust." I am most particularly grateful to the Graduate College and Dean Louis Katzner for providing me with Graduate Student Research Assistantships during the course of the book's composition. I thank my research assistants Mary Callahan Boone, Annette Wannamaker, Heath Diehl, Linda Rouse, and Kirk Richardson for their invaluable assistance. Each of them brought special skills to the task along with heroic endurance. I thank the English Department for its support in the form of course releases, and its former chair, Rick Gebhardt, for his support of my work. Thanks also go to my series editors, Philip Brett, Susan Foster, and particularly Sue-Ellen Case, for their helpful advice and comments.

Inasmuch as a book such as this one is always a dialogue among various scholars, I am very grateful for my conversations with Margaret Lourie, Jill Dolan, Heath Diehl, Herbert Blau, and Jonathan Boyarin. I particularly want to thank Elin Diamond, who has accompanied me on my journey from the very beginning and whose responses to the book have been generous and enlightening. Local colleagues Ellen Berry, Vida Penezic, and David Anderson have been important parts of this conversation as well.

There are people who helped sustain me during this project: special thanks go to my friend Mary Edwards for her enduring support and unflagging encouragement, to my parents Mollie and George Patraka who believed in the book, to Kathy Ruffer who listened, and to Cindy and Michael Peslikis who took care of Fang when even a small, affectionate terrier was too much.

Portions of this book appeared first in academic journals and anthologies. I thank the journal editors and publishers for permission to use this material in revised form: "Situating Genocide and Difference: The Cultural Performance of the Term Holocaust in U.S. Public Discourse," *Jews and*

Other Differences: The New Jewish Cultural Studies, ed. Jonathan Boyarin and Daniel Boyarin (U of Minnesota P, 1997) 54–78; "Spectacles of Suffering: Performing Presence, Absence, and Historical Memory at U.S. Holocaust Museums," *Performance and Cultural Politics*, ed. Elin Diamond (Routledge, 1996) 89–107; "Fascist Ideology and Theatricalization," *Critical Theory and Performance*, ed. Janelle Reinelt and Joseph Roach (U of Michigan P, 1992) 336–49; "Feminism and the Jewish Subject in the Plays of Sachs, Atlan, and Schenkar," *Performing Feminisms: Feminist Critical Theory and Theatre*, ed. Sue-Ellen Case (Johns Hopkins UP, 1990) 160–74; "Lillian Hellman's *Watch on the Rhine*: Realism, Gender and Historical Crisis," *Modern Drama* 32.1 (1989): 128–45; "Contemporary Drama, Fascism, and the Holocaust," *Theatre Journal* 39.1 (1987): 65–77.

SPECTACULAR
SUFFERING

INTRODUCTION

Theorizing a Holocaust Performative

No term is fixed forever in its meaning, unless it has become invisible through disuse. Rather it constitutes a set of practices and cultural negotiations in the present. Thus the narrative of making meaning out of the term "Holocaust" continues. The public performance of the term among Jews is multiple, varying in different cultural sites for differing political agendas and pedagogical purposes. The search for the best term to designate the Jewish genocide outlines an attempt to mark both its historical specificity and its uniqueness. This uniqueness has been linked to the extent of the perpetrator's intentionality, the degree to which the state apparatus legalized the devastation, the measure of its use of "technological weapons of destruction" (Stannard 151), and the number of people killed. But every genocide, in the particularities of its specific history, is unique. And while each genocide is known by this distinct history, it is also understood in the context of other genocides, even though these relationships are not ones of simple analogy or equivalence.

While both the terms "Holocaust" and "genocide" were originally conceived (or reinvented) to respond to the actions in Europe against the Jews during the 1930s and 1940s, genocide quickly took on the status of a generic, both describing the persecutions of other groups during this period and providing a means for defining actions against groups that would constitute genocidal destruction. Moreover, however proprietary the claims on the use of this term have been in some quarters, the evocative power of the term Holocaust has begun to extend its use tropologically to contemporary considerations of the destruction of groups other than Jews. Perhaps this is because "genocide" functions as a delimiting generic, while "Holocaust" brings with it all the protocols of the unspeakable, the incommensurate, and a sense of unlimited scope to pain and injustice. Or perhaps "Holocaust" connotes not just the violent moment of near elimination of a whole people, but also all that goes into it: the beginning of terror and of circulating discourses of oppression and exclusion, the construction of a state apparatus of oppression and the disinformation it produces, the incarcerations, the annihilation, and then the revolting denials and cleanups. The entire array of cultural, social, and political forces amassed to effect genocide are historically embedded in the term Holocaust.

The terms used to signify the attempted extermination of European Jewry constitute a varied history. Yehuda Bauer defines the Holocaust as the English name "customarily used . . . for the planned total annihilation of the Jewish people, and the actual murder of six million of them at the hands of the Nazis and their auxiliaries" ("Place" 16). The word Holocaust derives from "the Greek word for whole-burnt" and is meant, presumably, to sug-

gest the extent and the "manner of the death of the Jews of Europe" (Ezrahi
2). Yet, as Sidra DeKoven Ezrahi points out, the notion of "burnt offering"
to which the term is connected "raises problems through the sacrificial con-
notation that it attaches to the death of the Jews of Europe which is consistent with a prevailing Christian reading of Jewish history" (2). By contrast,
she suggests that neither "*hurbn*"—the Yiddish word for the Nazi genocide
connoting the violation of the continuity of life within the community—
nor "*shoah*"—the Hebrew word connoting "widespread, even cosmic disas-
ter," waste, and desolation—associates the victims with ritual sacrifice (221).
But, while English-speaking scholars critique the term Holocaust with its
connotations of sacrifice for a purpose, of placating God with the mysteries
of our suffering, they have generally agreed to use the term to refer to the
Jewish genocide because of its function as a stable, recognizable historical
referent.

During my own Brooklyn childhood in the 1950s, "the war" often designated the Jewish genocide, and "refugees" commonly signified those whom
we now call Holocaust survivors. Jim Young notes that "because there was
no 'ready-made' name in English [like *hurbn* or *shoah*] . . . writers and historians [in the 1950s] who perceived these events separately from their World
War II context, were moved to adopt a name by which events could be known
in their particularity" (*Writing* 86–87). Only in the 1960s, as G. F. Goekjian
notes, did the term "'Holocaust' gradually displace 'genocide' as the proper
name of the Nazi destruction of the Jews" (213–14). He uses the term "proper
name" to suggest a proprietariness against which he will argue for applying
the term genocide (and not massacre) to the history of the Armenians at the
beginning of the twentieth century. But in doing so, he also clarifies how the
term genocide itself "was coined by Raphael Lemkin [in 1943 to serve as] a
signifier for what was described as the 'unspeakable' fate of the Jews" (213).

Bauer points out that Lemkin originally had two notions of genocide: 1)
"the total 'extermination' of a people," and 2) the "extreme deprivation, destruction of educational institutions, interference in religious life, general
denationalization and even moral poisoning" of a group ("Place" 20). The
first notion emphasized the end product of annihilation, i.e., destruction of
the group, while the second emphasized the process, i.e., persecution, that
often leads to this end and can occur over a short or long time period. By the
time of Lemkin's 1944 book *Axis Rule in Occupied Europe*, these two aspects
of genocide had come together so that Frank Chalk and Kurt Jonassohn
could summarize Lemkin's definition of genocide as "the coordinated and
planned annihilation of a national, religious or racial group by a variety of
actions aimed at undermining the foundations essential to the survival of the
group as a group" (qtd. in Stannard 279). This formulation, by the way, is
currently being contested for its omission of the political, social, and sexual
from what constitutes an imperiled group.

The reiteration of the term group might suggest an essential or reified identity that erases difference within a particular community and thereby connotes a problematic aspect to such large, if necessary, formulations of genocide. It also could occlude the history of everyday interactions and similarities between perpetrators and victims that are mutated or rendered invisible by the perpetrators. Still, these notions of "group" point to the way that, as part of the process of genocide, the perpetrators construct a malignant collective identity for the victims. This identity dehumanizes through its erasure of the multiple and divergent ways members of a particular community define themselves as well as through its distortion of the ways in which members define the bonds among them. Perpetrators enact a totalization of a group identity upon the victims, a total rejection of alterity.

If the narrative practices surrounding the history of the term Holocaust are evolving, so too are their historical referents. Though the domain of the Holocaust is mass death, the narrative(s) created about it need not make it an immobile, tomblike place, nor create an inert body of knowledge intended only to conserve and preserve. Even producers of public discourse on the Holocaust can actively engage in redefining this space so that, as I show in the last chapter, the seemingly standard definition of the Holocaust as relating solely to Jews comes under interrogation at sites as formal as Holocaust museums. And while I do not mean to be facile about the terrible stakes involved in memorializing these events, a narrative space for producing knowledge of the Holocaust—one that would construct its consumers as actively engaged in producing meanings—might be a powerful means to prolonging remembrance.

Even if some contemporary groups do deliberately use the term Holocaust in a way designed to compete with or even erase the referent of Jewish history and suffering, if we assert an exclusive, proprietary claim over the term in response, we run the risk of magnifying one current perception: that the discourse of the Jewish Holocaust functions as a kind of controlling or hegemonic discourse of suffering that operates at the expense of the sufferings of other groups. Moreover, even when the term Holocaust is applied to other genocides, it need not become the kind of "proper name" that must erase the original referent to Jewish history. A good academic model for how this would work can be found in David Stannard's *American Holocaust: Columbus and the Conquest of the New World*. Stannard contends that the perpetrators of the American Holocaust against indigenous peoples drew on the same ideological wellspring as the later architects of the Jewish Holocaust, namely developments in Christian history and ideology.[1] Instead of borrowing the term Holocaust as a gesture against history, Stannard manages a deeper historical rendering that validates the specificity of the Jewish Holocaust by enunciating it through the genocide of other groups. He creates a space in which he sees the Jewish Holocaust as an effect of certain ideological happenings, but also as a cause since he writes in its wake. Stannard's model suggests that if Jews crave the historical specificity of the Holocaust, then to follow one path of that logic is to create relationships. Connecting the Holocaust with other struggles and other points of oppression may make it less possible to view it as an isolated and therefore nonrepeatable event.

Still, I think so much of the history of the Jewish genocide, the meanings attached to it, even the ethical, cultural, and linguistic protocols of where to look for meaning about such events, is so deeply embedded in the word Holocaust as to make the Jewish genocide a paradigmatic frame for other genocides located through use of the term. Pursuing the larger outlines of scholarly work on the Holocaust as one extant model for writing about genocide may yield the most promise for the projects of other groups.

Certainly fifty years of repeated attempts to memorialize, to witness, to inform, and to "understand" the events of the Holocaust account for part of this embeddedness of the Jewish genocide as a paradigmatic frame for "Holocaust." Nonetheless, to say that we can "know" or "understand" anything about the events of this Holocaust is problematic, since the material history underlying the term is so grounded in a sense of goneness. This is not to minimize the importance of survivors of the Holocaust: we want to honor and cherish their testimony and their palpable presence, but we should not make them stand in for the dead. Although I use the term "absence" elsewhere in the book, I use the neologism "goneness" here because it more completely reflects the definitiveness, the starkness, and the magnitude of this particular genocide by dictating the scope of what and who has been violently lost, including succeeding generations that cannot be. Murder and cruelty on a mass scale are what distinguish this goneness from the historian's problem of documentation and recovery. Goneness is inconceivable but its effects are palpable, particularly the inevitable desire to articulate, negotiate, mark, and define.

Representation, too, inevitably is about goneness, is itself a mark of goneness, and, in the case of the Holocaust, is the way in which we continually mark a spectacular and invisible absence in order to remember who once was and what once happened. Those who would represent the Holocaust necessarily make manifest the struggle with a content predicated on its own goneness. Representing the Holocaust, then, is inevitably an ongoing struggle, an ongoing performance. That this is so need not dispel our horror or prevent our judgment of the actual historical events in which these representations are grounded.

The struggle to represent the Holocaust in its goneness clarifies the limitations of representation in general. Representation (viewed as a process) assumes that there is a fixed set of norms or a closed narrative that can be translated, made "real," through its own reiteration. Representation, however, is also an object, one that is always a reconstruction, a pre-framed, pre-narrativized set of practices that attempts to make visible certain events, practices, and/or beliefs assumed to be fixed, essential, and pre-existing. This is not to suggest that all representations constitute a closed system for producing knowledge wherein the representation and its own reiterative nature are somehow elided. In fact, in this book I have consciously chosen texts that point up the struggle between (the object of) representation and (the process of) reiteration, such as Joan Schenkar's *The Last of Hitler*, Peter Barnes's *Laughter!*, Deb Margolin's "O Wholly Night," and Leeny Sack's *The Survivor and the Translator*. I suggest that the relationship between representation and reiteration must be posited as a risky struggle (between object and process, between history and memory) that has certain consequences.

If representations of the Holocaust in performance allow us to mark the goneness of the actual historical events, they also provide an opportunity to celebrate and mark the goneness of what we want never to exist again—Nazism and the Holocaust—even as we want to create relationships to other events and cultural conditions in the past and to a present in which genocide has not disappeared. This, too, is inevitably an ongoing performance. Chapter 2 ("Reproduction, Appropriation, and Binary Machinery: Fascist Ideology and Theatricalization") offers a way to use theories about fascist ideology and their theatrical representations as a means of recognizing certain larger structures that portend this particular imposition of power.

That the goneness of the Holocaust can never be a fixed set of norms, or a closed narrative that can be wholly represented in the present moment, inherently foregrounds the constructedness of representations of these events. Or, as Leeny Sack articulates her own effort to reiterate the experience of the Holocaust in performance, "I sit inside the memory of where I was not" (124). Representations of the Holocaust inevitably stage this sitting inside a place to which we cannot return. Our representations are fueled by the desire to pursue what we can neither see nor find, and so we compulsively return to the Holocaust with a need to repeat, to recover, to say, and to iterate that which is gone. To argue that theatrical representations of the events of the Holocaust reiterate the actual historical events, then, is not to argue that these representations re-embody or reenact the Holocaust.

Reiterations, by definition, are ritualized repetitions (Butler, *Bodies* x), rearticulations, reformulations (Butler, *Bodies* 15) "not contrasted with the real, but *constitut[ing]* a reality that is in some sense new" (Butler, "Performative" 278). This is precisely why the term reiteration produces its own instability, its own constructedness, its own partiality as a repeated act. This "new" in relation to representing the Holocaust, however much it constitutes a process of remembering, is always a danger and a threat, a sorrow in time and a locale for misrecognition. A reiteration of the Holocaust in performance reveals itself as a re-construction, fractured from the "real" by the reiteration's historical fixity in its present moment. Theatre reiterates the Holocaust, then, by announcing itself as performative.

In *Bodies That Matter*, Judith Butler conceives of the performative as "that power of discourse to produce effects through reiteration" (20). For Butler, the performative negotiates the terrain between discourse and its material effects. Because it is reiterative *and* performative it constitutes a reality that is in some sense new. There is little place for material history and its determinations in Butler's account. In relation to the Holocaust, however, a historical real—and its goneness—presses on discursive effects. For this reason, I must reconceive a performative for the Holocaust to account not only for the goneness, but also for the historical real undergirding it.

One of the central issues discussed in the varied uses of the performative circulating in contemporary critical theory is its link to the live, embodied, disappearing moment of performance. In her introduction to *Performance and Cultural Politics*, Elin Diamond clarifies her sense of the intersection of performance and performativity: "Performance, as I have tried to suggest, is precisely the site in which concealed or dissimulated conventions might be investigated. When performativity materializes as performance in that risky and dangerous negotiation between a doing (a reiteration of norms) and a thing done (discursive conventions that frame our interpretations), between someone's body and the conventions of embodiment, we have access to cultural meanings and critique" (Diamond 5).

If, as Diamond suggests, the intersection of performance and performativity reveals itself a point of entry into the production of cultural meanings, some of the larger questions of this book situate themselves at this intersection: What might a Holocaust performative look like? What is the doing and the thing done in risky and dangerous negotiation? What kinds of questions might the theoretical working through of this negotiation allow us to ask in order to illuminate the events of this particular genocide that are unrepresentable and outside the parameters of representation itself?

According to this model of the performative, the "thing done" is a kind of yardstick, a system of beliefs and presuppositions that has taken on an authority and become a hegemonic means of understanding. The "thing done," then, represents particular discursive categories, conventions, genres and practices that frame our interpretations, even as we try to perceive the present moment of doing.[2] As we are in the doing, then, there is the pressure of the thing done. The doing is not knowable without the thing done, and the thing done is all the discursive conventions that allow us to think through a doing.

Diamond's formulation (of the doing and the thing done) allows me to specify the special characteristics of the Holocaust performative. In relation to that particular genocide, I identify the thing done as *the thing gone* (and not just categories and conventions). It is the goneness of the Holocaust that produces the simultaneous profusion of discourses and understandings; the goneness is what opens up, what spurs, what unleashes the perpetual desire to do, to make, to rethink the Holocaust. I suggest that the history of the Holocaust and its goneness shifts the balance between the performative "doing" and "thing done": that is, the absoluteness of the thing done weighs heavily on any doing in the Holocaust performative. The Holocaust performative acknowledges that there is nothing to say to goneness and yet we continue to try and mark it, say it, identify it, memorialize the loss over and over. This is the doing to which Diamond refers, the constant iteration against the pressure of a palpable loss and not merely a set of discursive conventions. With proliferation comes, inevitably it seems, denial, resistance, appropriation, trivialization, and misrecognition. In this book, I am studying this terrifying, powerful absence and the profusion of discourses it produces.

When either the "doing" or the "thing done" in a performative changes, then the relationship between them alters as well. Because the Holocaust performative intensifies the pressure of the thing done on the doing, the performative relationship (between the goneness of the actual historical events of the Holocaust and its proliferation of meanings in discursive and representational paradigms) cannot be a "traditionally" postmodern one of play per se or of destabilization. Moreover, "subversion" and "transgression" (which the term "performative" frequently connotes) of discursive conventions are complicated and problematized by the Holocaust. As a result, in the Holocaust performative, play is limited by accountability: in this sense, one's interpretation makes one accountable to goneness.

The Holocaust performative, then, not only marks the gap between the goneness of events and our desire to represent; it also demands an added dimension of accountability. By this I mean that the Holocaust disallows the kinds of questions, methodologies, reading strategies, theoretical paradigms, and observations that we typically might deploy in relation to representation, forcing us to ask new questions and re-ask old ones. What are our own stakes (including not only scholars and playwrights, but also readers and spectators) in thinking and writing about these events? A Holocaust performative predicated on accountability leaves room for the kinds of ethical questions raised by the introduction of atrocity into representation. Uses of atrocity suggest that injustice cannot simply be moralized against (as in instances of "horrality," which I discuss in chapter 5), or made "right" (read avenged) within the parameters of representation in order to placate our own pleasure in looking. Such representations potentially disallow the kind of accountability which we must feel towards those whose absence can only ever be marked.

By accountability I don't mean normative gate-keeping about what can and cannot be included in discussions of the Holocaust, what is and is not allowed to be shown, by whom and to whom. I mean rather an acknowledgment that representation, artistic and critical, is always a site of struggle between history and its representations, between desire and loss, and between the unmanageable and the manageable. Accountability is not the same as reverentiality: accountability leaves room for critical inquiry, for debate, and risks being more invitational to other scholars. I do mean to allow space for questions of sex and gender (which have, in the past, too often been ignored by Holocaust scholars). But in our interpretive doings—that of the critic, the performer, the spectator/reader—the Holocaust is a rigorous taskmaster. It puts the whole enterprise of writing about these events in question. We necessarily ask ourselves: Why do this at all? Why this theory? Does it enable us to frame new questions that will be fruitful to our enterprise or are they merely fashionable?

My own sense of accountability to the events of the Holocaust and those who suffered in it challenges my critical assumptions and theories. This emphasis on accountability reflects my struggle between the conserving position of reverentiality and the more postmodernist position of theoretical play; accountability is a double-sided commitment that allows me critically to examine both positions. In the Holocaust performative, then, these two positions (of reverentiality and play) comment upon each other: it is postmodernism that sees the deadness of that reverential gesture toward the Holocaust, but it is the Holocaust (and its goneness) that marks the point at which discursive play becomes a screen to keep the dead at a distance.

For me, one of the single most persuasive visual expressions of accountability for the writer occurs in Art Spiegelman's *Maus*. Early in volume 2 (*Maus: And Here My Troubles Began*), Spiegelman portrays himself sitting at his drafting table,[3] trying to work on volume 2 of his comic book *Maus*, which focuses on his father's imprisonment in Auschwitz. Surrounding him, on the floor, is a sea of naked corpses. He recites statistics about the death of particular groups of European Jews and tells us about the suicide of his mother, who was a survivor of the Holocaust. But he also satirically includes "visits" (actual or remembered by him) from entrepreneurs who want to capitalize on the success of the first volume of *Maus*. Surrounding himself and his drafting table with bodies clearly does not serve to instantiate authority or lend prestige to Spiegelman's enterprise of writing about the Holocaust; rather, the pile of bodies marks the responsibility of all the writers who write for the present, in the present, for the living, but who also must write to and for the dead. They loom around us as specters, questioning any profit or success we may attain in the process of writing about them. They demand accountability and in being accountable, we keep the specters not alive but "real."

The questions that I pose in this book are inflected by the problematic of accountability. I seek to interrogate some of the deepest assumptions that ground my own work. Hence I challenge my own critical commitments to feminism in chapter 3, "Feminism and the Jewish Subject: Holocaust Theatre and the Politics of Difference and Identity." Here I explore the intersection of feminism and "Jewishness," suggesting that this relationship is problematized by the magnitude of goneness. As this chapter goes on to point out, however, this problematic does not cancel out the richness to be gained when our Holocaust methods of approach are considered in relation to a revised model of the strategies offered by gender and sexuality (as well as race and class). Instead I assume that intersecting the goneness of the Holocaust with modes of analysis based in identity categories can reframe how both sets of strategies and political commitments are deployed. The question I pose in this chapter, then, is not "how might we read the Holocaust as gendered?" but rather "how does gender matter in relation to the Holocaust and its history of goneness?"

The question of how gender "matters" in a situation of genocide is haunted by the alternative question of why it should "matter" in such instances. How can I hold my own desire to ask certain kinds of questions about the role of gender accountable not only for the knowledges that it produces but for the knowledges that it occludes? For instance, my critique in chapter 4, "Lillian Hellman's *Watch on the Rhine* and 'Julia': Realism, Gender, and Historical Crisis," of how gender is more traditionally reconfigured in Lillian Hellman's contemporary response to the crisis of Nazi victories throughout Europe is haunted by the context of what was then happening to many Europeans and most particularly to European Jews. Against my own gender critique of this play, I still imagine, correctly or not, Hellman's horror of living in that particular moment of history, when what was happening to European Jews could not serve as a persuasive strand of the argument to involve the United States in war. Would not a form such as realism, because of its very ability to cover over its own ideological positions with a seeming transparency, be precisely the form in which to embed one unspoken crisis within another, more ideologically acceptable one?

This last question suggests a larger challenge in the book to certain of my critical investments in the efficacy of performance over theatre, and of experimental Brechtian forms over realism. This obliges me to consider work across the spectrum of genres and conventions in theatre and performance that inhibits spectators from passive consuming and fascination. In Peter Barnes' Brechtian work *Laughter!*, for instance, I explore the efficacy of leaving the victims offstage and putting onstage white-collar workers who, despite their willed refusal to acknowledge it, are the middle managers for the death camps. In relation to Charlotte Delbo's presentational choral piece, *Who Will Carry the Word*, I examine how the choral refrain on the impossibility of our understanding the concentration camp narrative effectively comments upon the absence of the historical real itself. Leeny Sack's performance piece, *The Survivor and the Translator*, uses the metaphor of translation to underscore the difficulty of representing the experience of the Holocaust, even, as is the case here, for the close relative who translates, as well as the difficulty for the survivor herself of translating her experience into words. In so doing, Sack foregrounds the layers of translation that intervene between both the performer and us in relation to goneness. Finally, Donald Margulies' realist play *The Model Apartment* raises the question of how realism itself can be reconfigured to disrupt the very narrative of expectations that come from the form, in this case by making us persistently uncomfortable about how we conceive of survivors. Margulies thereby offers additional insight into the damaging consequences of goneness.

In speculating on which forms and even which plays work "best" at representing Holocaust history, in marking the playwright's struggle to represent *both* material events and goneness, I am invoking the Holocaust performative. Again, the question is, how do theatre and performance texts work to situate an event like the Holocaust in history when the event itself has no analogue? In chapter 1, "Shattered Cartographies: Fascism, the Holocaust, and Tropes about Representation," I identify certain kinds of tropes (i.e., figurative modes of analogizing) that I see at work in a number of Holocaust plays (e.g., translating the word, eating the word). As I read the plays through tropes, they take on a self-reflexive quality, calling attention to those textual features that enact the struggle with representation. I suggest that reading through tropes can, at least, frame our understanding of how plays and performances engage with the problem that this history is always unmanageable and the representation only ever partial.

Chapter 1 also constructs tropes to signify the historical practice of fascism and the way language in plays and performances is used to construct and resist it. Chapter 2, "Reproduction, Appropriation, and Binary Machinery: Fascist Ideology and Theatricalization," furthers this exploration by taking up the question of how we account for the specificity of fascism in relation to the Holocaust without precluding a recognition of contemporary manifestations of fascist practices. To understand the fascist practice of Nazism more fully also means examining the relation between sexual orientation and Holocaust history. Martin Sherman's *Bent*, then, clarifies hidden aspects of fascist practice in its struggle to extend the rubric of Holocaust victims to gay men.

Because performance is so heavily grounded in the presence of live bodies, it is a particularly useful site for investigating our accountability to the unmanageable injury and injustice done to bodies in the Holocaust. In chapter 5, "Theatre of Injury and Injustice: Staging the Body in Pain," the question of which strategies work best to show the performed body in pain is haunted by the question of whether we should show representations of that body at all. What is so gripping about physical suffering and bodily pain under circumstances of injustice that would make it worth this constant unearthing? What could we know through the body in pain that would make it worth staging?

Asking these kinds of larger questions about representing Holocaust history led me to look at forms other than theatre and performance texts to see how they posed and responded to such questions. Most particularly, I felt the need to explore what was at stake in a massive pedagogical practice that intervenes in public discourse about the Holocaust, namely the two recent U.S. Holocaust museums (which I discuss in chapter 6, "Spectacular Suffering: Performing Presence, Absence, and Witness at U.S. Holocaust Museums"). The ambition and scope of these projects dictates that I cannot merely be dismissive (reducing these efforts to "shoah business" or a "theme park" approach), even when the strategies of the designers are highly problematic. I am obliged to recognize the risks these museum designers have taken, and to develop a model to distinguish "pre-scripted" sites for interpretative performance from sites that allow for multiple interpretation. What is at stake here is the potential of these museums to offer thousands of people the opportunity to change from spectator/bystander to witness and to become performers in the event of understanding and remembering the Holocaust.

However, the problematic of accountability also spurs me to examine the relationship between a Holocaust museum and the country in which it is located and its history of oppressive suffering. For the United States, I locate the museums in relation to a local history of racial suffering and genocide, most particularly to the history of slavery. I suggest how the museums do or do not address this history and use the commitment by the United States to Holocaust museums as a way of addressing why, at least on the national level, other museums devoted to local occurrences of genocide currently still do not exist.[4] Finally, for the book as a whole, accountability directs me not to dismiss one mode of conveying meaning—the traditional/narrative/monolithic/complete/canonical—for another to which I am predisposed—the postmodern/metanarrative/multiple/incomplete/experimental. Instead, I've wanted to keep the two modes in a productive tension, clarifying how each shapes the engagement of readers and spectators and speculating on which mode works best in particular contexts or historical moments.

A particular burden that Holocaust scholars and educators face in the late 1990s is determining precisely what constitutes knowledge of the Holocaust and what constitutes its transmission. Since pedagogy is itself an area of accountability, it is not surprising that some of these debates take place in the public school system. On March 5, 1992, the *Bowling Green Sentinel Tribune* contained an article about a controversy that erupted when officials "at Westlake Elementary in Thousand Oaks [California] awarded a second-place prize in the annual oratory contest" to a fifth-grade boy who "put on a swastika and mustache and delivered a speech portraying Hitler as a victim of mistreatment by Jews." As part of the response to this masquerade, the school brought in Renee Firestone, a survivor of the Auschwitz death camp, who told children of her experience as a child at Auschwitz to counteract the effects of the earlier performance.

Firestone's talk resulted in the protest of a parent who, on condition of anonymity, complained to reporters that "school officials were giving too much time to the Jewish perspective." He buttressed this by the seemingly humane argument that "he feared Mrs. Firestone would not talk about Nazi atrocities against non-Jews" (by which he meant against the majority of Germans, and not against homosexuals, gypsies, leftists, and other Holocaust victims) and that "it's too one-sided." He went on to claim that "the parents should be discussing this but the kids should go and play" (thereby implying the earlier performance of Hitler by a child was still in the realm of "play"). He added, "We're being Holocausted." By turning a noun denoting extermination into a verb denoting an imposition, he implied that references to the Holocaust by Jews perform a one-sided, "Jewish" perspective for a presumably Christian, presumably unwillingly manipulated audience.

In these performances of the Holocaust—that of the fifth-grade boy, of Mrs. Firestone, and of the parent's public pronouncement—the question of accountability is deeply embedded. By bringing in a Holocaust survivor, the school system acknowledged its institutional accountability to the history of the Holocaust. True, the presence of Mrs. Firestone kept the boy's narrative from existing only in the realm of "child's play." But Mrs. Firestone's presence is haunted by the question: What happens when there are no living survivors, no "real" performers of this history left, and we must replace the living body of the survivor with videos of survivor testimony to counter future generations of young Hitlers? How can Mrs. Firestone be a match for those who increasingly feel "Holocausted" when she disappears and they do not? However harsh this question, it still means that those of us who are committed to preserving an accountable narrative of the Holocaust must continue to (re)shape, (re)define, and (re)articulate this narrative in relation to the stark landscape of goneness.

The questions I pose in *Spectacular Suffering* have been reframed over time to keep them in dialogue with larger cultural shifts. First, the increasing scholarly interest in representations of pain and the body, genocide, atrocity, torture, and suffering, and in the ways in which contemporary events of this nature have captured the awareness of growing sections of the population, however intensely mediatized these representations have been. Second, the shifts within Holocaust studies that redefine and expand who constitutes its victims (and perpetrators) as well as the rising tide of denial of these very historical events. Third, the development of a burgeoning field of

Jewish cultural studies that refracts gender, race, sexuality, and class through the prism of Jewish ethnicity while inviting the analyses that these categories, under the umbrella of culture studies, bring to matters "Jewish" in both high and popular culture (Boyarin, *Jews and Other*). Finally, as mentioned above, the consolidation of the Holocaust as a crucial signifier of not only Jewish but human suffering and atrocity as well as resistance by various groups seeking to foreground other histories of suffering and genocide. This resistance emphasizes the inadequacy of positing a monolithic spectatorship for works about this history; there are not only obvious differences from country to country but within generations and cultural identities, especially those that are racially inflected.

The ordering of the chapters in *Spectacular Suffering* approximately reflects the chronology of their initial composition, although all have evolved over time. The book thus builds on the two opening chapters, with their focus on the exact topic of dramatic representations of fascism and the Holocaust, to enlarge the discussion by considering further issues (such as gender in the next two chapters), by including other genres as a context (such as mass culture forms in the chapter on pain), and by opening out earlier questions to new arenas (the educational museum and public discourse in the final chapter) and broader projects in performance studies. Each chapter is also framed by different theories and questions so that each can be read independently. Chapter 1 deploys Hayden White's theory of tropes in relation to history and brings in Roger Griffin and Slavoj Zizek's ideas on fascism; chapter 2 uses theories about fascist ideology by Saul Friedlander, Eve Kosofsky Sedgwick, and Alice Yaeger Kaplan; chapter 3 opens with a discussion of Donna Haraway and Katie King to contextualize its questions about gender, and responds to debates in Jewish feminism articulated by Jenny Bourne and Alisa Solomon; chapter 4 uses Bertolt Brecht's critique of realism and his theories of historicization, refracting them through Elin Diamond's re-theorizings of Brecht into a gestic feminist criticism; chapter 5 opens with theories by Jean Francois Lyotard and Elaine Scarry and frames subsequent discussions with ideas articulated by Klaus Theweleit and Julia Kristeva; finally, chapter 6 grounds its analysis in Michel de Certeau's distinction between "place" and "space."

Reading, like writing, is a performance. To read this book is to bear performative witness to the events of the Holocaust. I am grateful to be able to share the burden of witness with the reader. Since there can be no catharsis in the reading of a book responding to the Holocaust, no "golden nugget" of knowledge to take away, but only a continual process of critical engagement (between scholars and readers, between playwrights and performers, between performers and spectators, between museum architects and museum-goers), the book must offer an exit, just as the United States Holocaust Memorial Museum affords the possibility of exit on every floor of

its exhibits. The closing chapter, on U.S. Holocaust museums, offers an opportunity for closure to the process of reading, even if there cannot be closure to the narrative of, to use the title of one of Jim Young's books, *Writing
and Re-writing the Holocaust*. My desire is not to entrap you in the book and
its painful content but rather to enable you to witness it and engage with it
and its struggle with the history of the Holocaust. There is no end to the
questions. There is no end to the need for engagement. And when we feel
the need to depart, we leave through the door marked "exit," always aware
that the narrative continues to be written after our departure.

1

SHATTERED CARTOGRAPHIES

Fascism, the Holocaust, and Tropes about Representation

> These are things that are never spoken
> Because no one can understand it
> And no one can help.
> About this
> Don't think.
> Don't speak.
> Nothing can help.
> —Leeny Sack, *The Survivor and the Translator* (151)

In *Tropics of Discourse*, Hayden White distinguishes between two groups of historians: "Those who think that language can serve as a perfectly transparent medium of representation, who think that if one can only find the right language for describing events, the meaning of the events will *display itself* to consciousness," and those historians, by contrast, whose work displays the "ironic recognition that any given linguistic protocol will obscure as much as it reveals about the reality it seeks to capture in an order of words" (130). It is, I think, still possible to analyze experience, material experience, without ignoring the complicated relation between experience and language—even if the ways we connect one thing to another or use one thing to represent another create meaning in themselves and are thus ideological, even if our identification of the field of inquiry *before* we interpret it constitutes an act of interpretation in itself. To complicate matters further, if on one level language cannot represent any experience directly, some experiences, such as fascism and the Holocaust, are even less available for representation, are especially resistant to logical, linear description.

The Holocaust exceeds the parameters of our frames of reference. The horrific events represented by the term Holocaust are so inconceivable that, to refer back to the epigraph to this chapter, they can never be spoken, understood, or ameliorated. In regard to representing the Holocaust, then, tropes are a way of mapping what cannot be mapped. By trope I mean the figurative mode of analogizing, i.e., the displacing and distorting in language of an experience by means of comparison or assimilation to other experience. Hayden White asserts that tropes function to structure not only poetic language but language in general. What he calls "the deterministic power of figurative language use" (150) is in part how it "tells us what . . . to look for in our culturally encoded experience in order to determine how we should feel about the thing represented" (91). Thus the connections made or not made between things are ideological in themselves—a phenomenon that is especially pertinent to fascism and how it is conceived in relation to both anti-Semitism and the Holocaust.

The first section of this chapter investigates some of the larger tropes that inform conceptions of the Holocaust, from David Rousset's trope of "the *univers concentrationnaire*" for the death camps to white supremacist tropes of denial of the "'Holohoax,' a gigantic hebe soap opera" (Cockburn 7). It explores the rubrics that configure analyses of fascism, such as that of "generic phenomenon," as well as the consequences of "disciplining" Nazism and fascism within European history, but the Holocaust and anti-Semitism within Judaic studies. Finally, it considers some of the larger ways of structuring plays and performances about fascism and the Holocaust— such as that of focusing on a single "important person," a representative family, a set of generic characters, or a group configured within a socioeconomic matrix. The second section of the chapter surveys tropes found in particular plays and performances that refer to the struggle to convey the Holocaust, to aspects of fascist practice, and to our own role as consumers and resisters of such translations.

Figuring Fascism and the Holocaust

Despite the common use of the term fascism to describe repressive, authoritarian behavior, the definition of what constitutes fascism is ideologically contested within the field of history. Is it a "generic phenomenon," or must fascist regimes be limited to Italy and Germany? Is it an aberrant convulsion of the mid-twentieth century or a practice that recurs in different guises? Is fascism the product of monopoly capitalism in times of economic distress, a ruthless method of modernizing accompanied by extreme nationalism, or, as more conservative historians propose, a reaction against modernization? How crucial is the criterion of extensive mass organization of a people for the definition of fascism? Is the model of Germany, with its web of Nazi organizations and Nazified preexisting ones, the sole model? If so, Spain, Portugal, and certain Latin American countries have had dictatorships but weren't fascist. For some conservative historians, these Latin American countries can then be classified as "potential liberal democracies," while fascism, manifested only in Italy and Germany, can be located next to communism under the umbrella of totalitarianism. Is any right wing political movement that identifies itself as populist and situates itself by its hostility to both left and capitalist ideology (while pillaging both) fascistic (Allardyce; Arendt; Cassels; Germani; Mosse, *Masses*; Nolte; Rabinbach; Turner; Weber; and Woolf)? Finally, if it performs the relations that characterize many forms of domination, how might fascism, with its biological determinisms based on interdependent sexisms and racisms (Bock), be connected to patriarchy? A grotesque caricature or a logical extension?

Roger Griffin's *The Nature of Fascism* continues the project of identifying generic elements of fascism that are contextualized by specific, historical accounts, defining fascism as "a genus of political ideology whose mythic core in its various permutations is a palingenetic [i.e., obsessed with 'new birth'] form of populist ultra-nationalism" (44). For Griffin, the rise of fascism marks

> an imminent turning-point in contemporary history, when the dominance of the allegedly bankrupt or degenerate forces of conservatism, individualistic liberalism and materialist socialism is finally to give way to a new era in which vitalistic nationalism will triumph. To combat these rival political ideologies and the decadence they allegedly host (for example the parasitism of traditional elites, materialism, class conflict, military weakness, loss of racial vitality, moral anarchy, cosmopolitanism), fascist activists see the recourse to organized violence as both necessary and healthy. (44)

Fascism, then, gives rise to "a new national community" (45) that can only be maintained in practice by "the maximum totalitarian control over all areas of social, economic, political and cultural life" (44). While Griffin offers this broad definition of fascism, he qualifies it by suggesting that "no matter how much [various manifestations of fascism] share the same structural core in terms of psychological predisposition, even they will have their own idiosyncratic motivations and rationalizations for investing their yearning for rebirth in an actual fascist movement" (199). Unfortunately, to some degree, Griffin situates Nazism's intense anti-Semitism as a part of this "idiosyncratic." As a result, although numerous references to anti-Semitism appear throughout the book, there is only one reference to the Holocaust, and this is a critique of contemporary revisionism and denial in response to Holocaust history.

If how we define fascism and what we connect it to are ideologically significant, then what we keep separate from it is similarly significant. Traditionally, studies of Germany and the Third Reich have been situated within the discipline of European history, while most often the Holocaust has been relegated to Judaic studies. This common practice of treating the two topics as two distinct phenomena avoids important questions. For example, if, as Hayden White asserts, an antihistorical attitude underlies Nazism, a sense of "the irrelevancy of known past to lived present" (37), how is this related to the Nazi effort to erase not only European Jewry, but any memory of them and their history? In *The Sublime Object of Ideology*, Slavoj Zizek's insightful analysis of the role anti-Semitism plays in fascism exemplifies how critical it is to interweave the history of the Holocaust into any analysis of fascism.

For Zizek, "*fantasy is a means for an ideology to take its own failure into account in advance*" (126). In relation to fascism, this happens in an especially lethal way: "the 'Jew' is the means, for Fascism, of taking into account, of representing its own impossibility: in its . . . presence, it [i.e. the 'Jew'] is . . . the embodiment of the ultimate impossibility of the totalitarian project—of its immanent limit. . . . The whole Fascist ideology is structured as a struggle against the element [i.e. the fetishistic embodiment of the 'Jew'] which holds the place of the immanent impossibility of the very Fascist project" of "a totally transparent and homogeneous society" (127). For Zizek,

> in the anti-Semitic vision, the Jew is experienced as the embodiment of negativity, as the force disrupting stable social identity—but the "truth" of anti-Semitism is, of course, that the very identity of [this] position is structured through a negative relationship to this . . . figure of the Jew. Without the reference to the Jew who is corroding the social fabric, the social fabric itself would be dissolved. (176)

Fascist ideology and practice can only ever exist in dialectic tension with fascism's Other and, I would suggest, "the Jew" represents a frequent grounding Other for fascism. Even in 1998, if one looks at U.S. white supremacist documents on the web, denial of the Holocaust and expressions of anti-Semitism manifest themselves as a critical, founding enunciation, and are commented upon at length, even if the central aim of such documents is racism (most particularly aimed at African Americans) and homophobia. One way of exploring this reiterated anti-Semitism and its concomitant assertion of Jewish conspiracies (often manifested in the acronym ZOG for the "Zionist Occupied Government" of the United States) comes with Zizek's assertion that

> In Nazi ideology, all human races form a hierarchical, harmonious Whole (the "destiny" of the Aryans at the top is to rule, while the Blacks, Chinese, and others have to serve)—all races *except the Jews*: they have no proper place; their very "identity" is a fake, it consists in trespassing the frontiers, in introducing unrest, antagonism, in destabilizing the social fabric. As such, Jews plot with other races and prevent them from putting up with their proper place—they function as a hidden Master aiming at a world domination: they are a counter-image of the Aryans themselves, a kind of negative, perverted

double; this is why they must be exterminated, while other races have only
to be forced to occupy their proper place. (128–29)

To the degree, then, to which the historical events of the Holocaust convey
both a place of Jewish identity and the lethal consequences of fascist thinking, the denial of the Holocaust becomes a critical move for white supremacists (even if, as in the case of South African apartheid, anti-Semitism is not
always essential to the operations of racism and white supremacy). Thus, to
the extent that any account of not only Nazism, but of fascism regards genocidal anti-Semitism as an idiosyncratic by-product, this account will miss
the crucial operations of anti-Semitism in analyzing fascism in general.

In the play *Laughter!* (1978), Peter Barnes makes visible the machinery
of anti-Semitism at work within fascism. Barnes uses the physical absence of
Jewish characters, as well as their abstracted presence in the bureaucratic
discourse that hides the implementation of the Holocaust, to underline the
dialectic relation between fascism and Jews as "embodiment of negativity"
(Zizek 176). The Auschwitz section of *Laughter!* uses a historical perspective
to connect the public spectacle of fascist ideology with the publicly denied
mass production of death by depicting how Nazism set the stage for the
development of a centralized, bureaucratic state, "based on solid middle class
values" (44)—a state depicted as a machine reflexively perpetuating murder
to maintain itself. Moreover, it can be asserted that plays [e.g., Edward Bond's
Summer (1982), David Edgar's *Destiny* (1976), and Stephen Lowe's *Touched*
(1979)] that portray aspects of fascism by analyzing "historical pattern focused through the ordinary" (Roberts 129), and by showing "the cumulative
making of history through daily lives," refute fascist ideology in their basic
premises.

Furthermore, the subject of the Holocaust further compounds the
troubled relation between history and representation. In his introduction to
the groundbreaking anthology *The Theatre of the Holocaust*, Robert Skloot
points to the dangers for artists of cheapening, trivializing, or exploiting the
subject of the Holocaust (11). One response to these dangers is a preference
for art that directly documents the testimony of survivors; but this, too, has
its perils. As Susan Sontag cautions when she discusses films about fascism
and the Holocaust in *Under the Sign of Saturn*, to "simulate atrocity convinc-
ingly is to risk making the audience passive, reinforcing witless stereotypes,
confirming distance and creating fascination" (139). Although this warning
does not refer directly to the impact of dramatic performance, the danger of
passive fascination is only compounded by the presence of live bodies onstage.
It may be that theatricalized works on the Holocaust—works that foreground
the medium—might avoid the perils of this kind of simulation and clarify
events without neutralizing the unbelievability of their horrific violence and
brutality. In *The Other Kingdom*, David Rousset constructs the idea of the

univers concentrationnaire for the death camps, "a universe apart, totally cut off, the weird kingdom of an unlikely fatality" (41) into which millions were displaced. Trying to stage this other kingdom inevitably results in a kind of additional displacement since, in a Holocaust play, the discursive and material referents to that onstage universe would, in our universe, be resistant to the ways we order experience.

In *The Holocaust and the Literary Imagination*, Lawrence Langer calls for an "aesthetics of atrocity" (22), which Skloot describes as disallowing a "distracting and destructive kind of pleasure" (12) while promoting a sense of credulity and even complicity in the reader or spectator. But if language, as Hayden White asserts, uses tropes to structure experience and if, as Harold Bloom suggests in *A Map of Misreading*, the trope is the linguistic equivalent of a psychological defense mechanism (91), it is difficult to imagine how art, insofar as it is linguistic, might resist those defenses. And if dominant discourse is an ideological effort to come to terms with problematic domains of experience, to incorporate them into conventionalized notions of "reality," "truth," or "possibility," how can we prevent it from repressing and rendering invisible a tangible reality of physical privation, torture, and death? The problem of finding a language for describing the Holocaust also reveals the problem of situating an event that may have no analogue in history but nonetheless is history.

Denial of the Holocaust and of the commitment to memorialize these historical events can also be tropological, including figures that relate to emplotment or genre. Thus, *Insaturation*, a racist American publication, called the Holocaust the "'Holohoax,' a gigantic hebe soap opera" (qtd. in Cockburn). The use of the term soap opera may reveal as much as it offends. In *Loving with a Vengeance: Mass-Produced Fantasies for Women*, Tania Modleski identifies elements in the form of the soap opera (87–107) that recall attempts to make meaning and find a language for the Holocaust. Modleski characterizes soap opera as encouraging identification with numerous personalities and as emphasizing interpersonal relationships, intimacy, and continuity rather than action and setting. In soaps, the enigmas proliferate and each day brings further complications that will defer resolutions and introduce new questions. According to Dennis Porter, "unlike Aristotelian drama, with its imitation of a human action that has a beginning, a middle, and an end, soap opera is entirely composed of an indefinitely expandable middle" (783). Unlike melodrama, it does not contain an ending that justifies the suffering of the good and punishes the wicked. It is full of interruption, psychic fumbling, repetition, and shifts in point of view. It is about disorders that resist ordering, including the "wrapping up" of a narrative line.

Of course, this kind of mass culture form depends mainly on infinite manipulations and permutations of plot, but it does suggest the degree to which texts dealing with the events of the Holocaust might well resist a regulated and orderly narrative. Stephen Spielberg's film *Schindler's List* (1993), for example, diffuses the centrality of its characters into diverse groups of people, among whom it shifts back and forth, rather than insisting on the logic of following the fate of one or two specific, though "representative," families. Modleski's characterization of the soap also recalls that while the events of the Holocaust, or indeed, any genocidal actions, are and should be part of the events of public history, to those experiencing them, these horrific actions were perpetrated in, and indeed became, the everyday domestic world, grotesquely replacing the one from which the victims were deliberately evacuated. Finally, the story of trying to represent and make meaning out of the Holocaust itself, both futile and inevitable, is an endless narrative.

What kind of story does Modleski propose as the opposite of a soap? She uses Laura Mulvey's analysis of cinema for her reply: it is the classic (male) narrative film structured "around a main controlling figure with whom the spectator can identify" (367) and achieve, temporarily, the illusion of mastery. The quasi-fascistic character of this narrative structure appears not only in films but also in television shows, any number of which offer identification with the powerful and the lure of what Hamida Bosmajian calls "romantic-demonic heroics" (55), despite their moral pieties. To the extent that a strategy of containment is inherent in this structure (thereby limiting responsibility for perpetrating genocide to a few oversized characters), inevitably it comes to haunt even serious, ironically constructed, single protagonist plays about fascism.

Two examples are John Antrobus's *Hitler in Liverpool* (1983), where a pre–World War I Hitler is depicted absorbing his ideas and rhetorical strategies from the British and from the expatriate German colony in Liverpool, and Michael Burrell's *Hess* (1980), a monologic performance of Hess's rationalizations with frequent accusations addressed to a British and American audience on the basis of colonialism and Vietnam. Though innovative in their techniques, both plays still assert the traditional idea of history as an examination of important people or leaders. This also is true of Bryan Wade's *Blitzkrieg* (1973), with its camped-up sadomasochism between Eva Braun and Adolph Hitler, its literal-minded equating of power practices with sexual practices.

Moreover, since all three of the above-mentioned plays focus on the interiority of their historical figures, they fail to reveal one crucial aspect of fascism: it strives to achieve social order, stability, and control through the evacuation of individual interiority and the negation of difference. Individuals become agents of the state, their only purpose to serve and represent the larger goals of the fascist project. And, as Zizek notes, this configuration of power necessitates that "the 'Jew' appears as an intruder who introduces from outside disorder, decomposition, and corruption of the social edifice— it appears as an outward . . . cause whose elimination would enable us to restore order, stability and identity" (128). Leni Riefenstahl's film *Triumph of the Will* (1934) contains two mass Nazi rallies: in one rally, each follower carries a flag in front of him; in the other, each follower holds a shovel. These displays symbolically perform this evacuation of interiority while the highly visible repeating props denote a homogeneous body, serving the state, which is threatened by an outside force.

In contrast to the focus on a single Nazi protagonist in the Antrobus, Burrell, and Wade plays, Joan Schenkar's *The Last of Hitler* (1982) includes a deliberately fictionalized construction of Hitler in a landscape of collective mind where ideas slide from one character to the next. The way all these characters participate in the machinery of anti-Semitism deflates the demonic stature of the Hitler figure in the play. For *The Resistible Rise of Arturo Ui* (1957; written in collaboration with Margarete Steffin in the early forties), Bertolt Brecht translates Hitler into Chicago gangster Arturo Ui, defusing his mystique (and the "dangerous respect commonly felt for great killers")[1] by locating him in a socioeconomic matrix of other people, motives, and decisions. For *Destiny* (1976), David Edgar includes a panoramic cast of Britains from all classes and political perspectives to document the rise of "Nation Forward," a new party signifying the nucleus of a fascist movement. Edgar's purpose was to show "why large numbers of ordinary people, often people heavily involved with the Labour movement, become attracted to an ideology which is self-evidently obscene," an ideology resonant with racism based on "blood," extreme nationalism, and notions of international conspiracy (qtd. in Itzin). Another strategy for locating the operations of fascism appears in Howard Barker's *The Loud Boy's Life* (1980). Here, Barker ironizes the focus on an important political person. He emplots the rise and fall of a reactionary, proto-fascistic British politician as a satiric or pseudo-tragedy: Ezra Fricker's "flaw" is his adherence to constitutionality. And instead of splicing in the dreams of the political figure (and psychologizing the character), Barker splices in "Fricker's London," a series of descriptions for a television program made by Fricker, which reveal his ideology in the context of local places and events.

Generic titles such as "Daughter," "Male Customer," "SS-Man," and "Old Woman" for the ordinary Germans of Heiner Mueller's *The Slaughter* (1978) represent the structuring that contrasts most sharply with the single "important person" focus. By means of a fragmented, condensed, presentational, and discontinuous text, the characters for whom, as Mueller notes, fascism "was normal, if not the norm," become the willing executioners of those in closest proximity for the sake of profit and survival. These generic figures sliced from various kinds of structures (familial, commercial, military) work together to convey the catastrophe of fascism lived by people in the everyday. Set at the very end of World War II, *The Slaughter* denotes the rupture and final ruination of every expectable "meaning" attached to these generic

relationships. Generic characterizations enable Mueller to avoid the construction of either abstract or "representative individual" characters so his
work can enact the erosion of subjectivity into the violent, raw grotesque.

Finally, in three plays I'll discuss in more detail later, the trope of "the
mind of Hitler" is countered by scatology. In Barnes's *Laughter!*, a Third
Reich bureaucrat asks "what do you call someone who sticks his finger up
the Fuehrer's arse?" The answer: "A brain surgeon" (55). In Schenkar's *The
Last of Hitler*, two nurses use a proctological instrument to "find Hitler" in
an unconscious Dr. Reich. And in George Tabori's *The Cannibals*, a cynical,
self-justifying SS guard asserts "there is a Fuehrer in the asshole of the best
of us" (262). In fact, the play denies this assertion in its portrayal of moral
engagement by death camp inmates sustained at great cost. Still, this recurrent excremental trope gives the lie to the clear blue sky, transcendent above
the clouds, which symbolizes Nazi consciousness at the outset of *Triumph of
the Will*.

Tropes in Individual Plays

Claude Lanzmann's film *Shoah* addresses the problem of language, experience, and the irreducibility of what is being portrayed, through the multiple languages of the speakers (two of which are not languages Lanzmann
understands), the interpreters for most of the transactions, and the additional translation represented by the subtitles. In effect, Lanzmann makes
clear that Europe, not just Germany, is the context for fascism by deploying
this trope of translation. In the plays I consider in this section, tropes constitute the bridge between art and the events of fascism and the Holocaust.
While the contemporary plays under discussion create figures for fascism
and the Holocaust, such as fascism as pathology or disease and the concentration camp as Hell, they also contain figures about language in relationship to the process of re-presenting this history and figures about language
that signify the historical practice of fascism and the way language is used to
construct and resist it. As I read them through tropes, the plays take on a
self-reflexive quality, calling attention to those textual features enacting the
struggle with narrative in relation to presenting this history. How do we
recreate via the language of theatre events that are horrifically unthinkable?
How might the use of certain kinds of linguistic tropes illuminate the struggle
with a history that is outside of any intelligible frames offered by representation? And what might we learn from the deployment of such tropes about
the struggle to render such unimaginable events?

Because autobiographical performance art so heavily relies on the use of
language to convey the "meaning" of a particular piece, most deployments
of this form suggest an increased availability to (and a freer flow of informa-

tion about) material experience. This mode of representation traditionally presupposes that because the experiences being related to the audience emerge from the experiences of the performer, material experience is more easily translated through language. Yet in Leeny Sack's, *The Survivor and the Translator*, the form of autobiographical performance heightens the spectator's awareness of the complexities and contradictions of translating history, experience, and memory into language.

Central to this piece is the way that Sack creates and confronts Holocaust history by performing in the present moment. Sack herself describes the piece as "A solo theatre work about not having experienced the Holocaust, by a daughter of concentration camp survivors" (123). The Survivor of the piece is her grandmother. Sack's performance is fragmented, repetitive, incomplete, and punctured by failures in "translation" at every level, including her grandmother's own constant circular failures of memory (How could extreme trauma and abuse be told in a linear, completely remembered way?). Thus the trope of translation functions to underline: first, the difficulty of putting the experience of the Holocaust into representation; second, the difficulty of imagining this experience for the spectator, even for the close relative who translates; and third, the difficulty for the survivor herself of translating her experience into words. Sack also uses fragments from other authors in the first half of the piece to augment the multiplicity of narratives and cultural contexts for Holocaust history and experience, rather than insist on one relationship with one Holocaust survivor, although that comes across very powerfully.

Her position as the Translator is marked continually for the audience by her wearing of earphones as if she were always responding simultaneously to another voice that we cannot hear: "The story I tell was slipped under my skin before I could say yes or no or mama" (124). Some of the piece is in Polish, an insistent pointing to the source of this experience in another language and, metaphorically, to a set of referents impossible fully to conceive and extraordinarily painful to relate: "Something like this you can't describe. . . . There weren't days" (145). Sack locates this resistance to translation in a doubled discourse because she simultaneously performs the crucial necessity to translate, the effort to work out an inexorable historical moment to which she has a direct relation, and the desire to affirm her own legacy as translator. Moreover, for Sack, the failure of language is sometimes more articulate than precise language would be: Her grandmother describes the Nazi crematoria as "Machines for burning people. . . . They ruined by machines" (142).

The most optimistic conceptions of translation—the sense of the explanatory, the clearly elucidated and the accurately rendered—cannot function for Sack's performance piece. "How," for example, Sack asks her audience, "can you describe a smell?" (132). More accurate is the sense of changing, transferring, or transforming from one place, state, or form to another: the performance enacts a kind of bearing witness to the very limits of the process of translation (even as we absorb information) and to its inevitable deformations and inadequate equivalencies. The trope of translation reminds us not only of the limits of translation in reference to Holocaust history, but of the weight and labor of translation itself, foremost for the survivor, then for the performing interpreter, and, finally, for us in the position of spectators.

If Sack's performance piece uses the trope of translation, Charlotte Delbo's play *Who Will Carry the Word?* (1972; English 1982) uses the trope of carrying to denote her struggle with representing the Holocaust. The play concerns the determination of French women political prisoners in a death camp that one of them should survive to carry back to the world their history of atrocity and slow death. The text of the play dwells on the inability to carry, to "bring back" certain words and experiences of the Holocaust in their horrific context even as it attempts to perform this very context. The trope of carrying extends to visual figuration since the women carry—support each other psychically, morally, and physically as in the roll call scenes where whoever falls is killed. The performed text also addresses to us the question of who will carry on or take over the weight of this story.

Delbo, herself a survivor of such a death camp, might have opted for the more personal "I" narrative often deployed in the venue of "autobiographical performance." As a survivor of the concentration camps, she would certainly have the authority to sustain that voice (and it is the voice she uses when writing prose on the same subject). Yet here she chooses to recreate this history using a choral structure of shifting voices. This chorus utilizes its multiple voice ("ces paroles" [the words] in the French title) to negate a scriptural, authoritative text (as implied by the English title, "the Word"). This choral rendering enlarges our sense of the scope of the victims and underscores the fortitude and magnaminity of their group effort to survive. Language in this play, then, is imaged as a carrier, a medium of transmission from a place where the borders between being alive and dead have collapsed and the words expressing the simplest things—cold, thirst, hunger, tiredness—have a different meaning in the context of an invisible, inhuman otherworld. Thus *Who Will Carry the Word?* clarifies how even multiple voices, in multiple contexts, fail to convey the experience of the concentration camp to an audience.

Sack and Delbo use tropes of translation and carrying to demonstrate how language covers over material experience, even as they attempt to reveal traces of that history in their struggle between language and the Holocaust. In George Tabori's *The Cannibals* (1968), denial of the history of the Holocaust is imaged as a kind of linguistic cannibalism, as when "savages eagerly desire the body of a murdered man so that his ghost may not trouble them" (265). The figure of eating language appears in the play, implicitly asking us how much of the suffering and violation of others we consume, render invisible, suppress, by and through language.

The central image of *The Cannibals* is a dinner party in a concentration camp, performed by two survivors and the sons of the men who did not survive. References to food saturate the play to denote the intensity of physical hunger and to create sites for moral choice. Except for the two survivors, the prisoners choose not to eat the body of a dead inmate even when an SS Officer orders them to eat or be gassed. The choice, don't eat and die, or eat and die spiritually, is obviously more extreme than our own dilemma. Yet *The Cannibals* dedication to a "small eater" suggests that while we might have to repress some recognition of atrocity to live, we must carry more than we eat.

The trope of eating that Tabori uses suggests consumption (and hence repression) of the material history of the Holocaust. The trope of licking, as expressed in David Hare's *Licking Hitler* (1978), refers more directly to what of fascism must be "tasted" in order to defeat it. *Licking Hitler* depicts a World War II British "dirty tricks" unit broadcasting to Germany. In contrast to eating, "licking" suggests that we take only a little, a consumption of small quantities. Yet in a slang usage, licking connotes the defeat of one person/group by another. In this play, the title slides between these two meanings, suggesting that in order to lick (i.e., defeat) Hitler, one must lick (i.e., place the tongue on the cultural and discursive body of) Hitler and Nazism.

Like a number of contemporary British playwrights, Hare was influenced by Angus Calder's *The People's War: Britain 1939–45* (1969), which asserted that beneath the rhetoric of common cause, the war gave the British elite an opportunity to consolidate their privileged status. Hare's *Licking Hitler* reinforces this premise by implying that the dirty tricks used with impunity by a few to create disorder correspond to the activities of those who, in his words, "carve up provincial England" (66) after the war. An officer in this unit declares that the British must bring "the same vigor, the same passion, the same intelligence" to our side as "that great genius Joseph Goebbels" brought to his (48). Same indeed: the smears and innuendoes used in the faked radio conversations between two German officers incorporate the rhetoric of fascism—red-baiting, anti-Semitism, and obsession with disease, corruption, sexual perversion, and eugenics—in order to create chaos and undermine German morale.

But the generating of "sharp vicious rumors" becomes an enthusiastic game divorced from human consequence, challenging the World War II heroics of schoolbook British history. As Nancy Banks-Smith states on the play's book cover, "smear, slander and character assassination" create a "plague of lying" that "festers and infects everyone." The lie of the dirty trick is

connected to the "inveterate lying" that insists on a humane, egalitarian politics from which it proceeds. The perils of "licking Hitler" also extend by
analogy to forms of art that play with and sensationalize the language and
ideology of fascism, ostensibly to undercut it.

Both Hare's *Licking Hitler* and Joan Schenkar's *The Last of Hitler* (1982)
configure fascism and its concurrent anti-Semitism through the trope of
plague. In both plays, words projected over the radio signify transmission of
a pathology. Schenkar's play is organized around a group of escalating motifs
shifted from character to character to reveal the process by which we project
onto the Other that which is most feared, identify it as contagious, and image ourselves as its victims. Countering the pathology Nazism attached to
Jews and other victimized groups, and taking Hitler's construction of the
threat of the Jewish Other literally, Schenkar makes her characters subject
to contamination: They not only project "Jewishness" onto each other, they
"catch it" like a disease. The discourse of anti-Semitism materializes on the
bodies of those who speak it so they become their own hated, fear-filled
projections. Thus there are no actual Jewish characters in the play, only the
"suppositious" imaginings of Jews (in burlesqued stereotypes) that the characters invent, "catch," and become. What's left is an engineered absence at
the heart of the play that evokes the historical reality of the Holocaust.

Schenkar implicates her audience in the infectious humor of death in
this send-up of 1940s American radio shows. The play is staged in a huge
radio console with two miked broadcasters ensconced amongst cathode tubes
at the top of the set. In *The Last of Hitler*, Schenkar uncovers fascism in 1940s
America without ever abandoning the particularity of American references
and patterns of speech. Focusing on the role of mass culture, Schenkar depicts waves of bigotry, paranoia, and hatred projected over the airwaves to
grow in our brains. The giant radio is thus culture within a medium in both
senses and the play can be read as a surreal work staged in a collective brain
where all associations are possible.

The most riveting visual image in Schenkar's play is that of Dr. Reich
and the six-year-old skeleton Edmond in a tableau recalling an Edgar Bergen/
Charlie McCarthy routine. The cynical, accusing, and rumor-mongering
dummy spews forth a repertoire of tasteless jokes. On one level his performance suggests the perils of the communication of ventriloquism: he is an
innocent skeleton held by a crafty actor who speaks for him. But the impres-
sions derived from this exchange are more ambiguous: Is Edmond dead,
alive, or ghost; child or adult; dummy, autonomous, or even ventriloquist;
performer or performed upon? *The Last of Hitler*'s portrayal of ventriloquism
is not at all simple, especially since the hate-filled dummy has Hitler's childhood history. In one interpretation, it could image how the repressed elements of a people are projected onto a leader who speaks for them. What
intrigues me, moreover, is how this ambiguous performance highlights a

shifting space between people and leader, a kind of reciprocal projection that suggests the multidirectional web of transactions among an authoritarian leader and his followers.

Schenkar's use of projected language differs from its use by Robert MacDonald in *Summit Conference* (1983). Set in 1941 in the Berlin Chancellery, MacDonald's play depicts Eva Braun and Clara Petacci meeting at the same time as Hitler and Mussolini confer. After the first third of the play, MacDonald projects the consciousness of the two fascist leaders onto the two women, who then involuntarily speak as Hitler and Mussolini about fascist policies and future plans. As dummies, Braun and Petacci become straight men: reflecting in their performed parody neither their circumstances nor their gender—no dimension of response, for example, to the woman-hating speeches MacDonald plants in Braun's mouth. Thus the play exploits its two female characters and the trope of projection for the theatricalized novelty of displacement. I suspect that some of the appeal of Wallace Shawn's play *Aunt Dan and Lemon* (1985) also stems from the novelty of female fascists (including an intellectual seduction with sexual undertones of a young woman by an older one) unmediated by an analysis of the ideology of fascism in relation to gender.[2]

In the plays discussed above, linguistic tropes help us (as readers and spectators) understand the struggle to represent the Holocaust as well as fascist practice in the descriptive language of theatre. In Peter Barnes's play *Laughter!*, the idea of concrete, descriptive language is itself inverted: concrete language is equated with symbolic letters and numbers, and death itself is double coded for safekeeping from consciousness.

"Tsar," Part I of *Laughter!*, depicts Ivan the Terrible, who, by acts of terror and violence, created "the first centralized, multi-national State in the West" (26). This historic development paves the way for Part II, "Auschwitz," where Barnes focuses on the relation of fascism to the modern state, to the institutionalized, bureaucratic organization of incarceration and murder. The play effectively demonstrates Roger Griffin's assertion that "Once fascism takes power and forms a *regime*, factors other than ideological zeal (for example, fear, opportunism, conformism, cynicism, gullibility, sadism, the effectiveness of social control, or the absence of practical alternatives) will motivate many to . . . collude with the new regime without any intense affective commitment to its ideology or policies" (184).

Set in 1942, in an office "in WVHA Department Amt C," the play presents Hitler as a picture wreathed in Christmas holly while ordinary civil servants fuel the death machine. Cranach, head of this office administering the concentration camps, insists "everything has to be written down. It's the basis of our existence" (28). Instead of writing as an act of keeping the Holocaust in history, here written language functions to denature. The language of termination is so abstracted—"I don't mince words. I've always believed in calling a CF/83 a CF/83" (28)—that it neutralizes the significance of information and precludes the imagining of atrocity.

The language of coded numbers plays a powerful role in ordering the production of death:

> Future cases of death shall be given consecutive Roman numbers with consecutive subsidiary Arabic numbers, so that the first case of death is numbered Roman numeral I/1, the second Roman numeral I/2 up to Roman numeral I/185. . . . Each new year will start with the Roman numeral I/1. (38)

That each Roman numeral codes another horrific way of dying is obscured by the literalizing of the numbers and wiped out in the yearly summing up. That "CP(3)m is CP(3)m" (65) *only* and not the new concrete crematorium flues signifies the reduction of human consequence to neutral, manipulable elements within a closed circuit of meanings. Crime becomes the "unauthorized" and the "unsigned," danger means "redundancy" and "compulsory retirement," and conflict equals interoffice struggle: "Kyklon B isn't being used to kill rats but to discredit this department" (32).

A passage in Jean Baudrillard's "The Precession of Simulacra" further illuminates what Barnes depicts:

> [In the] passage to a space whose curvature is no longer that of the real, nor of truth, the age of simulation thus begins with a liquidation of all referentials—worse; by their artificial resurrection in systems of signs, a more ductile material than meaning, in that it lends itself to all systems of equivalence, all binary oppositions, and all combinatory algebra. (254)

Baudrillard uses the image of the map as an example of how industrialization has resulted in what he terms an age of "simulation." Whereas the "territory" once preceded the drafting of maps, he suggests that the rise of industrialization and its insistence on mass-produced objects has led to a "hyperreal" space where the map precedes the territory. In other words, the "real" referent (i.e., the territory) is erased and the mass-produced maps (i.e., the simulations) come to stand in for the "real." In the case of Barnes's play, the characters make mass-produced numbers stand in for the "territory"; this numerical mapping erases the actual liquidations over which these characters preside.

What Barnes makes visible through the language of numbers and letters is the practice of divorcing the real from its referent. "CP(3)m" stands in for the crematorium, much as Roman numerals stand in for those sent there. The language of numbers and letters, then, becomes "hyperreal" (in the Baudrillardian sense) in that they have no referent in the "real" and instead take the place of that referent as "reals" in and of themselves. Obliterating "the territory" allows the characters to obliterate the material consequences of what occurs bureaucratically. Thus the coding of the mass-produced deaths of genocide makes the deaths themselves invisible. Barnes's play creates one of the most extreme examples of simulation, refuting, by implication, an argument that Nazism was a resistance to modernism and modernization; for the modernity of Nazism resides in its mass production of death. Barnes's play implies the potential of other modern state bureaucracies for criminal action.

In response to criminal speech, the language of jesting functions in *Laughter!* as the social gestus of reconciliation and denial. The office workers turn their own privations—lack of food, their children and lovers killed in war, the climate of repression—into jokes. Even the moral conflicts between Christianity and Nazism become a humorous gesture of accommodation: "Obedience is regarded as a principle of righteous conduct. So I look on National Socialism as Catholicism with the Christianity left out" (35). The play is also a demonstration of how, for the spectator, laughter creates complicity with the characters and diverts attention away from engagement with important issues. As the Author character in clown dress tells us at the outset of the play, "laughter confuses and corrupts" and is "an enemy of resistance and change" (2).

In order to defeat this new order of bureaucrats, Gottleb, a vicious "old style" Nazi SS, confronts the administrative simulation of reality with a grotesquely vivid account of Auschwitz accompanied by a staged simulation of death. The comedy emplotment of the play cracks open as the language cracks open, as the file cabinets on stage crack open to reveal:

> a vast mound of filthy, wet straw dummies. . . . They spill forward to show all are painted light blue, have no faces, and numbers tattooed on their left arms. . . . two monstrous figures appear . . . [and] hit the dummies with thick wooden clubs . . . [to] the splintering sound of a skull being smashed. (64–65)

Cranach wards off this vision with a joke based on a point of language: "He was lying. I could tell, he used *adjectives*" (66). The file doors then slam shut, a simultaneous staging of the process of repression and the recontainment in language of what has spilled out in bodies and words.

If in Barnes's play language contains the atrocity of the Holocaust and fascist practice perpetrated by the office workers in the play, Edward Bond's *Summer* points to the ways in which certain kinds of discourses (and relationships) surrounding fascism reassert themselves in the present to create a situation that can be neither redeemed nor resolved. Xenia, who lives in London, returns to an unspecified East European country and the coastal town her family once dominated economically. Marthe, her former servant, presides over Xenia's previous home, now turned into vacation apartments. During World War II, this home had been frequently visited by Nazis. The privileges accorded to Xenia as a result enabled her to save Marthe from the mass execution perpetrated on the townspeople in retaliation for their acts of resistance. Xenia wants Marthe to acknowledge both her act of kindness to Marthe and her pain at the violent ejection of her (kindly) father from his place by the postwar regime. Marthe refuses.

In *Summer* a former German soldier and prison guard also returns as a tourist to the islands that were World War II concentration camps, where local "people [were] shot every day . . . for months on end" (26). The German justifies the events of fascism in an essentializing language. War is inherently "harsh," and "had to be" because "men are animals"; thus the soldiers were not "enemies" but "defenders" against "scum" who destroy culture. This culture becomes essentialized in the "poignant" symbol of the "woman in white," a young woman (actually the young Xenia) seen by the soldiers on a balcony who came "from the same class as our officers" (34–38). As the quintessence of upper class standards of beauty, fragility, and purity, she "saves" men from themselves in the act of being defended (even if she, herself, is unaware of being seen). Thus the iconizing language of fascism that situates itself in hierarchies of class, race, and gender is present even in the language of the ordinary German soldier. It is, most particularly, Bond's way of indicating the symbolic labor upper class women perform, albeit involuntarily, within a fascist economy.

Found on another German soldier who worshipped this symbol of white transcendence is a photograph depicting "six or seven naked women standing [huddled] in a group in a field" at whom "a gray figure pointed a rifle" (27). The agony of the imminent death along with their vulnerable nakedness is exploited as sex just as the girl in white is rendered sexless, demonstrating the binary oppositions that are fully connected to death-dealing practices. If the individual person of the girl is erased in her superior status, the other side is the dehumanization of other women—for Bond, who is a socialist, inevitably women of other classes.

But what should we make of Bond's "To the Audience"? This poem in the program for the British production of the play states that "communication is possible," for language can draw "a lesson" in words that are "the truth" (from Bond's notebooks on *Summer*, qtd. in Roberts 103). Locating the meaning of kindness in the geography of class is a major project of *Summer*:

> When you have so much power you might as well be nobody. Necessity takes over. Factories and banks aren't run by kindness. They run on their own laws. The owners and owned must both obey them. The kindness of one person to another can't change that. . . . Your family [an upper class one]

made the people who loved and respected them confuse kindness and justice. That is corrupting. You can live without kindness, you can't live without justice or fighting to get it. . . . The state of injustice is always a state of
madness. (23)

By drawing a triangular relationship among Eastern European capitalists,
fascists, and working-class people, the play suggests that upper-middle-class
entrepreneurs are always going to be reconfigured in close relation to fascists. Located this way by use of a series of tropes, upper-class kindness is an
act of privilege determined by unjust economic relations. This speech represents an act of "judging" with "precision," demonstrating the possibility of
"reformed human consciousness" (qtd. in Roberts 136) as embodied in language. By implication, the speech suggests that behind the problem of
language's inherent unreliability, one may locate a material and ideologically
sustained injustice. In this context, it might be argued that language resists
fascism when it locates the meaning of events within the relations of class.
Nevertheless, in realizing this focus on class relations, Bond's text makes no
mention of Jews whatsoever. The Holocaust play that fully intersects a class
perspective with issues of ethnicity has yet to be written.

Each character's perspective in Bond's *Summer*, no matter how deeply
felt, is presented as largely produced by their classed position in relation
to the events of fascism and the Holocaust. While C. P. Taylor's play *Good*
(1982) is not about class per se, it does target the rationalizing language
of the educated middle class and its ability to justify increasingly violent and
inhumane behavior. *Good* concerns the progressive descent of literature
professor John Halder into the elite of the SS. Halder's rationalizing appropriates and distorts the language of psychoanalysis. For example, he tells a
Jewish friend understandably terrified of the Nazis that he is merely "in an
anxiety state," and is "being engulfed in a subconscious storm" (44). He in-
terprets his own aligning with the Nazis as "breaking from the emotional/
physical umbilical cords that tied me to my mother" (32). "Anxiety state"
and "emotional umbilical cords" become Halder's own set of pseudo-
psychological tropes by which he denies his activity to himself. Halder
also appropriates the language of humanism and intellectual discourse to
support fascist practice:

> The highly individually centered philosophy of Judaism . . . pushed Western
> literature in a direction which almost entirely ignored man as a social animal
> . . . [and the] point of view of the fulfillment of a culture, or a nation as a
> whole. (51)

By the time Halder has become a "humanity expert" for the death camps, he
is proclaiming that the "philosophical problem" is that "we have confused

subjective fantasy concepts like good, bad, right, wrong, human, inhuman . . . as objective, immutable laws of the universe" when they are, in fact, products of "Jewish moralists" (85).

But *Good* contains a "detour," a trope that creates meanings deviating from and undermining the literal level of the text and Taylor's admittedly worthwhile project to show that "the atrocities of the Third Reich" were "not a simple conspiracy of criminals and psychopaths" (xii). In 1930, Nazi ideologue Alfred Rosenberg asserted that "only man must be and remain a judge, soldier, and ruler of the state" (qtd. in Mosse, *Nazi Culture* 40). However, in contrast to this Nazi ideology of male power, Taylor uses the strategy of gendered language as a central means to evaluate Halder in the text. Repeatedly, Halder is accused of having become a "Nazi Cunt"—a label that absolves him of direct responsibility for fascist practice by suggesting that he is a whore of the Nazis, not a Nazi. In 1933, another Nazi ideologue, Engelbert Huber, asserted that "The German resurrection is a male event" (Mosse, *Nazi Culture* 47); if anything, Halder is a "Nazi Prick."

If detours, such as the one in *Good*, sometimes result from the overlaying of tropes, playwrights do occasionally avoid their use to prevent cutting down the history of atrocity to assimilable size. For example, in the middle of Joan Schenkar's *The Last of Hitler*, a play characterized by the quantity and flux of its tropes, the two broadcasters begin to read statistics, noting European country, number of Jews killed, and percentage of the Jewish population that represented. The baldness of this citation seems a resistance on the part of the playwright to clothing this facticity in figurative language. So, too, the character Emmanuel Lieber in Hampton's *Portage to San Cristobal* recites over short-wave radio to five Nazi hunters the names of specific people, the atrocity committed against them and the place where it happened. Lieber's language represents an attempt to construct not metaphors or examples but an unending, memorializing litany to the dead that is all encompassing.

Many of the contemporary plays and performances I've included express their authors' awareness of the problem of putting experience into language, from the ironic pie in the face at the Author figure as he rails against comedy in *Laughter!* to the agonized search of Delbo's characters to find the words to convey what happened to them. Moreover, those plays and performances that are most reflective about the limits of language extend their tropes most vividly into visual figuration and so best use the resources of the theatre, perhaps because these texts do not pretend to simulate; instead, with their tropes about transmission from experience into language, they can concentrate on getting audiences to accede to the material reality of the events of fascism and the Holocaust. Thus they reinscribe the Holocaust in history, if only in the history of the consciousness of spectators, and enable us to explore our responses to these events.

Furthermore, most of the plays and performances reflect the provisional nature of the ways in which these events are presented and to what they are compared. By deferring intellectual or emotional resolution, this theatre invites us and other writers to continue the discourse, to examine the relationship of these events to ourselves, to our present, and, by implication, to our transition into the future. These plays and performances imply an understanding of history as a text, a dynamic recreation. Moreover, they suggest that how we use language and its tropes in itself constitutes history, especially in terms of the uses of power and the ways we organize experience. Perhaps the history of the repression of atrocity and the abuse of power in language is also the history of what has been and can continue to be done with impunity, especially if the vastness of the scope of its inhumanity subverts our sense of order and our concept of our capabilities. Who disappears from our reality and what disappears in our language are connected.

In addition, the plays and performances enlarge the concept of what constitutes fascist practice both in geographical terms, e.g., the British locale in *Destiny*, and in theoretical terms by relating certain practices—such as essentializing, appropriating, and denying the referentiality of language—with their fascist potential. They suggest areas for further exploration that I take up in other chapters: how our fear of the Other and what the Other will have or take from us is transformed into murderous terror; how a rigid arbitrary construct can be applied with dangerous flexibility; or the way simultaneous, contradictory lies obscure what is happening rather than raise questions.

At the same time the plays and performances testify to the historical reality of both atrocity and abuse of power, they articulate the limits of language and historical knowledge, as currently conceived, to express it. And they push against the limits of language to open up a new space for representing experience, despite the recognition, as Hayden White notes, that rewriting any set of tropes will obscure as much as it reveals. Finally, the works I've discussed suggest our ferocious attempts to resist knowledge we do not want, dangerous information that transgresses the boundaries of established order, even if it is these very boundaries and their limits that help create the horrific events outside them.

2

REPRODUCTION, APPROPRIATION, AND
BINARY MACHINERY

Fascist Ideology and Theatricalization

Among the areas for further exploration noted at the end of chapter 1, I want first to take up a fascist ideological practice that produces simultaneous contradictory lies, which obscure events rather than raise questions. Four plays—Thomas Bernhard's *Eve of Retirement*, Joan Schenkar's *The Last of Hitler*, Peter Barnes's "Auschwitz" section of his trilogy *Laughter!*, and Martin Sherman's *Bent*—are especially pertinent to exploring the theatricalization of fascist ideology and its dualistic operations. I frame the analysis of these plays with several contemporary theoretical works that uncover the logic of a contradictory and obscuring dualistic discourse in fascist ideological practice: Saul Friedlander's *Reflections of Nazism*, Eve Kosofsky Sedgwick's "Privilege of Unknowing: Lesbianism and Epistemology in Diderot," and Alice Yaeger Kaplan's *Reproductions of Banality: Fascism, Literature, and French Intellectual Life*. Friedlander identifies the juxtaposition of aestheticized political dualities, especially that of "the kitsch aesthetic and the themes of death," as critical to the operations of fascist ideology (1). Sedgwick asserts that

> A defining feature of twentieth-century fascisms . . . will prove to have been a double ideological thrust along the axis of same sex bonding or desire. . . . In a knowledge-regime that pushes toward the homosexual heightening of homosocial bonds, it is the twinning with that push of an equally powerful homophobia, and most of all the enforcement of cognitive impermeability between the two, that will represent the access of fascism. (121)

Kaplan investigates how fascism

> works by binding doubles, a process that leads to persistent blindness to the fascist machinery in theories that insist on deciding between two parts of fascism. . . . Splitting and binding in fascism empty its language of the kind of content or consistency that usually helps explain political doctrines. (24)[1]

Thus all three theorists describe what Kaplan calls the totalizing "polarity machine" of fascist ideology—a machine that would, in Klaus Theweleit's words, fuel "the fascist process of appropriating and transmuting reality" (89).

According to Judith Butler, "the subject is constituted through the force of exclusion and abjection, one which produces a constitutive outside to the subject, an abjected outside, which is, after all, 'inside' the subject as its own founding repudiation" (*Bodies That Matter* 3). The larger structures of fascism seem to be predicated on the "simultaneous, contradictory lies" of racial anti-Semitism, homophobia, virulent anticommunism, sexism, all serving to normalize the Nazi subject. This isn't to analogize these processes of Othering: as Butler notes, we need to "resist the model of power that would set up racism and homophobia and misogyny as parallel or analogical relations," thereby missing their specific histories and the ways each of "these vectors of power" requires and deploys the others (18). But the ideologies of racial anti-Semitism are so deeply rooted in fascism that the system enacts a compulsory reiteration of Aryan/Jew as constitutive, a "founding repudiation" without an origin (despite all the myths of the Aryan past) that must be reiterated, performed in acts, over and over. The binary constructed in this "founding repudiation" is so wildly, violently exaggerated that it must continually escalate its claims to maintain itself. And racial anti-Semitism is so critically constitutive that its reiterative acts must be obsessional and lethal: genocide of the Other is not a "by product" of Nazi fascism; it is always there, inscribed in the core of its founding.

We need a multidirectional mapping of the process of Othering: one that moves in many directions, drawing lines of relation among seemingly disparate events and practices. To this enormous task this chapter offers a way to use theories about fascist ideology to map theatrical strategies in plays that purport to represent fascism. Mapping these strategies means locating those plays that constitute an intervention into fascism—plays that not only show how the binary machine of fascism works, but suggest what is obscured (the "cognitive impenetrability" that Sedgwick discusses) by the erection of these binaries. Conversely there are plays whose reproduction of fascism's binary process risks enacting the structures of fascism they seek to illuminate.

I also want to map those plays that stage a "dangerous history" for contemporary spectators in relation to fascism. By "dangerous history" I mean the use of history in theatre to create a political critique of the present by revealing repeating or resonant structures in the past. Such a critique need not directly assault spectators to challenge their conceptions of "how to respond." And the representation needs to challenge the safety of local conditions and structures in a considered way—one that, in this case, might reveal present or potential fascistic structures or suggest ways in which they might be mutated or recycled by the slippery operations of a fascist machinery in a postmodern context.

Such works refuse to make the either/or choices about fascism Kaplan describes—choices that allow fascist ideology to "pass" under a certain limited rubric—e.g., fascism as exclusively antimodernist or as exclusively right wing—that safely contains/explains it. Nor do they, in Friedlander's terms, offer interpretations that easily turn "into a rationalization that normalizes, smoothes, and neutralizes our vision of the past" and so cancels the threat of history. Those that do so Friedlander calls "voluntary or involuntary modalities of exorcism" which replicate the Nazis' maneuvers to "neutralize their own actions" (59). Friedlander also identifies an opposite kind of danger which he connects especially to 1970s films about fascism. While intending to interrogate and subvert fascism, these films actually betray an underlying logic that reproduces fascism's aestheticized dualities uncritically. This aesthetic reproduction is especially dangerous in light of Kaplan's insistence on fascism's own aestheticization of politics and domination.[2]

To clarify what Friedlander identified in this "new discourse that replicates fascist ideology," it is necessary to explore his contention that Nazi aesthetics and the power of its appeal lay in the juxtaposition of two contradictory series. The effect of these series was to create a contradictory response: fascination, terror, ecstasy, and the "simultaneous desire for absolute submission and total freedom" (xv). These effects were accomplished by yoking, on the one hand, love of death ("a ritualized, stylized, and aestheticized death" [15]), nihilism, pessimism, primordial myth, blind destiny that leads to inevitable destruction, apocalypse, and universal conflagration, the leader as superhuman object of desire, and pseudo-spirituality exploiting esotericism and mystery with, on the other hand, kitsch emotion ("a simplified, degraded, insipid but all the more insinuating romanticism" [12]), including nostalgia, sentimentality, the everyday invested with legend, and the leader as Everyman representing petit bourgeois codes of respecting "the established order." What Friedlander is claiming is that these works basically reconstruct the danger of fascism's impermeable binaries.

Austrian playwright Thomas Bernhard's *Eve of Retirement* (German 1979; English 1982) takes the risk of reproducing this aestheticized discourse of fascist ideology in theatre by deeply inhabiting it in order to expose it. The play depicts a claustrophobic, perverse, incestuous familial conspiracy of two sisters and their SS brother—former concentration camp overseer and currently Chief Justice about to retire. Instead of presenting the more abstract ideological aspects of the fascist brother's relation to his sisters, Bernhard literalizes it sexually. This representation differs from Theweleit's understanding of how "sister" functions ideologically as he describes it in *Male Fantasies*:

The "sister," viewed as a love object, serves to define the *limits* of possible object choices. Anything beyond her name is uncharted, dangerous terri-

tory, yet she herself is taboo. What this all comes down to, again, is that
no object seems attainable and no object relations seem capable of being
formed. (125)

Bernhard grotesquely magnifies the literal possibilities of brother and sister
sexual congress to underscore what is latent in this incest taboo. More generally, he deliberately reinscribes Nazi ideology into the rhetoric of a sick
family to emphasize its perverse psychological dimension. His trio's obsessive interest in and desire for death and chaos intersect with compulsively
repeated cliches, especially those about nature. Nostalgia for a romanticized
German past and ideals of heroism and destiny intermingle with a ritualized
fixation on purity versus filth, on poison, putrefaction, degeneration, corro-
sion, depravity, and decay. The intersection of kitsch and horrific destruction is exemplified by the photo album the trio peruses, which alternates
pictures of family holidays with images of the concentration camps and those
killed in them. Finally, there is a paranoid aestheticizing in their frequent
references to ghastly atmosphere, horrible house, abominable pit, crushing
monsters, insanity, and fanaticism—all of which function to screen and transform their past into a Gothic narrative (as if something "happened" to them).
Risking reproducing fascist aestheticizing in this self-conscious way, Bernhard
creates a potential space for a parodic reenactment in the present moment
that may instill a troubled recognition in its current audience. As Jeanette R.
Malkin states in "Pulling the Pants Off History: Politics and Postmodernism
in Thomas Bernhard's *Eve of Retirement*": "Bernhard parodies the shared,
official 'memory' of a Nazi past through image and icon, while . . . forbid-
ding forgetfulness by giving voice to 'hidden' taboos, to 'unspoken' (yet still
active) national texts, by confronting the audience with the conflated facts,
memories, taboos and emotions of a still present past" (119).

　　Still, there is always room for debate about the efficacy of a postmodern,
self-conscious, ironic political strategy that seeks to tap its target audience's
unconscious, its ugliest and most repressed obsessions, by reproducing them
in a jarring way. According to Denis Calandra, "The thematic material of
[*Eve of Retirement*] could be the substance of any number of Post-World War
II German plays; but whereas someone like Heiner Mueller forces the audience to face the brutalities of German history and its continuing present
influence, Bernhard's satirical thrust leads to a general misanthropy" (149).
He even attributes Bernhard's relative success with theatre audiences in Germany to "the middle class German's penchant for self-criticism to the point
of self-hatred," as well as to this theatre-going public's "latent masochism"
(140)—an attribute Friedlander observed in delineating his aestheticized
dualities. True, the family trio in this play produces guilt-ridden accusations
that revolve around words like infected, disgusting, perverted, abominable,

vicious, brutal, violated, despicable, and dangerous. Yet I think there is something problematic about extending the self-hatred of the characters in the play to the German viewing public at large. Such an extension implies a monolithic identification on the part of the audience with the brother's relativistic assertion that "There is a criminal in each of us" (172). This implication that a kind of essential fascist lurks in the heart of every German obscures the reality that fascism is a set of ideological practices with more than one locale.

But there is something luxuriant if also agonized in the loathsomeness of Bernhard's portrayal of Nazism. His language is so overloaded that it risks devouring the parameters for judgment or even recognition, and so positioning spectators, like the sister Clara whose ritual role is to judge her siblings, as silent and paralyzed. Even if spectators reject the brother's equally relativistic claim that "we are all victims of the war" (176), they may sink into a fascinated revulsion for a theatricalized fascism in which theatre becomes the characters' own self-conscious aesthetic system rather than Bernhard's means of undoing them.

Both Bernhard's *Eve* and the next play for discussion, Schenkar's *The Last of Hitler*, are ironic, ritualized, parodic; both intertwine the comic with the perverse in order to insinuate a relationship to a fascist mentality—Bernhard for a German audience and Schenkar for an American one—to which its audience would not willingly assent. Both use recognizable references to the past to produce an aura of complicity and continuity in the present. Both include heavy doses of anti-Semitism while excluding actual Jews from their plays. As noted earlier, Butler maintains that the subject is "constituted through the force of exclusion and abjection, one which produces a constitutive outside to the subject, an abjected outside, which is, after all, 'inside' the subject as its own founding repudiation" (*Bodies That Matter* 3). By excluding actual Jews from the stage, both plays try to make visible not only the constructedness of the abject other by the fascist, but its true location within those who construct it. And, finally, both risk reproducing Friedlander's aestheticized dualities to suggest the addictive lure of fascistic modes of thinking in the present.

Friedlander also identifies the aesthetic perils in representations based on "Nazism as an unlimited field for a surge of the imagination, for a use of aesthetic effects, for a demonstration of literary brilliance" (xvi). In *The Darkness We Carry: The Drama of the Holocaust*, Robert Skloot identifies a kind of exploitation in which there is more enjoyment by the playwright of "grim speculations" and more desire "to provoke theatrical excitement" than there should be (70), certainly suggesting a specifically theatrical, dangerous way of presenting history. One example Skloot gives of such a work is Joan Schenkar's 1982 play, *The Last of Hitler*. Perhaps, at times, the play does radiate a sense of fascination with its own willed villainies, even if it resolutely attempts to deconstruct the mystifying demonic associated with them. Still, having written about this play before, I would like to suggest some contexts for understanding what Schenkar is trying to do.

Alice Yaeger Kaplan speaks of the way fascist ideology mutates according to the political tensions of the moment and the way fascist language appeals "at different emotional registers at different moments of fascism's history" (24). She describes a process of recycling old and new human reflexes to serve a politics of destruction (32). Thus language is not only "emptied" by fascism; fascism recycles and appropriates ideas, practices, and material history from multiple contexts to reclaim them within its own economy of meaning. If Schenkar's work is a kind of circus of sliding metaphor, it is this mutating, flexible, recycling reproducability of fascist ideology in language that she is trying to capture and subvert. In *The Last of Hitler*, Schenkar undercuts both the way metaphor continually reinscribes itself and the conserving structure of metaphoric equivalences, hence its addictiveness. She achieves this effect by using metaphors parodically, slightly altering and skewing them as she repeats them to create a theatricalized endgame for the metaphors that fuel fascist ideology. This technique opposes, in Friedlander's terms, fascism's use of the language of "accumulation, repetition, redundancy," and "the circular language of invocation" to create a kind of hypnosis (21).

Moreover, Schenkar's central metaphors of emplotment are, I think, more pointed and effective than those of, say, James Schevill's (1975) *Cathedral of Ice*, another "circus of metaphor" piece that, like Schenkar's, is vengefully iconoclastic, and suggests, as hers does, the United States as a ground for fascist ideology and anti-Semitism. *Ice* is metaphorically emplotted in a "Dream Machine" that creates eerie comic and serious dream images relating to contemporary themes of power in the context of the history of the Third Reich. The Hitler/Narrator tries to control its images, but cannot. The dream machine, however, is a somewhat vague, ambiguous conceit; by contrast, Schenkar stages her piece within a giant brainlike 1940s radio. On stage, the huge radio console is framed by a radio proscenium; embedded in the radio are the two miked broadcasters who are contemporary and therefore self-consciously present "The Last of Hitler" radio show. The radio speaker hangs over the top of the stage like an immense, malignant mushroom and the giant radio tubes glow with fluorescent pink light as if organic and growing. From this radio emerge all sorts of broadcasts with fascist potential.

Thus Schenkar's central conceit locates her work among the specific, historical shifts in representation created by radio along with silent film at the beginning of the twentieth century (and the way these two, taken together, separated hearing from seeing for the first time, as Kaplan notes). Russell Berman's foreword to *Reproductions of Banality* describes "the radio

[as] . . . the field in which the fascist demagogue . . . appropriates the modern mass media as part of the resistance to modernity" (xxii). Kaplan further elaborates the historical function of radio:

> With the advent of radio and the transformation of all the political figures into disembodied "speakers," wooing the public on microphone, the 1930s became a veritable festival of oral gratification. Fascist regimes weren't the only ones that "used" voice . . . not . . . all disembodied political voices were fascist but . . . the machinery of the media gave birth to a new kind of ideological vulnerability. (23)

This machinery offered unprecedented possibilities for oral slogans and the cult of the recorded, amplified voice. Kaplan goes on to assert that

> what fascism transforms is not the means of production or distribution of wealth in the state, but the technical means by which the state reproduces its own legitimacy before individuals. When fascism took power, it took charge of the imaginary, using the most advanced sophisticated agents of representation available . . . new elements in the "design" of everyday life that few knew to take seriously as political forces. (34)

As a relatively new technology, the radio created enough awe and fascination to be seductive to its listeners. The newness of the sheer mass of listeners to whom it simultaneously communicated conferred a certain authority on radio as well.

Schenkar's use of radio evokes this historical moment of disembodied voice, intertwining it with the effects of radio on 1940s America. In doing so, the play theatricalizes the creation of subjectivity by newer media forms. Investigating radio's potential to become, in Schenkar's words, "a vast circulatory system transmitting poisons to infected cells" (159), she emphasizes the power of broadcasting, of the voice in the dark, to convey language undiluted by visual imagery penetrating our domestic spaces. Since we need not stop our everyday activities to hear it, what is heard insinuates itself into the very fabric of our lives. Throughout the play, characters who obsessively listen to radio repeat the phrase "I heard it on the radio" as a kind of validation of any popular sentiment they express—a direct transmission from the cultural brain to theirs. It is as if the voices on radio become a single, coherent, authoritative Voice: outside the Voice lurks the terrifying landscape of infectious difference, "the impure" of fascist ideology. *The Last of Hitler* puts spectators at risk because it historicizes the fascist potential in twentieth-century media technology and because it insists on breaking down the borders between twentieth-century American colloquial culture and fascist practice.

Schenkar's use of the paradox of staged radio theatre reveals something fundamental about the nature of the medium of radio that couldn't be exposed through this medium itself. Thus I want to raise a more general question given fascism's use of twentieth-century media innovations: how well can the much older form, drama, represent this use, or is it precisely this older form that can frame and interrogate the effects of mass culture and our complicity in responding to them? An even larger question that haunts this chapter: To what degree can theory, in this case theory about fascist ideology and practice, be theatricalized and performed? Certainly, plays themselves express ideological structures in their content and form, whether deliberately or not, and certainly scholars have traced expressions of theories in plays. But am I reversing the process by wanting dramatists self-consciously to dramatize theoretical ideas?

One play that does powerfully theatricalize theorizing about fascism is the "Auschwitz" play from the 1978 Barnes trilogy *Laughter!* When Kaplan explores one aspect of the polarity machine in fascism's abstract/literal dichotomy, she argues:

> Just as the regime art practiced by the established fascist state is cloyingly unimaginative, consolidated fascist ideology relies more and more on literal characterization and representations of its chosen negativity. Nazism partakes in the actual extermination of its projected negative fantasy in the concentration camps. [Moishe] Postone . . . argues that the work of the camps was to render the Jewish people—the threatening and the abstract—into a nonpeople, into abstracted shadows (skeletons) of humanity. Camp administration "proved" that Jews were "reducible" by ritually wresting from the masses of exterminated bodies all that remained on them of use-value, such as clothes, gold fillings, hair, and so on. (31)

This reductive literalizing and its horrific results are the repressed visual text of "Auschwitz." Barnes's drama is set in 1942, in an office where ordinary civil servants administer the concentration camps while denying the literal of what they do through the abstract, distancing languages of writing, numbering, and jesting. But at a critical point late in the play, the file cabinets crack open and slide away to reveal "a vast mound of filthy, wet straw dummies. . . . They spill forward to show all are painted light blue, have no faces, and numbers tattooed on their left arms. . . . Two monstrous figures appear . . . [and] hit the dummies with thick wood clubs." Each [uses] a "large iron hook, knife, pincers and a small sack" to tear at the corpses to recover gold teeth, false eyes, and jewelry from the corpses (64–65). Thus this scene is poised on that horrific moment of "reducibility" Kaplan describes. And the denial by the office workers of what they see, then, suggests not the evil banality of Arendt's imaginationless Eichmann, but the willed refusal to imagine material suffering at any cost in order to construct the facade of the everyday around evil. Instead of limiting the expression of fascism to political events, Barnes, with his "ordinary" office in "Auschwitz," dramatizes the fascist ideology implicit in the culture of the everyday, in the characters' relationship to a lived experience they perceive as expressing their private, apolitical selves. The dangerous history of this play marks the cumulative historical ability of the everyday to create the institutionalized, bureaucratic organization of incarceration and murder.

And "Auschwitz" is also dangerous in the way it delineates the changing sociohistorical context of fascist practice by theatricalizing how a more established, "civilized" fascist bourgeois culture feeds off an earlier, more visibly violent populist form, making it into a kind of covert, respectable industry. Many plays dramatize the beginning phases of fascism; some dramatize fascism in a kind of eternal present despite frequent historical references. But, as Kaplan notes, fascism's "history corresponds to a topological shift":

> After an initial, rallying period, during which a left-sounding movement appeals to a populist petty bourgeois, the movement's power is consolidated in formal bureaucracy; populist ties are severed or dissolved into party ties and economic power passes back into the hands of the traditional capitalist channels. . . . The populist ideal mutates toward an elitist one. (33)

Barnes locates his play at the historical moment of that "topological shift," depicting a centralized, bureaucratic state based on solid middle-class values. He historicizes this shift of power in the opposing presence of the character Gottleb, a vicious "old style" Nazi SS officer who evokes the earlier, dramatically violent, "gathering" stage of fascism and who, at the end of the play, is defeated by the bureaucrats. They close "Auschwitz" with a macabre singing of "This is a brotherhood of man" from the American musical *How to Succeed in Business Without Really Trying* (1961). The use of the American musical marks this play's partial removal from a strictly German, forties locale, and reminds us of Barnes's insistent critique of capitalism as well as fascism.

Barnes's vision in *Laughter!* was not reassuring to his audiences and was "unsafe" by comparison with some of his other works, such as *The Ruling Class* (which took aim at that class and not the middle class). In an interview with Mark Bly and Doug Wagner in 1981, Barnes described the response to *Laughter!*:

> When we did *Laughter!* at the Royal Court, I used to go into performances, and I felt waves of hate coming out of the audience. They actively loathed it. Actively. It came out like steam. The actors used to say: "God we could feel it up on the stage." The British want a theatre of reassurance, one of affirmation. They do not want a theatre of disturbance. (45)

Joan Schenkar, too, offers her audience a theatre of disturbance. When I spoke with her in 1992 about *The Last of Hitler*, she told me:

> I'm interested in no escape, in really imprisoning the audience in a way—yes, taking prisoners . . . and in a way forcing them to enter these nightmares. . . . So what I'm always trying to do . . . is make two things happen at once, which is to keep this humor going so people are laughing and underneath it keep this dreadful subtext going in which the thing at which people are laughing is too awful for words. . . . I mean in the best of all possible productions I've made you laugh at something dreadful, just dreadful.

I watched the play several times and there were always some people who fled the theatre. Both Schenkar and Barnes pose terrific challenges to their audiences by means of a disturbing and even savage comedy. Both, in their own ways, ask audiences to become implicated in fascist ideology and its operations, to be caught by surprise in something we might want to condemn but do not want to understand quite that well.

By contrast to these two plays, the 1984 semi-documentary German film *The Wannsee Conference* announces itself as more focused in its scope, more realistic, more historically accurate. Like Barnes's work, it focuses on the horror of the bureaucracy of death, but the film elaborates more on the agency of those who perpetrated it. It neither "familializes" fascism nor frames it within eroticized perversity, but instead portrays with chilling banality an eighty-five minute conference attended by third-tier Nazi civilian and military governors from throughout Europe and presided over by Reinhard Heydrich, head of the Nazi Security Police. In the comfortable Berlin suburb of Wannsee, on January 20, 1942, the "Jewish Question" has become purely a question of logistics—of implementing the "Final Solution" as efficiently as possible. The audience for the film is at risk because the film refuses to locate fascism in a demonized, charismatic, manipulating figure who hypnotizes his followers. Instead we are faced with banal, competitive, rather jovial bureaucrats, none of whom wants to be saddled with "all the work" of implementing genocide. One meaning of "banal" is "open to the use of the entire community," "a common, shared place." The shared, banal place at Wannsee (whether it is expressed by fear, rationalization, self-congratulation, officiousness or contempt) is the commitment to Jewish genocide. The journey to this shared place of genocide, then, becomes all the more dangerous and risky precisely because it represents a jockeying for power within and among various parts of the Nazi political machine, depicting a grotesque obsession covered over with the normalizing aspects of the bureaucratic everyday. The film exposes the obscene underside of collegiality when employed in the service of genocide. It is the lethal juxtaposition of Jewish genocide being negotiated and implemented in the everyday that makes the proceedings so chilling.

According to the film's producer, Manfred Korytowski, this documented meeting actually functions to obtain for the SS "the approval of the ministries so that everything would be legal and they would all be in it together. Nobody wanted to make the decision themselves. Heydrich wanted them all gathered together at this conference . . . making it legal and binding" (Ryan A13). The meeting not only consolidates the authority of the SS, it evacuates the legitimacy of non-Aryan human groups; in Lyotard's words, "being one of the race grants not only the right to command, but also the right to live" (*Differend* 101). Thus the audience faces an historical demonstration of the unlimited amount of state violence that can legally be put at a state's disposal. The deliberate, seemingly neutral precision of the film's documentary-style realism itself serves to underscore the horrific nature of the event. This documentary-style realism also tricks the viewer into assenting to the veracity of an imaginative recreation, however dependent the film was on transcripts of the actual meeting. One might suppose that such a tableau— mostly "talking heads" around a table—would be appropriate for theatre. But it is the circling of the camera amongst the faces, creating a narrative of complicity, that gives the work much of its power. My preference for *Wannsee* raises the question of whether I am trying to impose on drama a desire for a semi-documentary form that film can accomplish better. More pertinent for the discussion of Sherman's *Bent* that follows, what can theatrical realism accomplish?

Earlier in the century, Walter Benjamin, considering the relation of theatre to newer media, asserted that only commercial theatre's position is usurped by newer technological media. Such forms as epic theatre could use these media strategically both to learn from them (e.g., appropriate such techniques as montage) and to "enter into debate with them."[3] But despite Benjamin's (and my own) preference for works that use Brechtian techniques, there are conditions under which the traditional techniques of realistic identification may be useful. Responding to the powerful impact of the American TV series "Holocaust" for West German viewers, Andreas Huyssen states:

> In post-war German drama, the socio-psychological need for identification with the Jews as victims clashed to varying degrees with the dramaturgic and narrative strategies of avant-garde and/or documentary theater. The historic evolution of dramatic form and the canon of political educators emphasizing document, rational explanation, and social theory had bypassed the specific needs of spectators. (114)

He opens to debate the notion that a "cognitive rational understanding of German anti-Semitism under National Socialism is *per se* incompatible with an emotional melodramatic representation of history" (95). I think where an audience resists applying realism's normalizing concepts of what it means to be "human" to a particular "category" of humans, the form can assimilate a group that the audience resists acknowledging. But the group is inevitably assimilated from the point of view of its victimization and the suffering entailed by an intense desire to be "just like us" where "us" is hegemonic. The politics of identification, in such a case, involve a deliberate reinscribing of the dominant order on the marginal group.

Martin Sherman's 1979 play, *Bent*, which focuses on a particularly horrific historical moment in gay oppression, fits this rubric.[4] The play responds to two resistances from heterosexual audiences: one, that of their difficulty acknowledging the "humanness" (i.e., lack of difference from themselves) of male homosexuals; and two, that of their historical unwillingness to admit homosexuals to the canonical list of those who "count" as victims of Nazi genocide. To respond to the first resistance (i.e., to acknowledging "humanness"), *Bent* reveals "a culture that isn't just sexual," as John Clum puts it, and "affirms 'traditional family values' with only one minor difference: it validates homosexual love within the framework of heterosexual marriage" (178). I partly agree with Clum's assertions, since realism tends to emplot everything within parameters of the familial.[5] But perhaps he overstates his case by suggesting that Sherman's play "affirms 'traditional family values'" since *Bent* centers on a homosexual "couple," and not a "traditional" family. The play would fully adhere to the familial presuppositions of realism only if the homosexual men were celibate *and* not in a relationship with each other, or closeted *and* engaged in a heterosexual relationship, or dead. What is so novel about this realistic Holocaust play, then, is that the locus of loss is not the family and its reproduction, but rather the relationship that develops between two homosexual men amidst a horrific situation.

To respond to the second resistance (i.e., to admitting homosexuals to the canonical group of victims of the Holocaust), Sherman portrays both the excruciatingly cruel and murderous treatment of homosexuals by the Nazis and acts defying the Nazis by gay men. But to drive home its point, the play creates an unfortunate hierarchy of suffering among the various groups within the camp (Max connives for a Yellow Star so he will be treated better than he would be if wearing a Pink Triangle).[6] If the play itself represents a necessary foregrounding of oppression on the basis of sexuality in the Holocaust, it should not have to diminish the suffering of ethnic groups in order to achieve its aim. But this hierarchy cannot easily be jettisoned from the text since it serves as the grounds for the obligatory realist narrative of moral growth. Sherman effectively reconceives the usual realistic gesture of moral growth in *Bent* as commitment to another man and as "coming out." Yet in the context of the Holocaust, this "coming out" narrative with its presupposition of moral growth—signaled at the end of the play when Max takes off his jacket, with its Yellow Star, and puts on the dead Horst's jacket, with its Pink Triangle—has problematic consequences: it makes Jews stand in for heterosexuals in the narrative of "coming out."

The most dangerous history *Bent* creates for its resistant spectators occurs in the play's second half, which constructs homosexual love and its passionate expression in language as not only unrelated to fascist homosocial
practices but resistant *to* fascism. But in *Bent*'s earlier scenes, a problematic
effect arises from the play's many agendas (some, no doubt, resulting from
the dearth of plays on this subject). These scenes portray the central character, Max, as drunk, stoned, promiscuous, brawling, and attracted to homosexual fascists, one of whom he calls "my own little storm trooper." Although
this storm trooper is almost immediately victimized himself—being shot by
Nazis in Max's apartment—the portrayal still leaves room for an interpretation Eve Sedgwick identifies as:

> The dangerously homophobic folk-wisdom now endemic in both high- and
> middle-brow culture that . . . sees a sexualized "decadence" from whose im-
> age the supposedly answering image of fascism is seen as inseparable [thereby
> encouraging the hallucination, and here she cites Richard Plant 16] "that
> the incomprehensible Nazi crimes could be easily explained: the Nazis were
> simply homosexual perverts." (123)

Plant, in discussing this sexualization, takes us right back to Friedlander's
discourse by citing the 1969 German film *The Damned* (*Gotterdammerung*) as
one of the worst offenders. This identification of Nazis as homosexual per-
verts allows us to distance fascism from our (heterosexual) selves as well as
reinforce "this culture's distaste, not for fascism, but for homosexuality itself" (124). Separate from outright homophobia, this confusion of the homosexual with the violent homosocial is partly engendered by what Theweleit
refers to as fascist "filiarchy," in which fascists secure their patriarchal dominance as sons, not fathers.[7] But the text's twinning of two different homosexual historical moments, as part of the play's agenda for its gay audience,
may accidentally contribute to this impression. As John Clum notes:

> The Holocaust provides a background of brutal oppression. But the real
> issue of the play is self-oppression manifested in behavior that would be
> considered typical for an urban gay man in 1979. . . . The opening of
> *Bent* . . . is purposely ambiguous as to its time period [in order to comment
> on] . . . some of the more common elements of the gay world, circa 1979.
> Fashionable S & M is interpreted as cruelty, a result of one's own self-ha-
> tred; promiscuity is presented as an evasion of intimacy; sex is seen as a stage
> in the progress toward emotional intimacy. (175, 176, 178)

Thus, despite *Bent*'s painful detailing of the violence and terror to which
Max and other homosexuals were subject under the Third Reich, I wonder
whether the play actually provides spectators with what Sedgwick refers to

as an "availability across the society of values or language or worldviews that would explicitly allow these strong [sexual] charges [of homosexuality] to be respected, felt through, legitimated, and inhabited, not to say loved" (121). As Clum suggests, despite the theatrically electrifying "talking sex" scenes between Max and Horst, the "availability" to spectators is constructed on a desexualized liberal defense of individual rights in tandem with the appeal of the motif of doomed love, rather than on any challenge by specific sexual practice to the sex-gender system as presently constructed. Jill Dolan makes this point even more vigorously: *Bent* unwittingly reconfirms the dominant culture because "gay male sex must be expressed furtively, described but not performed, and must culminate in orgasms of affirming emotional love rather than physical transport" so that "sex is exiled to a nonphysical plane" ("Practicing" 268). Which is only to say, especially in light of the publication of Plant's *Pink Triangle*, that we need more plays about homosexuals, the Holocaust, and fascist ideology—a project that seems especially urgent given, for example, William F. Buckley's rumored demand for the tattooing of people with AIDS.[8]

I would like to see a play that put in relation to fascism and homosexuality Sedgwick's version of binding and splitting, which she describes as

> a very heightened foregrounding of same-sex bonding (especially male) to the individual and societal mind: heightened in its visibility, in its perceived problematicalness, and not least importantly in its investment with a charge specifically of "sexuality," [combines with extreme homophobia] . . . to produce the cognitive and ideological *apartheid* around homosexuality that will provide the undergirding of any new fascism. . . . Fascism is distinctive in this century not for the intensity of its homoerotic charge, but rather for the virulence of the homophobic prohibition by which that charge, once crystallized as an object of knowledge, is then denied *to* knowledge and hence most manipulably mobilized. (121)

If the polarity machine of fascist ideology underscores the *difference* of homosexuality from heterosexuality, fixates on it along with a violent homophobia, then realist works that create human identity through the erasure of difference would be the least likely to be able to dramatize these operations.

In terms of the polarities of fascist ideological practice noted at the beginning of this chapter, the realistic structure of Sherman's *Bent* may prevent it from theatricalizing the complexity of fascist ideology in relation to homophobia, but it certainly dramatizes the grotesque effects of the polarity machine as expressed in the splitting off of homosexuality in a murderous discourse of Otherness. Bernhard's *Eve of Retirement* risks reproducing the aestheticizing discourse of fascist ideology in order to expose the claustrophobic consanguinity of its binaries. Schenkar's *The Last of Hitler* "works over," mutates the polarities in order finally to disintegrate them, portraying one mass medium as it produces and transmits these polarities as well as underscoring the way fascist ideology is embedded in its modes of representation. Barnes's *Laughter!* succeeds in theatricalizing the way fascist ideology appropriates and mutates to appeal to different needs, constituencies, and emotions at different historical moments. His use of a group configuration (the work gang) within comedy allows him to avoid the individual protagonist configuration common to "serious drama" and so to theatricalize the drama of fascist ideology in relation to lived experience among a range of individuals. *The Last of Hitler* and *Laughter!*, one in its surreal comic form, the other in its Brechtian comedy, theatricalize and so frame the relation of the everyday to fascist ideology—a relation that realism, though ostensibly providing details of both history and everyday life, obscures, even when the effects of ideology is the play's apparent subject. Locating fascist ideology as they do allows Schenkar and Barnes to eschew the faulty proposition that representing fascism as the most horrifying and bizarre Gotterdammerung will in itself lead to an understanding of fascism, Nazism, or "the mind of Hitler" without these metaphors being yoked to the most banal compliances and back turnings, to everyday self-deceptions that serve an implied fascist ideology. Ideally, a theatricalization of fascist ideology must not only mark the fluidity of the fascist dichotomies and highlight their construction within representation, but it must also ask for what purpose and to what effect it does so.

3

FEMINISM AND THE JEWISH SUBJECT

Holocaust Theatre and the Politics of Difference and Identity

> They say at the ends of time
> birds with madmen and children
> will have the gift of prophecy
> but I myself don't see
> understanding them
> Listening does not
> make me say
> they awaken
> a light
>
> —Liliane Atlan, *The Carriage of Flames and Voices* (205)

In "A Manifesto for Cyborgs: Science, Technology, and Socialist Feminism in the 1980s," Donna Haraway includes the following critique of certain feminisms:

> Beyond either the difficulties or the contributions in the argument of any one author, neither Marxist nor radical feminist points of view have tended to embrace the status of a partial explanation; both were regularly constituted as totalities. Western explanation has demanded as much; how else could the "Western" author incorporate its others? Each tried to annex other forms of domination by expanding its basic categories through analogy, simple listing, or addition. Embarrassed silence about race among white radical and socialist feminists was one major, devastating political consequence. History and polyvocality disappear into political taxonomies that try to establish genealogies. There was no structural room for race (or for much else) in theory claiming to reveal the construction of the category woman and social group women as a unified or totalizable whole. (78)

Haraway's parenthetical "or for much else" could, I suggest, contain the situation of "Jewishness" and Jewish women in relation to these totalizing feminisms. In that case, when "taxonomies of feminism produce epistemologies to police deviation from official women's experience" (74), and, implicitly, from the feminist theory that grows out of it, Jewish women's experience and its relation to feminist theory would be among these deviations.

Haraway's powerful theorizing about exclusions within feminism has been one of several critical points of departure for current feminist theorists. In *Theory in Its Feminist Travels*, Katie King maps the varied terrains of feminism using the trope of "lacquered layering" (2):

> the layerings of instance, of political meanings constrained in particularity, lacquered over so finely that they are inseparable and mutually constructing while distinct. Superimposed (overlapping and nonoverlapping) histories specify age cohorts, cohorts from specific political movements, marked and unmarked racially constituted collectivities, the varieties of identities deployed and constructed within identity politics, people from shared historical moments, geographical unities, and those traveling between, or inhabiting several such groups. Over and over these cohorts specify themselves as "the feminists." Teasing out the threads that connect some and distinguish others is part of mapping out the geography through which "theory" travels. (2)

She goes on to note that "naming a *particular* cohort for each object is not always appropriate or possible within this analysis: it's the *investments* that matter the most to me" (6). These investments, inflected by context, history, commitments to other identity categories and so on, produce varieties of readings and positionings under the general rubric of feminism.

When I first began to think about writing this chapter on the plays of Nelly Sachs, Liliane Atlan, and Joan Schenkar, someone told me that what I should make visible in their work was the erasing of a gender discourse in representing the subject of the Holocaust. Although I am aware of the crucial work of feminist scholars and artists dedicated to placing the Holocaust experience of women in history, I was troubled by the idea that my purpose in writing about the pained attempts of these playwrights to reveal the landscape of the Holocaust—what Sidra DeKoven Ezrahi calls "the elusive and spiritually unedifying subject of large-scale physical suffering and submission to death" (33)—should be to focus on their lack, their flaw, their deviation from a standard notion of feminist theatrical treatments that foregrounds the analysis of sexism and gender. Speaking as both a feminist and a Jew, I refuse. Just as feminism resists being subsumed to a totalizing postmodernism, I want to resist subsuming the plays of Sachs, Atlan, and Schenkar on the Holocaust to a totalizing feminism that elides historical differences. How can I, for example, simply mark Nelly Sachs's passionate response to atrocity—her mystery play reconstruction in *Eli: A Mystery Play of the Sufferings of Israel* of a traditional Jewish community, including its conservative gender relations—as a way of "nostalgically naturalizing" a "virulent form of oppression"? In so doing I would be appropriating another perceptive analysis of Haraway's (91) without noticing that this context makes it trivial and perhaps a little obscene. My own distress here, when I can comfortably critique nostalgic resurgences of sex-gender asymmetries in Lillian Hellman's anti-fascist play *Watch on the Rhine* (in Chapter 4), outlines the tensions between my commitments as a feminist scholar and as a scholar of the Holocaust—tensions I have avoided previously by dealing with the two fields more or less separately.

In pursuing this argument I am not insisting on some kind of "special case" status for my work, nor am I justifying texts that erase women's experience in the Holocaust. I agree with historian Joan Ringelheim that "even a cursory look at studies about the Holocaust would indicate that the experience and perceptions of Jewish women have been obscured or absorbed into descriptions of men's lives" (741).[1] Nor am I ignoring the intersections of female or feminist and Jewish identities staged in these plays. Rather, I am asserting that the feminist critical strategies I have employed in other analyses must be seen through the prism of a Jewish critique in relation to this historical event of annihilation. Such a Jewish critique constitutes part of the cohort investment (to use King's terms here) of Jewish feminism. To exemplify the way investment produces differing readings, I briefly turn to three examples from three Holocaust plays by women. In each case I note a possible feminist analysis and then suggest how that reading might shift in response to a feminist Jewish subjectivity and the weight of Holocaust history in producing this site for speaking, reading, and writing.

Drawing on a biological notion of female identity for *Eli*, Sachs privileges the mother in her focus on the rebirth of an East European Jewish village. One dazed young woman with a child on her arm recounts how "in a hole in the earth I bore it, in a hole I suckled it—Death took its father, me he did not take, saw the milk in my breasts and did not take me." Although she "can't bear the light any more" but "mounds of earth [she sees] dancing," her symbolic importance to the regeneration of the Jewish community is marked at the end of this scene when Sachs blots out the bodies of the dancers in "the glare of the evening sun"; "Only the Young Woman with her child stands out clearly in the light" (19–20). This biological emphasis on rebirth culminates in the transcendental text at the end of the play: appearing in divine circles above the head of the dying murderer of the child Eli is "the Embryo in its mother's womb, with the primal light [of God] on its brow" (50). In response to this reduction of women to their biological and traditional roles, I must still consider that the mass murder of the Jewish population is the ground for Sachs's construction and resonates passionately in each of these images in the play.

A gendered analysis of Liliane Atlan's *Mister Fugue or Earth Sick* (French 1967; English 1987) would focus on the girl child Raissa's central role in creating a resistant discourse in response to the journey of four children toward Rotburg, and death. The following passage foregrounds Raissa's metaphoric imagination, her insistence on infusing her fantasy with the material conditions that torment the four, and her refusal to construct herself submissively even in relation to the other (male) children:

> *Raissa:* Look there's a big city with trains and lots of lights. Lots of noise. Iona, you're the train. Mister Fugue [a soldier named Grol caught trying to hide them and sentenced to death, whom the children name Mister Fugue] you'll be the garbage can. Abracha, you're the sea, make sea sounds. . . . Tamar, you're the cat, go meow. Got it? Good. I need a rope. Well all right, Yossele, be the rope. Okay, so the cat and me, we're digging through the garbage, picking out things we can eat. I'm the owl, the bat, the hyena and god in heaven, it's all the same, I'm digging through the garbage. . . . You're not smart, Yossele. Just a frayed rope. I'll put a match to it. That way, human beings, you won't be able to call [god] by tugging on it. And if you do tug on it, you'll burn. . . .
> *Yossele:* What if you played becoming a little girl, a pretty little girl, Raissa, good and gentle.
> *Raissa*: I spit on pretty little girls. I prowl around, I dig through garbage cans. I hear trains passing, I'd like to catch them. I hop one. The train wants no part of me. No use crying, this train's going to Rotburg. The whole earth is Rotburg. (75–76)

Raissa's "blacker than night" awareness makes Mister Fugue lose what he calls his stupidity as she initiates him into the horrors of this desolate Holocaust landscape. The Nazi Christopher's sadistic obsession with these children focuses especially on Raissa, who sings while being beaten and who refuses to bury Iona alive. Her resistance so enrages Christopher that he shoots Iona and thus gives him a quick death. For Christopher, Raissa is "that Bitch" he identifies as leading their resistance "from the inside." Even when another child, Abracha, calls her "a bad woman" for not complying with the children's vision of future life, she responds by asserting her authority over their narrative: "The real article, you idiot, the real article. I'm the only one who's held up. Me, I saw the black and didn't build walls of fakery or music to hide it, and I still haven't fallen, and I can damn well betray you all at once if I want to, because that's how it is, I allow it" (100). Out of this material I can build a narrative of Raissa's struggle against the verbal and physical incursions that all the males in the play make against her as a female. But in doing so I am aware of foregrounding what, in the overall sense of the play, is backgrounded by Atlan. She sees the children as the last Jews of a ghetto engaged in a group strategy for endurance of terror and pain. The play eulogizes them and their culture, albeit in a fragmented or painfully satiric way.

Joan Schenkar's play does incorporate elements of a gender critique. In *The Last of Hitler* (1982), Schenkar links fascism to the dangerous, overweening imagination allowed to men under patriarchy and the destruction wrought by it. Dr. Reich, the male doctor figure in this play—a figure Schenkar associates with patriarchy in works such as *Signs of Life* (1980)—tries to locate the emotional plague of anti-Semitism through logic and scientific discourse; in doing so he cannot apprehend either its sources or his own fascistic qualities. Those victimized by Reich's fascistic medical regimentation, the unseen but often-mentioned Dionne quintuplets, are females required to perform their victimization over radio and in public until they perish. Another female performer is victimized on "The Mary Lee Taylor Cooking Show." While demonstrating how to cook a kosher chicken, Mary Lee gets cooked in her own oven and eaten by the more violently anti-Semitic John Cole. This suggests in a grotesquely comic way how women as "sympathizers" with other cultures become "chicken," i.e., oven food, along with the Jews. Although sexism is depicted in *The Last of Hitler*, it is not foregrounded as it is in Schenkar's earlier play *Signs of Life*. *The Last of Hitler*'s gender critique is embedded in the staging of the anti-Semitic discourse of the Other—its infiltration into mass culture and the complicitous response of its listeners—so it operates more marginally in the text.

These examples illustrate that a gender analysis succeeds, in Haraway's terms, only to the extent to which it offers itself as a partial explanation. More generally, an analysis interweaving feminism and "Jewishness" is positioned within two sets of identity politics that resist two constructions of dominant discourse—the discourses of sexism and anti-Semitism. Feminist theory began to specify the difference of Jewish women positioned in this way in the late 1980s. For example, in an effort to interweave the subject positions of feminism and "Jewishness," Julie Greenberg asserts:

> There is a growing body of feminist Jews who care deeply and mutually about being both Jews and women. We are not willing to compromise on either identity and are equally committed to fighting anti-Semitism among feminists and sexism among Jews. . . . [T]here is not a Jewish self separate from a female self. Being a Jewish woman . . . is a totality and all experience is filtered through that integrated reality. (180)

In response to the difficulty of this project, Greenberg unfortunately employs the same totalizing notion of identity for "being a Jewish woman" that I critiqued through Haraway, thereby canceling out the tension between the two identities she merges. Judith Plaskow's solution to this conundrum configures a similarly essentialist identity: "The situation of the Jewish woman might well be compared to the situation of the Jew in non-Jewish culture. The Gentile projection of the Jew as Other—the stranger, the demon, the human not-quite-human—is repeated in . . . the Jewish understanding of the Jewish woman" ("The Right Question" 226). While I appreciate Plaskow's effort to work out this relationship, her formulation of "the Jewish Woman" equates two discourses on Otherness too simply. Moreover, the Holocaust is not about Otherness within Judaism but about the Jew as Other: Jews were killed as Jews though they were victimized as women in the process and their deaths were often accelerated by their gender.

Here I do not mean to refute the many provocative assertions of Jewish women's marginalization within Judaism found in such anthologies as *The Tribe of Dina: A Jewish Women's Anthology* (ed. Kaye/Kantrowitz) or *On Being A Jewish Feminist* (ed. Heschel). These two books laid the groundwork for tracing the particular investments of Jewish feminism. Indeed, the work of these scholars themselves has evolved, become more precise, over time. For example, in 1992, Plaskow wrote in *Tikkun*:

> Jewish feminism not only offers a wide-ranging critique of the subordination of women in Jewish religious and institutional life, it also offers a vision of a Jewish community organized to enable the participation of all its members, a Jewish history made whole, a revitalization of Jewish God-language, a broader definition of the Jewish family, and a new sexual ethic. It invites Jewish men to a reconsideration of their own Jewish humanity, its contours and its meaning. ("Jewish Feminism" 76)

Plaskow is now working through the consequences for "Jewishness" of this developing Jewish feminism. But my studies of the treatment of the Holocaust still convince me that Jewish feminist attempts directed at critique and re-vision need to take the Holocaust into account in their theorizing or risk being erased by the magnitude of this event. Or, at least, given my engagement with the Holocaust, I need to do so.

The problem, then, is to locate "Jewishness" for women in regard both to the Holocaust and to the possibility of a collective identity that relates to that history. Cynthia Ozick asserts that "The point is not that Jewish women want equality as women with men, but as *Jews with Jews*" (136). Even if I disagree with her politics and believe many Jewish women want both and more, I have to note what she goes on to say:

> The point is the necessity—*having lost so much and so many*—to share Jewish history to the hilt. This lamentation—*having lost so much and so many*—produces not an analogy or a metaphor, but a lesson. . . . The nature of the excision [unnoticed by the vigilant Jewish mentality developed in the aftermath of group loss] is this: a great body of Jewish ethical thinkers, poets, juridical consciences—not merely one generation but many; in short, an entire intellectual and cultural organism—has been deported out of the community of Jewish culture, away from the creative center. . . . And this isolation, this confinement, this shunting off, is one of the cruelest events in Jewish history. (136–37)

Basing her analysis on the events of the Holocaust as they affected Jews,
Ozick tries to create a feminist Jewish politics of loss and collectivity. Yet,
despite her understanding of the loss, there is no agreement on what is "the
center of Jewish culture." At the same time, she risks essentializing "Jewishness" at the cost of nearly erasing gender difference. Finally, Ozick's formulation does not question the hierarchical aspects of insisting on an equality
based on the most elite areas of a culture rather than on the damaging effect
of sexism on the lives of ordinary Jewish women.

Thus while Ozick begins to suggest that grieving and critique are not
mutually exclusive, she does not go far enough. Located, as it is, within the
boundary of Jewish relations among Jews, her formulation would leave no
room for the kind of outwardly focused progressive Jewish feminist politics
Melanie Kaye/Kantrowitz identifies when she notes that "some of the most
hopeful developments in Black-Jewish relations have been among feminists"
("Class" 100). Nor would there be room for the kind of activities that challenge the conservative Jewish establishment from the margins such as the
efforts of Jewish feminists, both American and Israeli, to organize to end the
occupation of the West Bank (See "Special Section: Jewish Feminists Organize to End the Occupation"). Kaye/Kantrowitz's question "Given [the] lack
of agreement about even such basics as the nature of Jewish experience and
identity, the parameters of anti-Semitism, how are Jews supposed to work
politically *as Jews*?" ("To Be a Radical Jew" 275) begins to suggest a Jewish
feminist politics of differences within Judaism that rests more on specificity
and material history than on essentialism.

But how does Holocaust history figure into this question? Is there something about the Holocaust as a historical event that makes it necessary for
progressive scholars, more than their counterparts in the past, to take their
Jewishness into account? In recognizing the need for Jewish feminists to
take the events of the Holocaust into account, some feminist critics have
suggested that we have deployed Holocaust history as an a priori narrative
of victimization that operates as a founding claim of identity. The stiffest
challenge to the intersection of Holocaust history and identity politics comes
from Jenny Bourne:

> The holocaust haunts the feminist Jewish psyche like a spectre that cannot
> be laid to rest. Jews are permanently under a sentence of death and must,
> therefore, judge their actions in that light. Attempts at our genocide are
> inevitable. History repeats itself not as farce (as Marx would have it), but as
> prophecy. We live in an imagined world of our impending destruction and
> strike out lest we be struck. (16)

Somewhat contemptuously, Bourne constructs "a feminist Jewish psyche"
that responds to the events of the Holocaust by configuring a repeating,

cyclical threat of Jewish genocide existing outside time. By projecting our knowledge of past suffering into an abstract, ahistorical moment, we sink into a kind of psychic self-absorption. Bourne goes on to assert that identity politics inflected through Holocaust history have allowed Jewish feminists to "escape" from "material realities" and contemporary political crises:

> We [Jewish feminists] refused, that is, to take a stand on the crucial and painful contradictions posed by the material realities of the Middle East, and opted instead to internalise those contradictions into a crisis of Jewish feminism, to be resolved on the basis of our complex identities. Politics required us to take a stand on the issue, metaphysics allowed us to escape it—but feminism allowed us to conflate the political and the personal, the objective and the subjective, the material and the metaphysical, and escape into Identity Politics. (4)

Certainly Bourne's rigorous critique of identity politics, here in relation to Jewish feminism and Holocaust history, operates as a strong caution about how not to intersect the two. But Bourne herself cannot imagine "how Jews can work politically *as Jews*," nor that there can be a political commitment born out of a feminist Jewish subjectivity, nor that the history of the Holocaust could be used by Jewish feminists to make political connections to the suffering of other groups. Or, as Diana Fuss states in her critique of Bourne, Bourne does not herself "historicize or contextualize notions of 'identity,' 'politics,' and 'identity politics'" enough to explore "under what historical conditions and for what specific groups might an adherence to identity politics *not* signify a 'stunted' or 'self-righteous' politics" (127).

Part of the legacy of oppression, in particular the genocide of a group, is precisely that the injury and injustice inflicted will haunt and define the present. That is why the inclusion of a monologue on the Holocaust and a monologue on slavery are critical for Anna Deavere Smith's performance piece *Fires in the Mirror* (1993). When two groups whose identity is anchored in a history of suffering collide, as they do in Smith's depiction of African Americans and Hasidic Jewish Americans in *Fires in the Mirror*, the collision is excruciatingly painful and violent. It is precisely because of the power of these narratives of suffering that, however useful Bourne's reminder of the crucial effects of material inequity or the dangers of identity politics, her critique is too dismissive and simple. Moreover, it is worth noting Fuss's point that "[t]o insist that essentialism is always and everywhere reactionary is, for the constructionist, to buy into essentialism in the very act of making the charge; *it is to act as if essentialism has an essence*" (21). Instead of regarding the category of essence as "immediately apparent and naturally transparent," Fuss wants to make room for an analysis that asks "*who* is utilizing it, *how* [is] it deployed, and *where* [are its] effects concentrated" (20–21).

Cultural critic Alisa Solomon, who is engaged precisely in theorizing a more varied terrain for Jewish feminism, exemplifies a working through of Fuss's questions (and, by implication, comments on Bourne's critique of whether Jewish feminism can respond to contemporary struggles). In "Building a Movement: Jewish Feminists Speak Out on Israel" (1990), Solomon demonstrates historical specificity and makes Jewish feminism less a category than, as Judith Butler suggested for feminism in general, a coalition defined by "politically engaged actions" and the diversity within it. Solomon speaks from both a feminist and a Jewish historical consciousness in order to critique certain Jewish as well as Israeli (and also Arab) policies and practices. She takes the risk of a tactical essentialism, while marking political differences within a conception of Jewish feminism:

> Since the early 1970s, alienated and assimilated Jewish women have been joining with sisters more rooted in their Jewishness, to strengthen Jewish identity in all its diversity—as religious, secular, Ashkenazi, Sephardic or lesbian Jews—and from this position of strength, have been forging the foundations of a movement that can promote a just peace between Israel and Palestine. . . . Of course, not all Jewish feminists have been swept into this particular expression of grassroots activism—indeed most have not. Esther Altshul Helfgott (Seattle), a historian of Jewish feminism, speaks for many Jewish women when she says, "I do want to see an Israel where Arabs and Jews are one with each other, and I believe peace is a feminist issue. I respect what the women's peace groups are doing, but it's not my vehicle politically, right now." (43)

In this example, differences within the Jewish feminist movement, while not covered over, are articulated to each other in such a way as to promote joint political activities. Yet as Solomon goes on to note, this deployment of a tactical essentialism is not without its critiques:

> Jewish feminists who oppose the occupation while defending the right of Israel to exist within secure borders—the common position of the women's peace groups around the country—have gotten flak from all sides—from the "official" Jewish establishment that considers any criticism of Israel traitorous (in Minneapolis, one synagogue actually called the police on a vigil of three women); at all times, from other feminists and progressives who will not countenance any defense of what they call the "Zionist imperialist oppressor"; and from those Jewish feminists who just don't want to hear criticism of Israel or discuss the issue at all. Jewish feminist peace activists have had to fight this destructive either/or formulation on all three fronts. (45)

Here Solomon clarifies the vulnerability of people who are actively negotiating among a variety of political positions. While she directs us to track investments in relation to political commitments, she doesn't actually refer to the Holocaust. Which is only to say we need to keep working on this issue. I do not presume I can offer a formulation that encompasses the questions I am raising, but I am trying to outline some of the difficulties in answering them and suggest what such a project, this excursion into Haraway's parenthetical "much else," might be. One way of doing this is to look at the politics of Otherness as they apply to Jews in order to clarify why Jewish feminists have insisted on including their Jewishness as part of the construction of their feminism, why the Holocaust continues to "haunt" us in a personal way, and why the playwrights I will discuss foreground "Jewishness" over feminism in their Holocaust plays.

Even Haraway's statement that "gender, race, or class consciousness is an achievement forced on us by the terrible historical experience of the contradictory social realities of patriarchy, colonialism, and capitalism" (72) reminds me that the category "Jewishness" is not perfectly analogous to the other three. On the one hand, it *is* a category created by oppression in which a grotesque, anti-Semitic totalizing construction (of "Jewishness") creates an awareness forced upon Jews by (terrible) historical experience, in opposition to the actual diversity of people within this category. Yet the three categories Haraway mentions are abstract constructions that aid in understanding how oppression works systematically; they don't correspond to specific peoples. On the other hand, Jews not only theorize Otherness under the terms of their oppression, they also theorize "Jewishness" based on a specific history and a range of ethnic, cultural, and religious practices no matter how contested these are *within* Judaism. This kind of theorizing is not defined in terms of Otherness but in terms of its own multifaceted particularity. Such a self-conscious communal history and web of traditions does not have to be conceived monolithically in order to be asserted; nor is it defined by simply inverting the terms of the opposition of Otherness, reversing its valuations while staying within its binaries.

What is central (and different) is the threat of an alternate culture (not a subculture that can be appropriated over time by the dominant culture)—a historical collectivity resistant to the imposition of dominant discourse. It was this collectivity, this cultural body, translated by the Nazis into an implacable, biologically determined, and finally lethal difference, that was specifically being annihilated in the Holocaust. This paranoid rejection of difference is the very basis upon which Nazi ideology is constructed. Moreover, the irrationality of Nazi claims is inflected by the very fact that Jews are not visible ethnics, not a separate race, but can, so to speak, "pass"; Nazism translates these accommodations by Jews to earlier though continuing religious and cultural anti-Semitism into further proof of their dangerousness and so into further justification for death.

The Holocaust in this sense represents a definitional struggle where a subjectivity constructed within a different, already extant discourse is conceived as so threatening that not only must its discourse be annihilated and abused but so must all who produce it. Thus the huge radio speakers of Schenkar's play cancel out the individual Jewish speakers. For Christopher, the Nazi of Atlan's play, even four Jewish children's voices threaten the stability of fascism. And Sachs culminates her play with the words of the Voice, inscribed with a capital "V," to counter the destruction with divine authorization. The works of Sachs, Atlan, and Schenkar all locate themselves at the terminus of this murderous discourse of Otherness, privileging the loss of that Jewish collectivity in the Holocaust as well as the threat to it in contemporary anti-Semitism. Sachs responds to loss by reconstructing a Jewish discourse in simultaneous communal and religious narratives. Atlan theatricalizes the construction in language of that collective Jewish subjectivity in response to a fascist discourse and a material landscape that objectifies and bestializes. Schenkar focuses on fascist discourse in order to exhaust its obsessions through repetition, vulgarizing and domesticating it in order to remove its power as a mesmerizing demonology against which the listener is powerless.

While these playwrights foreground this loss of Jewish collectivity, none of the three chooses to do so within a documentary form. They do not assume the position of a memorializer faced with the imperative of transmission and its facticity, nor that of an investigative reporter. Nor do they become historians of these events, committed to a minimum of literary (in this case theatrical) intervention.[2] One way to account for this choice is to historicize the position of each playwright in relation to the Holocaust, as well as to the time in which each play was written.

None of the three is a survivor in the strict sense of the word. Sachs, originally "an assimilated young woman living in Berlin and writing neoromantic poetry," refound Judaism in response to the slaughter, and was forced to flee from Nazi Germany to Sweden in 1940 (Ezrahi 138). Thus when she wrote *Eli: A Mystery Play of the Sufferings of Israel* in 1943, she had only partial knowledge of the horrific extent of the destruction of European Jewry. In an impassioned response to what she did know, she dramatically recreates a community to return to and a village to rebuild when there actually would be fewer survivors to return and often nothing in Europe but wasteland awaiting them. She constructs her characters on a shifting ground midway between speaking spirits of the dead and rebuilding survivors. Many of their lamentation monologues focus on what happened in the Polish village before or as people were being taken away. Thus the play seizes this history as it was at its moment of disappearance. The time of the play's conception is also marked by Sachs's ability still to represent the murder of one child, Eli, as a symbolic event requiring holy retribution. By contrast her later poetry focuses on the deaths of children in the plural[3]—deaths too inconceivable in scope to be contained within a symbolic narrative. For *Eli*,

Sachs chose a kind of ritual, invocative poetic theatre where, as Elinor Fuchs points out, "the very rhythms of her verse summon up the Hasidic world, full of motion and music" (Fuchs xiii).

As children, Liliane Atlan and her sister Rachael were hidden during World War II away from their family (many of whom they knew had been deported) in a house in Lyon, France. Confined there, Atlan discovered an abandoned bathroom in the garden with a terrace and a window and there enacted theatre. Rachael was the audience and, in Atlan's words in an interview with Bettina Knapp, "I was the stage: the actors, the author. . . . Everything lived within me: I screamed, gesticulated, died. I would speak out my lamentations, my dirges, my psalms" (200). As she told Kathleen Betsko and Rachel Koenig in another interview, "The plays were always the same. There were many characters and they all died, one by one" (25). Her own experience of creating theatre pieces in an enclosed universe evokes her treatment, in the 1967 *Mister Fugue or Earth Sick*, of four children who stage theatre rituals in order to endure their ride in a huge wire cage at the back of a truck taking them from the ruins of a ghetto to be killed at Rotburg, the Valley of Bones. The techniques Atlan uses to portray the children's taking charge of their own chaotic, fragmented group narrative—a narrative they physically act out as they speak it—resemble the techniques of transformational theatre. Here Atlan uses these techniques as strategies of the characters rather than simply her own stage devices. According to the stage directions, "The children do not describe, *they see*, they live what they see. They do not search, *they find*, instantly," (56) and the loose narrative, shifting from one child to another proceeds faster and faster the closer time presses. Atlan's description of her characters as "no longer real children" places them and their excruciating experience, depicted in the text without a shred of sentimentality, outside the limits of conventional representations of childhood. That they are played by adult actors visually underscores the shifting space of their own self-identifications, especially as, out of an ironic, blasphemous agony, they create and live out futures based on shards of the past. By using adults to play children, Atlan also marks the loss of those children: there will be no children to play those parts.

Schenkar, the youngest of the three playwrights, is positioned by the American distance Ezrahi identifies as marking a separation from direct knowledge of East European Jewish communities and from a grounding in the specifics of the horror, "anonymity and routine of mechanized mass death" (182). Writing *The Last of Hitler* in the eighties, Schenkar uses a kind of skewed historicizing technique, looking at the present through the prism of a reinvented past, and incriminating both past and present in the process. Breaking a certain "Gentleman's Agreement," she places 1940s fascism in intimate relation to 1940s America without ever abandoning the particularity of American references and discourse, especially as expressed in radio mass culture. Turning references to the ovens, soap, and showers of the concentration camps into obscene innuendo, the playwright marks a kind of pornographic fascination with the paraphernalia of death from the American distance that obscures both its material reality and those subjected to it. In *The Last of Hitler*, the horror of the Final Solution is wedded to the horror that there is no "last of Hitler," no end to the plague of destructive Othering and thus no final solution to eradicate fascism. The challenge that this play directs to the audience, then, is to imagine its own voice in the dark, its own mental radio show, its own latent narrative of prejudice.

All three playwrights, then, have no direct knowledge of the Holocaust. They foreground the question of knowledge in their plays rather than offer Knowledge of the Holocaust. Eschewing realism, they do not present a story of the Holocaust as if they were recapturing it or offering "the truth." Instead they underline in the forms of their work their own partial ability to represent it. Sachs, Atlan, and Schenkar reject realism's inscription of the subject as complete, coherent, and rational. There is for all three writers no disruption in the landscape of the Holocaust that is containable within the borders of realism and, in terms of form, no social order to which to return. There is no secret to be disclosed or exorcised or exiled, no enigma resolvable by logic and linear narrative. Yet they do not substitute a purely formalist analysis that celebrates a postmodern, decentered and dispersed subjectivity unattached to the circumstances of its construction, the material conditions that necessitate this kind of representation. Instead, all three write what could be called mystery plays, each presenting an enigma without a solution.

Yet, even their mysteries are marked by history. Sachs's narrative of divine revelation is, as her postscript to *Eli* describes it, "designed to raise the unutterable to a transcendental level, so as to make it bearable" (52). This transformation is achieved when the divinity shining through Michael, a shoemaker character described as "one of the thirty six Servants of God who, unaware of it themselves carry the invisible universe," makes the murderer of the child Eli crumble into dust. But even the transcendent, divine text is affected by history since "The new Pentateuch, I tell you, the new Pentateuch is written in mildew, the mildew of fear on the walls of the death cellars" (29). The mystery of representation in *Eli* is located in the theological inscription of unspeakable material events onto the invisible, transcendent world.

For Atlan, within the unimaginable universe of desolation, nature—birds, cliffs, the sea—constitutes an enigmatic and fragile space that Mister Fugue tries to create metaphorically with the children. But the children fracture a transcendent text based on nature, as when Yossele says "Now God, he went crazy, he knocked around in the sea like a fish, in the air like a bird, nothing but barbed wire, he doesn't dare anymore to sit or stand, he steals passes, but he doesn't leave" (66). Thus they appropriate Fugue's imagery to project their own history onto both the natural and the divine. The divine text Sachs conflates in the Voice and the Embryo has been ruptured permanently in Atlan's work; only children and madmen are left to prophesize but remain inscrutable or unheard. An enigma of representation circulates through the play: What or who are children whose material experiences render them unrepresentable as children? This enigma deconstructs the ideology of the "real" child, with its patriarchal genealogy, even as the play mourns the severed connections of the last four inhabitants of this particular ghetto. In fact, in all three works, children become a site of the problem of representation. One of the major nonrealistic devices of these plays is the way they mediate between the histories of these children and their theatrical representation. In Sachs one child is holy, dead, symbolic; another, daughter of the murderer of Eli, symbolically sinks into death after hearing Michael play Eli's pipe. In Atlan, in addition to the children enacted by adult actors, there is the mythically childlike Grol/Mister Fugue and the deathdoll, Tamar, who, animated by the voices of the children to express their pain indirectly, stands in for a dead four-year-old girl. In Schenkar, there is the speaking six-year-old skeleton Edmond and the often-mentioned but never seen or heard Dionne Quintuplets. Thus, children become a site of the impossibility of representation, as underscored by these metaphoric, partial representations.

Schenkar, too, presents an enigma of representation in her play. Her physicalization in disease—the "emotional plague" of anti-Semitism the characters "catch"—counters the pathology of cancer that Nazism attached to Jews. The discourse of fascism and anti-Semitism litters the stage with distorted and grotesque versions of "Jewishness." The characters' heightened version of patronizing or joking anti-Semitic remarks or their endless, formulaic conversations about what is caused or run by Jews leads to "catching 'Jewishness'": during the course of the play, the characters transform into their burlesqued, vulgar stereotypes. There are no actual Jews on stage; Schenkar refuses to create an invented persona for this engineered absence at the heart of the play. All the Jews in the play are "suppositious," leaving only a gap, an emptiness at the center of the play that combines the historical reality of annihilation with the absence in representation created by the discourse of the Jew as Other. The characters' occasional, incomplete lament "I will never understand" marks the way even the determination of "what" or "who" is erased by this discourse.

In reaching for this enigma, Sachs, Atlan and Schenkar attempt to put the site of the Othered into play, to inscribe the site of erasure when, in the words of Atlan's children, "Nothing lasts save erosion, this is the code" (102). The impossibility of a certain kind of visibility as, in the Atlan epigraph quoted earlier, "I myself don't see," becomes the lament of these plays. And the partial understanding they have and offer—formally never promising to "awaken a light" but, at most, in Sachs's words, to "make the unutterable bearable"—becomes the politics of their work. Sachs and Atlan counter the erasure of the Jewish subject via a cultural imagining of sociality that serves as a ground for its reconstruction. If the events of the Holocaust are in part about wiping out Jewish subjectivity, then an imagined sociality constructed in language functions as vestigial evidence of a continual subjectivity under grave threat of extermination. In opposition to the social that has been annihilated in material terms, they depict the creation of imagined socialities of "Jewishness" in resistance to a fascist discourse that erases and defiles. There is no linearity in this process; the texts and the characters slide backwards and forwards in time to recover a past that doesn't exist for a nonexistent future in a present that is an unspeakable absence.

Sachs renders sociality chorally through generic characters whose individual narratives make up a mosaic. The need for the divine text marks how threatened the sociality is; thus Sachs inscribes the provisional nature of what she does by using myth, insisting on a kind of eternal possibility of beginning. The bodies on stage create a sociality in themselves, but also outline the distance between those bodies and what has been lost historically. Sociality is also under excavation, marked in the text by characters piecing together fragments from the everyday life of a vanished world, pulled from the ground. This archaeological undertaking, combined with the images of the baby born in a hole and the old man rescued from a mass grave, amount to an unearthing, deliberately reversing one directional signal of death to create this new sociality in defiance of history.

Atlan's child characters, injured and ill, construct themselves in language in a situation where the material is out of their control, including their very lives. Near the end of the play, Iona, digging his own grave and beaten with a stick by Christopher, still intones "They were dying, the mountains, they were spitting blood, they fell like old people and still, Lord of the Worlds, they danced, and us too, we're dancing, for Yossele and Raissa, you see, are getting married. . . ." From the truck Raissa responds "In the commandos' faces, alleluia," and the others repeat "Alleluia" as they dance wildly (93). In this scene, Atlan suggests that sociality is a collective, cultural construction in history, not just a static tradition, and is marked by its relation to the context in which it is being constructed. Thus instead of mourning the loss of a coherent, unified Jewish identity, Atlan reveals the very fragility of that provisional construction and the tenacity that the children nonetheless bring to this enterprise, making the weight of what has been done by the Nazis that much worse.

Both Atlan and Schenkar place their notion of a Jewish sociality in history by emphasizing either the material terms in which it is created or, for Schenkar, the particularity of the contexts that threaten it. In a contradiction of representation, Schenkar visually stages the means by which the 1940s radio show of anti-Semitism constructs its listeners. She explores the invasiveness of a simulated mass culture sociality that achieves its collectivity through bigotry and exclusion. The text shows how the false, negating sociality of anti-Semitism is always under construction, has to be obsessively reiterated, thereby emphasizing not its fragility but its tenacious ability to seep into the structure of everyday life by capturing its rhetoric. As transmitters of information and entertainment, forms of mass culture spread (as in the transmission over the radio airwaves of the pathology of fascism), shape (as in the certification of normality bestowed by stereotypes on those not contained in them) and contribute to (as in the dummy's obscene innuendoes) a discourse that appropriates Jewish sociality as a means of erasing it. At the end of the play, the figure of the Hasid, transformed into a devil figure as he was by Nazism, pulls the giant plug (which becomes a pitchfork) out of the radio, which becomes a crematorium. It is as if the grotesque formulations of the Other have become animated so as to annihilate the discourse that constructed them. The audience is left with the responsibility for imagining that absent sociality erased by fascism and its discourse of Otherness.

Having stated earlier that Jewish feminist critique and re-vision need to take the Holocaust into account, I'd like to conclude by exploring the importance of a gender discourse in representing the Holocaust and the necessity for Holocaust scholars to use feminist strategies in identifying and analyzing their texts. To begin with, if the works of Sachs, Atlan, and Schenkar privilege the loss of a Jewish collectivity over specific gender concerns, it is also the case that feminist theory is a crucial frame for understanding works that gender this collectivity.

The inadequacy of the prevalent analysis of Holocaust work because of the absence of this frame is exemplified by what happens when Ezrahi, in an otherwise perceptive and eloquent book, groups a series of texts that concentrate on the experiences of women in the Holocaust. When she discusses what has been referred to as "survival literature," she notes that "Most of these novels have been written by women" (67) but cannot theorize why. She can identify works such as Ilona Karmel's *An Estate of Memory* or Zdena Berger's *Tell Me Another Morning* as a "significant trend" (68), but without a feminist analysis, she has trouble identifying exactly what that trend represents. Even though she is responsible for pioneering the inclusion of work by women in the Holocaust canon, since no discourse linking feminist critique to the Holocaust is available to her, she must resort to male thinkers on atrocity and the Holocaust to frame her inquiry. These male thinkers foreground the "struggle to maintain integrity of self" and the resistance to "the debasement and disintegration of the individual" (72)—both gender-neutral concepts. Her analysis consequently subsumes the focus in these novels on bonding among women under the topic of individual survival strategies. The tension between this frame, which rests on an idea of "universal human responses to concentrationary oppression" (72), and her topic becomes evident when Ezrahi suddenly switches her generic pronoun from he to she (77), while still negating the particularities of gender in the "mutually sustaining groups" (79) she describes.

One of the recent projects of feminist historians of the Holocaust is to investigate gendered strategies of maintenance among women, especially cooperation and the creation of "families" of support. As I'll presently show, this project turns out to be complex and difficult. Moreover, there is, as yet, no Holocaust play I know of that focuses on the experience of Jewish women and how they configured themselves in response to oppression. Leeny Sack's *The Survivor and the Translator* does portray the atrocities visited upon Jewish women in the camps by Nazis, most particularly by SS women:

> So how looked a day. First of all not everyone could take it. So they fell. You came into the barracks so lay already lifeless women. Not because they were sick or something. Just. They were hungry. They didn't get to eat. They worked and they fell. . . . I'll tell you how it was. Terrible. We finished. . . . Returned nine hundred women to one block. . . . Could sleep there maybe three hundred. Four hundred. They were hungry. Didn't have where to stand. Where to sit. So those yells I still today hear. The screams of those poor people. . . . [S]o over everyone they [SS women] gave it with the whip on all sides. . . . Such sadism you can't imagine. (144)

As this passage suggests, the testimony of Sack's grandmother (the survivor) powerfully creates a landscape of terror, chaos, pain, and despair. Though it doesn't focus on bonds among women per se, it persuasively captures the unthinkable conditions under which such bonds were sometimes forged. There is, however, a play that portrays bonding among women political prisoners in Auschwitz. Charlotte Delbo's *Who Will Carry the Word?* (French 1972; English 1982), about French women political prisoners in a death camp determined that one of them should survive to carry back to the world their history of atrocity and slow death. *Who Will Carry the Word?* explores, to quote Ringelheim, "the strength in women's friendships, . . . sharing, storytelling, and conversations" (756). And it does so without ever celebrating these traits and behaviors in such a way as to obscure the horrific circumstances that necessitated them or the reality that most of these women died. Delbo, who herself is a survivor of a death camp, recreates this history using a choral structure of shifting voices, thus emphasizing not only the cooperation among these women under extreme conditions, but their collective passion to have the narrative of their experience memorialized.

What is still needed are more plays that explore the experience of Jewish women and the intersection of female and Jewish identity in the Holocaust. To use the title of Karmel's novel, the estate of memory of the Holocaust itself is incomplete without inclusion of what happened to women. In asserting this, Ringelheim asks:

> Why should ideas about the Holocaust as a whole exclude . . . women's experiences—exclude what is important to women—and thus make the judgment that women's experiences as women are trivial? These aspects of women's daily lives—vulnerability to rape, humiliation, sexual exchange, not to speak of pregnancy, abortion, and fear for one's children—cannot simply be universalized as true for all survivors. (745)

She also marks the way "maintenance strategies" among women were different. In earlier work Ringelheim focused on how these strategies related to their survival.[4] Yet because the intersection of feminism and "Jewishness" continues to be theorized, by the time of her 1985 article in *Signs*, Ringelheim is critiquing her own theoretical stance in earlier work for its totalizing "cultural feminist" approach. She asserts that "such uncritical valorization" of women's behavior in the Holocaust, including reclaiming the "values, ways of life, and skills" of women "as if they have not arisen within an oppressive situation" has the effect of "valorizing oppression" and "blunt[ing] or negating its effects" (756). "What," she asks, "does the transformation of female gender roles really mean in the face of the oppression and genocidal murder perpetrated during the Holocaust," especially in the face of how few women and men actually survived? (760).

Ringelheim's statement in the *Newsletter* of the Holocaust Project—a mural series by artist Judy Chicago who is "committed to emphasizing (though not isolating) women's experience in this project"—offers one way of answering her question:

> During the Holocaust women were victimized as women and not only as Jews; Jewish women were the targets of the Nazis *because* they were Jews. But they were attacked and used as women—as mothers, as objects of sexual derision and exploitation, as persons even less valuable than Jewish men because of the curious and damaging sexual division of labor. My own research shows that more Jewish women may have been deported and killed than Jewish men. Thus it is absolutely clear that there is a serious and deadly relationship between anti-Semitism and sexism. It can no longer be ignored if we want to understand the lives and deaths of women during the Holocaust. It is time to refocus and rearrange the politics of the Holocaust.[5]

I would add that the relation between anti-Semitism and sexism can no longer be ignored if we want to understand the lives and deaths of Jews during the Holocaust since women make up half its population. In line with her assertion that there is a politics in how the Holocaust is conceived and represented, it seems to me that the particularity of the differences within Judaism are where the strength of any critique of the Holocaust lies; a material approach, one that tries to understand specific conditions, specific histories, including women's, will help in the formulation of a contemporary discourse on the Holocaust. Ringelheim's not yet theorized "deadly relationship between anti-Semitism and sexism" in the Holocaust suggests a fruitful direction for a theory interweaving feminism and "Jewishness" in order to navigate the two sets of identity politics and the two discourses of Otherness within which a Jewish feminism is positioned.

4

REALISM, GENDER, AND HISTORICAL CRISIS

Lillian Hellman's Watch on the Rhine
and "Julia"

The U.S. Holocaust Memorial Museum in Washington D.C. contains a powerful narrative on the role of the American liberator/soldier in the events of the Holocaust. I examine that narrative here in relation to the question "How does theatre ideologically construct the site of the American liberator/soldier in a contemporary crisis?" The present chapter probes the consequences of this narrative in the early 1940s by examining Lillian Hellman's *Watch on the Rhine* (1941) along with "Julia," her memoir story in *Pentimento* (1973), in which she re-visions events of World War II after the "crisis of fascism" is over. I establish an intertextual relationship between *Watch on the Rhine* and the "Julia" section of *Pentimento* to illustrate how one text can historicize another by the same author. Rather than presenting a full-blown reading of "Julia," I use it to expose the limitations of *Watch on the Rhine* as a realist play, to show what is erased in the play and left out of history.

Watch on the Rhine's representation of history is ungendered, never estranging spectators from the relations of gender it represents; instead, the text operates as if asymmetric relations between the sexes were a given or point of origin, thereby omitting the struggles around gender present in other Hellman works. I explore what the text assumes these fictions of ideal gender relations are, how it reproduces and manipulates them, and how they are related to the play's antifascist polemics. In doing so, I hope to underscore what is at stake in a gendered analysis of both a historical crisis and a text that represents one. Using *Watch on the Rhine* I also investigate whether a realistic play using familiarizing, ahistorical structures can move spectators toward emotions and actions, without getting them to historicize, even when there is a concerted effort, within the family plot, to replace "psychology" with "politics."

Historicization in drama studies constitutes a dialogue of perspectives. To historicize a play is to understand it in its changing sociohistorical context and account for one's own critical stance toward that context, as well as to understand the role of its contemporary and current spectators. According to Brecht, who first theorized this problem for the theatre, historicized works construct spectators as historians who are able to look objectively at the complex material conditions and human contradictions within the play's events and, by extension, within their own contemporary history. Brecht, however, had no interest in gender as a specific social phenomenon, so gender as a cultural construction was not a historical context for him. In contrast, I assume that there is no ungendered history and seek to investigate not only how gender is thematized in *Watch on the Rhine*, but also how it is inscribed into the conditions of the play's production.[1] A gendered reading is not simply one option among many, but a necessity if a play is to be fully historicized.

Works of realism, in which the playwright purports to investigate social and material conditions, pose a particular problem to this concept of gendered historicizing because issues of gender are often reduced to emotional conflicts. These are the very plays that must be historicized, because the seamless unity of realism conceals the history of its own making, thereby suggesting that all the events that are depicted occur naturally and inevitably. This naturalization of events makes it difficult for the spectator to historicize and so recognize history as a place of differences, struggle, and choice. Since realism is the form closest to history as written, this observation has even wider implications. As Elin Diamond argues: "To understand history as narrative is a crucial move for feminists, not only because it demystifies the idea of disinterested authorship, but because *the traditionally subordinate role of women in history can be seen as the legacy of narrative itself*" ("Refusing the Romanticism" 95).

Watch on the Rhine

A gendered historicizing of realistic texts is crucial to an understanding of how these texts position their spectators seemingly within but actually outside of history. Hellman's *Watch on the Rhine*[2] exemplifies what is at stake when a gendered analysis is omitted for those realistic plays organized around the perception of a historical crisis. In response to the urgent threat of fascism, Hellman sought to infuse antifascist polemic into the ahistorical structures of a naturalized and nostalgic version of gender relations. To do so, the "unpatriotic" text of *Pentimento*'s Julia, who "prematurely" fights fascism in Europe, is repatriated in *Watch on the Rhine*'s portrayal of the heroic but depoliticized European Kurt (*Pentimento* hereafter cited as *Pen*). The plot of an imperiled family in America literally familiarizes the play and naturalizes an asymmetric relation between the sexes within marriage and family. The spectator is offered the seduction of the seeming logic, acceptability, and inescapability of female subservience. The play typifies a general trend, deliberate or unconscious, to resurrect gendered inequality in response to any perceived "ungendered" historical crisis, denigrating opposition to patriarchy by rationalizing regressive fictions about gender on the basis of this "larger" crisis.

A common patriarchal fiction of ideological neutrality is that, especially in the face of a "large" crisis, gender (as well as race, ethnicity, class, and sexuality) is not a determinant of history. This prioritizing on the basis of expediency often erases the historical contexts of race, class, ethnicity, and sexuality as well. By contrast, when gender is historicized as a product of alterable structures in history, spectators are given a perspective on gender to consider and evaluate against their own gendered history. To quote Elin Diamond, "When spectators 'see' gender they are seeing (and reproducing) the cultural signs of gender, and by implication, the gender ideology of a culture" ("Brechtian Theory" 84).

Watch on the Rhine serves as an especially clear example of this tendency because of its "datedness" as a "relic," because of the melodramatic contrivances that allow it to be easily dismissed from the more respected parts of the Hellman canon. The very obviousness of the play's message-laden rhetoric and didacticism obscures the sophistication and seductiveness of its use of the structures of realism, a form that gains much of its power from its seeming transparency. Unless one simply assumes that antifascist plays were, by definition, appealing to audiences in the forties, the powerful response to this one needs theorizing. Even the 1980 Broadway revival of *Watch* elicited an unusual devotion. Despite its decent reviews, the play was slated to close after five performances. Instead, money was raised from outside contributors, including other actors, and, as Peter Kihss related, "The director and designers waived all royalties. The cast agreed to work for the actors' minimum. The stage crew took a pay cut" (15), and the play was extended indefinitely. I attended one of the extended performances and was fascinated by the aura of devotion in the house, including that of the ushers who wept openly during parts of the play. Perhaps one appeal of the work rests on a nostalgia for what Julius Novick, in his review, calls "a real *play* play" (84). But Arvin Brown, the show's director, testified to its contemporary relevance, noting that "Today there is a watch on Iran and a watch on Afghanistan, a watch on Libya, a watch on Pakistan" (Kihss 15). That the play's notion of antifascism can be made generic, generalizable to any government whose activities are perceived to threaten us, suggests the way a work of realism, despite its specific use of historical detail, is often ideologically reconfigurable.

Indeed, throughout the history of its reception, the piece has performed more public ideological work than any other Hellman play. Both when it first came out, and now in the Wright biography,[3] *Watch on the Rhine* has been manipulated into "proof" of Hellman's independence from the Communist Party, the confirmation of her rejection of "party dictates" at the time of the Hitler/Stalin Pact (this defense itself reproduces the idea that

Hellman was secretly a "card carrying" Communist in order to refute it). In 1942 Roosevelt chose it for his yearly command performance and his first public appearance since war had been declared (*Pen* 193–94). He took this opportunity to tell Hellman he was confused by rumors that she "was so opposed to the war that [she] had paid for the 'Communist' war protesters . . . around the White House." Curiously, Hellman's other well-known work on fascism, "Julia," endured even more severe public manipulation. Yet, rather than analyzing the portrayal of resistance to fascism in the text, critiques most often focus on the accusation that Hellman appropriated the Julia story,[4] thereby discrediting Hellman's famous stand against the House Un-American Activities Committee, and perhaps more telling, undermining the credibility of her stinging analysis in *Scoundrel Time* (1976) of the behavior of liberals in the McCarthy Era.

Watch on the Rhine is a call to arms for "nice, liberal" (*Pen* 186) middle-class Americans, an exhortation to fight or help those who fight against fascism. The text's creation of an implicit state of war results in the only justifiable killing in all Hellman's plays and her most deliberate, unambiguous act of creating a hero. Her indictment of American innocence and isolationism takes place twenty miles from Washington, D.C. at the Farrelly country home.[5] According to *Pentimento*, *Watch on the Rhine* was originally set in "a small Ohio town." Hellman changed her locale to a more politically central one so that American ignorance of the threat of fascism could not be excused on the grounds of provincialism or distance from the center of power and information. Here Fanny Farrelly, widow of an American diplomat, and David Farrelly, her lawyer son, live a life that is "secure and comfortable in the American style" (Stark Young 498). Their houseguests are Teck de Brancovis, shady Rumanian ex-diplomat and refugee from failed European business deals, and his American wife Marthe who dislikes and fears him. In the play, Teck represents the cynical, manipulative, effete aspects of "Old Europe," which Hellman believed made it easy for the Fascists to take power. Teck is also a character onto whom American audiences can project all their anti-European prejudices, leaving the hero Kurt, as the New Man of Europe, free for admiration.

Enter, exhausted and shabby, Sara Mueller, the daughter Fanny has not seen for twenty years, her German husband Kurt, a professional "Anti-Fascist," and their three children. Kurt is carrying $23,000 "gathered from the pennies and the nickels of the poor who do not like Fascism" (*Watch on the Rhine* 278; hereafter cited as *WR*). After a ten-day stay, he learns his comrades in the underground resistance have been captured and he must return to Germany with the money to free them. But Teck has discovered that Kurt is on Germany's most-wanted list and blackmails him. In response, Kurt kills him to preserve his funds as well as the secret identity that will allow him to recross the German border safely. Fanny and David, finally comprehending the dangers of fascism, now manifest within their own living room rather than an ocean away, are disillusioned in their belief that America is a special world, immune to the tangle of European history. They commit themselves to being accessories to murder by delaying their report of the crime. After a tearful farewell to his family, Kurt leaves on his mission, knowing that this time he will probably never return.

In structuring these events, Hellman made hard use of her women and children: they provide the exposition, the tension, the comedy, the pathos, the audience for the "big speeches," the secondary plot complications and the mechanism by which the hero is kept offstage so that his purity remains unsullied by domesticity or the machinery of the plot. While Hellman always structured her plays around her female characters, this time she imbues this structure with a gendered pro-war ideology designed for the specific purpose of getting the American spectator to accede to United States participation in World War II. On the basis of the emergency posed by Nazism and for the sake of expediency, she reverted to a traditional model of gender relations, including female subservience wedded to conjugal bliss and familial devotion. In order to clarify, though not justify, this regression, it is necessary to look at historical events contemporaneous with the play and to pinpoint both how the historical crisis is represented and how the spectator in 1941 would have been positioned.

The stage directions (and program) situate the play in late spring of 1940. By 1938, Nazi troops had invaded Austria; Hitler had seized the property of Jews in Germany and begun interning adult male Jews in concentration camps; Japan had taken Manchuria and was continuing to attack China in a full if undeclared war. During 1939, Franco, supported by the Fascists, took control of Spain, Stalin signed a Non-aggression Pact with Hitler, Mussolini invaded Albania, and France and England declared war on Germany in response to its invasion of Poland. By the early summer of 1940, Hitler and the Nazis had already invaded and taken over Czechoslovakia, Denmark, Norway, Holland, Belgium, and France. The spectator at a performance of the play in April of 1941 could add to these events (and so have more extensive knowledge of current history than the play's characters) the German invasions of Hungary, Rumania, Bulgaria, Yugoslavia, Greece, and parts of North Africa, as well as the Japanese incursions into Indochina and Thailand.

According to *Pentimento* (185), Hellman's diary entries document that *Watch on the Rhine* was first conceived as early as 1938, a time of growing fascist aggression she had already identified as an urgent crisis.[6] While the events of either 1940 or 1941 could serve, at least theoretically, as sufficient grounds for historical crisis, and despite the claims that *Watch on the Rhine* had "all the timeliness of first page news" (Mantle) and "carried the blazing effect of a front-page headline" (Moody 120), the actual play refers to few specific events—events that after all could be read about in any newspaper. The perception of timeliness results more from the sense of emotional urgency the play projects along with an external context of rapidly shifting events. Moreover, the contemporary spectator of *Watch on the Rhine* did not assent to our retrospective view of an urgent historical crisis of international proportions: through the spring of 1941, eighty percent of Americans still opposed a declaration of war by the United States (Graebner 14). The dangers of fascist aggression may well have been obscured by an aura of optimism created by the improvement to American business from trade with warring nations, by the stability of South and Central America as markets for goods and as sources of natural resources, and, given the disillusionment after World War I, by the satisfaction that Americans had so far managed to stay out of what we continued to view as a European embroilment.[7] Thus the historical crisis that the text responds to is that the threat of fascism did not constitute a great enough crisis in 1938 or in spring 1941 for the play to move its spectators to struggle actively against fascism. To convince her audience that a crisis even existed, Hellman relocated it within the structure of the American family, basing the play's appeal on an emotional and ideological narrative of possession. Funneling historical events and the emotions connected to them into the fate of a family and a marriage, into the loss of a father and husband, served as a strategy for getting the spectator both to internalize and to internationalize what was now recreated as domestic crisis.[8] Indeed, when *The Village Voice* reviewer, Julius Novick, polled his mother about seeing the play, she replied "It was very consciousness-raising at the time. It really hit you" (84). The question is what exactly did Hellman hit her audience with?

Spectators of the play are positioned through a series of gendered, familiarizing metaphors that serve as its text more than its overt thematics, plot, or characters. Of course, the creation of distorting equivalences between two things that are not equivalent is implicit in the structure of metaphor itself, making it both a powerful and dangerous tool. But in the case of *Watch on the Rhine*, like so many other realistic works, the equations, displacements, and substitutions are seamlessly made, with whatever contradicts or disrupts them rendered invisible, often at women's expense. *Watch on the Rhine* positions its male and female spectators in a gendered way that offers them (more than simply different identifications) different seductions and rewards. This positioning creates a system of exchange that is flattering and exciting to audiences.

The marriages in *Watch on the Rhine* serve as a central way of positioning male and female spectators. And these marriages are metaphors for contrasting models of political relations between the United States and Europe. Marthe's marriage to Teck stands for the aspects of European culture that must be rejected, while Sara's marriage to Kurt stands for those that must be repatriated (along with Sara and Marthe) into an internationalized version of liberal American ideology. While the childless DeBrancovis marriage represents the depletion, cynicism, and amorality to which we as Americans resist connecting, the marriage of Kurt and Sara with its three children operates as a mediation, a bonding between the best of Old and New worlds, which is staged as loving and unshakable, and so challenges American isolationism in a tropological way. Marriage functions in a literal sense as a traffic in women as exemplified by Marthe's pretentious and opportunistic mother, who married her daughter to Teck for the sake of a title. And since Sara, in defiance, had to escape her mother's trafficking to marry the poor but admirable Kurt, the text marks mothers both as poor personal advisors and, on a metaphoric level, poor political ones, thereby forcing into the background the play's literal critique of the policies of male diplomats. This strategy prevents the process of historicizing by spectators, replacing the power of the public political with the familial.

In its use of transatlantic marriages to outline a desired response to international politics, the text itself traffics in women by creating a system of meanings in which the married female characters function as ideological commodities. The use of marriage as a metaphor creates an appeal to the male spectator residing in the notion that an adoring, faithful wife is the reward for politically and ethically correct action in the public arena. The female spectator is offered the idea that politically correct men are loving and humane and that the marriages the women make constitute politically important activity without additional action on their part in the public arena. For example, Marthe's switch of allegiance from her marriage to Teck to a romantic interest in David Farrelly operates as a sign of her growing political awareness of fascism's dangers and of the text's payment for his. For both it represents their rejection of their mothers and their mothers' power over them, past or present; the equation of this romantic choice with political awareness expands the danger of the mother and her independent actions into the international arena. Male authority is legitimated while female authority is displaced. The text then disarms the dangerous mother in Sara's scrupulous devotion to Kurt's ideals in her relations with her children.

The presentation of Kurt's worshipful children and admiring wife radiates an aura of nostalgia for an idyllic place outside history, pushing the world back to the uninfringed borders of an intact nuclear family and making its fragmentation the play's central crisis. In *Nostalgia and Sexual Difference,* Janice Doane and Devon Hodges identify the source of nostalgia in *nostos,* the return home (to an idealized past) and show how nostalgia operates not just as "a sentiment but also a rhetorical practice" (3). Metaphorically, *Watch* equates the return home with the referent of the nuclear family as authentic origin or stable center where "sexual differences [are] uncompromised by questions about the relation of these differences to ideology and culture" (7). As

a consequence, these familializing metaphors operate as an ahistorical structure of familiarity that underpins all the play's polemics and so extends out
to naturalize or dehistoricize all the history the text slips into it.[9]

Furthermore, in its reinscription of patriarchal structures and heterosexuality clothed in blissful marriage, *Watch* equates the family with the "good
people" whom fascism threatens and who must be re-covered by war. That
the threat in the household comes from Teck conflates his literal threat as an
opportunist and fascist sympathizer with the idea that outsiders to the family
are suspect and dangerous. The creation of the Farrellys as a Washington
diplomat family blurs the distinction between domestic, familial decisions
and national policy. Thus the nuclear family is established as the building
block of American liberal democracy, complete with an ideological shift away
from isolationism toward the idea that America must lead the world toward
democracy, individual rights, private property, and Christianity (Kurt even
quotes Martin Luther). Moreover, the political network of resisters who secretly consort to oppose fascism is reconfigured by the play into the nuclear
family, with women assigned secondary support roles. Nuclear family structures become so metaphorically integrated with taking political action that
characters outside these structures simultaneously are assimilated into nuclear
family and political awareness. Thus, David Farrelly, a bachelor, and Fanny
Farrelly, a widow, operate on the margins in this system. They are underused
commodities in the struggle against fascism and for the family who will be
reassimilated and reeducated, "shaken out of the magnolias" (*WR* 301) in
the course of the play. Peculiarly, given the frequent perception of the nuclear
family as isolated, protective, and self-interested, isolationism becomes a
metaphorical equivalent to isolation *from* the nuclear family. This equation
typifies the kind of clever, insinuating strategy Hellman is using.

These familializing metaphors suggest several gendered appeals to the
spectator in the context of impending war. Besides authenticating the traditional place of women, the text offers female spectators, in the absence of
their husbands, matrilineal authority (through their sons) but not the (presented as) dangerous matriarchal authority. Also, the text grants the female
spectator approval not for fighting fascism directly but for staying patrioti-
cally at home, ensconced in a civilian family that has assumed further moral
weight by its reconfiguration as a network of resisters. And even if the actual
departure of Kurt is presented as a painful, tragic event, the play still promises its male spectators authority over and ownership of a nuclear family as
well as the freedom to leave it for the moral adventure and heroism of war.

The opening of the 1943 film version of *Watch on the Rhine* refers to
"some men, ordinary men, not prophets, who knew [the] mighty tragedy
was on the way . . . and had fought it from the beginning. This is the story of
one of these men." This text informs the viewer to expect a gendered narrative of male heroism organized around a man who stands for courageous and

foresighted men. Neither the play nor the film leaves its historical marking of "the beginning" vague. Kurt's frequent references to the struggle against fascism in Spain, including singing the whole German Brigade song, foregrounds our failure to aid the elected socialist-liberal government against a fascist rebellion (supported by Hitler and Mussolini) which culminated in Franco's victory in 1939. Thus the play creates a fixed point of origin for the escalation of fascist aggression, with Kurt proclaiming "It would have been a different world if we had [won]" (*WR* 269). This temporal slide in the text to an earlier time elicits in male viewers an amalgam of guilt about the past and glorification of the future war as a form of expiation.

To facilitate the metaphoric overlapping of 1938 and 1941, of a civil war having international consequences with a domestic invasion, of brigade and resistance fighter with ordinary American soldier, the text erases the historical context of Kurt's political allegiances, thereby further essentializing the hero. Kurt's nine-year-old son Bodo comically parrots the language of class exploitation and revolt, so Kurt's possibly Leftist politics are present but safely contained by a humorous domesticating device. Moreover, when Teck reads aloud the Nazi's official description of Kurt as having neither "known political connections" nor "known trade-union connections" (*WR* 286), the spectator is assured by the Nazi hatred of the Left that Kurt's politics consist of that loose ethical conglomerate of fundamental human decencies that is the province of American democratic ideology. Hellman is negotiating between the leftist he would have been and the middle class discourse of this kind of theatre. Bodo also serves as a device for articulating the qualities of Kurt as "a great hero," asserting that in Spain, Papa "was brave, he was calm, he was expert, he was resourceful" (*WR* 247), and thus explicitly equating the (male) hero with the father. As "Papa," the hero is middle-aged, sensitive, frightened, exhausted, physically ill from torture and bullet wounds, and violence-hating. These traits heighten the pathos, widen the range of spectators who can identify with him, and strengthen the reproach by underscoring how far he deviates from the standard image of the young, healthy, strong, male hero. Metaphorically, the abused Old World, European Father must be protected and avenged by the New World, American Sons.

Brecht's Mother Courage remarks on what is required of soldiers: "Take it from me, whenever you find a lot of virtues, it shows that something's wrong" (148). The completeness of Kurt's virtues[10] conveys the text's anxiety about the power of the Nazis even if Kurt's anecdotes testify to how they can be defeated. At the play's end, Kurt's exit from America to rejoin the German underground serves as a paradigm of the male soldier-hero leaving his family to go off to war, just as his killing of Teck enacts the deliberate injuring of persons that is war's goal in a more anonymous way. That an individual decision by an antifascist can stand in for what is by now (in 1941) a matter of national policy is a revealing displacement. It works to enhance

the power of the ordinary male spectator by representing the historical process as an aggregate of individual, courageous acts outside specific institutional, cultural, or economic contexts. In this realistic play's system of
representation, coherent, unified subjects located within the family either
remain, as in Kurt's case, heroically unchanged or they learn (about the threat
of Fascism), decide to act, and so recover their identities—identities implicitly linked to the development of an aggregate national identity.

Since this identity is American, the European Kurt must be evacuated
from the text. The finality of his departure on a mission from which he is
unlikely to return—combined with his son, Joshua, being too young to follow—underscores the gap at the center of the play, which the contemporary
American hero/ordinary soldier is solicited to fill. When the Sergeant asks
Mother Courage "How can you have a war without soldiers?", she replies
"It doesn't have to be my children" (140). Getting male spectators to identify with a hero isn't hard; maybe creating a situation so urgent and a hero so
appealing and loving that the female spectator will accede to a subservient
role in his support isn't either, but creating a climate in which women will
relinquish their male children for the sake of war, the central agenda of *Watch
on the Rhine*, is definitely difficult. The female spectator is given a vision of
herself as courageous and mature, a heroine if she does not impede her sons
from joining the struggle. Made when we were at war, the 1943 film foregrounds this aspect of the text. Joshua is cast as older, and his revelation to
Sara that he will follow Kurt is bracketed off into a new final scene, set months
later. The two of them are in a bedroom, with Joshua tracing on a large map
the route to Germany that will lead him to his missing father—a route that
parallels the route of many of our soldiers. He insists that he will leave to
find his father/fight (the two become equated), that in his absence Sara must
prepare Bodo for the same fate and that she is "a brave lady." Thus becoming "Mother Courage" in this patriarchal economy rests not on protecting
one's children, on holding them back, but on offering them up, however
reluctantly, to the dangers of war. As E. Ann Kaplan notes about the uses of
maternal sacrifice in film, "investment in the pathos of lost Mother-son
bondings keeps the maternal melodrama from straying too far from patriarchal mandates" (126).

The playtext constructs its crises around the absences of fathers and the
responses of sons (suggesting the patrilineal authority of the realist text). No
accident, then, that early on a less committed David Farrelly images himself
as "a bad monument" to his dead father, Joshua Farrelly. Kurt's patriarchal
authority is facilitated by this evacuation of Joshua Farrelly in the text. The
gap allows Kurt's European, better-informed worldview to merge with
Joshua's without directly criticizing his authority or that of his American
liberalism. The portrait of Joshua looming over the living room transports
him to the symbolic realm of the Father, exemplifying the entire movement

constructed by the play toward the ideology of heroism and war conducted by men. Appropriately Sara says "Papa is going home" to explain Kurt's final departure even while the rest of the Mueller family has "come home" to America. As David N. Rodowick points out in his essay on the domestic melodrama of the 1950s, "the figuration of patriarchal authority need not be characterised by a single character . . . rather it defines the centre of a complex network of social relations. . . . The symbolisation of patriarchal authority can be played out across a purely imaginary figure [such as the dead Joshua Farrelly] . . . or indeed this function can be split, distributed across a number of characters" (271). For *Watch*, this distribution of patriarchy across characters includes Kurt Mueller, Joshua Mueller, and David Farrelly. Even the struggle against fascism can be configured as the struggle between two patriarchal systems, one evil and one benign.

Kurt's climactic speech can be seen as the moment of excess, of overstatement of its ideas, in which a realistic play unwittingly reveals gaps in the seamlessness that hides the history of its own making: "In every town and every village and every mud hut in the world, there is always a man who loves children and who will fight to make a good world for them" (*WR* 299). The familiarizing slide from town and village to individual mud hut promises heroism to each male head of household. It internationalizes the father/hero, firmly assuring the moral correctness of his mission while placing him "beyond politics," beyond even a specific history of events. While women are to give up their children to war as their patriotic commitment, in a curious appropriation of many mother's concerns, men's commitment *to* children is erected as their reason for fighting in war. Besides erasing both political action by women against injustice and their labor in the production of children, these lines literalize the absence of women in the text's representations of them.

E. Ann Kaplan notes that in the maternal narratives of the '30s, "to be healthy, the daughter must turn away from the Mother and discover identity through marriage—that is, through subordination to the male" (133–34). Indeed, Sara's rejection of her mother and her mother's values to marry Kurt twenty years earlier is the anterior action to the play. The reward for her choice parallels what Maria LaPlace, discussing *Now Voyager*, describes as the romantic ideal of women's fiction: "the ideal heterosexual relationship is always represented in terms of perfect understanding, a mutual transparency between the lovers, a relation of 'soulmates.' . . . The romantic hero is a 'maternal man' capable of nurturing the heroine; tender, expressive about his feelings, he does not hesitate to express his love and admiration" (159). In the portrayal of the relationship between Kurt and Sara, the text even promises the female spectator that the emotional intensity of this romance continues after marriage. As Sara tells Kurt in the final scene: "For twenty years. It is as much for me today—(Takes his arms) Just once, and for all my life. (He pulls her toward him)" (WR 300). Yet, the equality between men and women that is part of this ideal is not present in this marriage; the text justifies Sara's subordination to Kurt's authority on the basis of the political crisis of fascism as reconfigured in the home. The subject of romantic love in marriage is also echoed in a humorous way in Fanny's depiction of her marriage: "(Without turning, she points over her head to Joshua Farrelly's portrait) Thank God, I was in love" (WR 233) and "(shrieks) What! Your father bored with me! Not for a second of our life" (WR 247). There's even a competition between Fanny and Sara over whose marriage is the more loving, until Kurt halts it with an amused "Ladies, ladies" (WR 248). The housekeeper Anise humiliatingly recounts how a pregnant Fanny, jealous when her husband danced with another woman, faked the sounds of labor and spitefully screamed for three weeks, ensuring that this character has no matriarchal authority in the play but, instead, functions as the comic type of the sharp-tongued matriarch.

The text uses parallel comic and serious tracks not only in representing the women, as in the depiction of conjugal love, but also in depicting their relationships to their husbands' ideals. Fanny, who "always [finds herself] wondering what Joshua would have felt" (WR 236), boasts "I am proud to have Papa's convictions" (WR 260). Her parroting of her husband's ideas both allows them to be criticized indirectly and also infantilizes her, especially given the child Bodo's similar parroting of Kurt's ideas. The case of Sara is more complex. Twice in the play, Kurt cuts her off, once with a "Be still, Sara" (WR 253) and once to control her anger and interject a long narrative of his own. In response to this narrative, Sara says "I wanted it the way Kurt wanted it" (WR 253). Though never comic, Sara is no more a true speaking subject in the play than Fanny is. Her wifely function is to translate Kurt's point of view in his absence, to serve metaphorically as both an extension of and mirror for her husband. When Bette Davis played Sara in the film, Sara's centrality was expanded in that the camera never showed Kurt speaking without Davis as Sara, usually slightly behind him, intensely emoting in sympathy and support. This interpretation paradoxically heightened the character's subjection while making the star an inescapable focus.

If Robert Sherwood's 1940 play about the threat of fascism, There Shall Be No Night, has as its main female character a nearly speechless wife who is rarely without her apron, Hellman's strategy of making seemingly intelligent, mature women self-consciously speak their subordinate positions is certainly more seductive. But a devolutionary image of girlhood underscores both Fanny's and Sara's representations. Half in amusement and half in anger, David tells his mother, "Mama, I think we'll fix up the chickenhouse for you as a playroom. . . . and you can go into your second childhood in the proper privacy" (WR 235). And, included for the "self-effacing part" (Atkinson 1) of Sara is a gentle remonstrance from Kurt to "not be a baby" about enjoying her former, luxurious home. Moreover, praise for Sara culminates in David's and Kurt's evaluation of her near the end of the play as "a good girl" (*WR* 290). This larger, gendered narrative of infantilization includes the portrayal of Babette, Sara's daughter, four times described as "a pretty little girl." Babbie exults in American opportunities to cook, sew, and get new dresses, implying to the audience that, in contrast to war-torn Europe, America is a place where femininity still flourishes. Indeed, with Sara described initially as "very badly dressed" in mismatched clothes, much care is given to the scene in which Marthe brings out boxes of fashionable, expensive dresses secretly bought by Fanny for Sara and Babette. The reabsorption of the Mueller females into the discourse of consumerism serves as a confirmation of their repatriation into middle-class, capitalist America, with no parallel activity for the Mueller males. It is as if up-classing were a promise reserved for women, while the effacing of class differences is reserved for men fighting against fascism.

Watch on the Rhine capitalizes on the nostalgia for sexual inequality just at the edge of the historical moment when so many real women would shift into active industrial participation for the war effort. In one sense, then, the devolutionary women's line slides over the forties, erasing the competent, self-supporting image of Rosie the Riveter to anticipate the more restricted position of women in the fifties. But perhaps American responses to the war and its aftermath contained the seeds of the fifties with its suburban reproductions of "chickenhouse playrooms," just as the portrayals of women in this play do. Hellman's 1943 film script *The North Star* portrayed gun-wielding, torture-resisting Russian women and girls responding to invasion by the Nazis, thus reinforcing by contrast that, even when staged within the illusion of America invaded, *Watch on the Rhine* still had no space in form, content, or ideology for female resistance. In support of a formal declaration of war and acceptance of the archetypical departure of the soldier, the text sacrifices gender equality. So for the female spectator the play must create a situation so pressing, a mission so holy, that any role in it is glorified.

"Julia"

Describing the writing of *Watch on the Rhine*, Hellman said it was "the only play I have ever written that came out in one piece, as if I had seen a landscape and never altered the trees" while "all other work had been fragmented, hunting in an open field with shot from several guns . . . unable to see clearly, . . . hands empty from stumbling and spilling" (*Pen* 193). The "one piece" denotes the ease of reproducing ideology as consistent with itself and actual conditions, of not going against norms she challenged in other plays. The "open field" suggests some of the discontinuities and contradictions to a totalizing worldview, revealed in the process of much of Hellman's writing, including "Julia." Instead of the coherent, linear, realist narrative of *Watch on the Rhine*, "Julia" is a structural and thematic interplay of movement—the movement of women across Europe and the associative movement of Hellman's memory and reflection contextualizing in unpredictable ways. It is a text that foregrounds concealment and deception, both as the necessary language of the antifascist underground and as an indictment of those who denied the threat of fascism out of apathy and self-interest. As such, "Julia" oscillates between revealing and concealing Hellman's desire for Julia as a hero and as a beloved person of power and grace. Accordingly, language is never transparent in the text; the writing is self-reflexive, calling attention to its own textual strategies.

The events depicted in "Julia" occur through 1938, so "Julia" is a pre-text to *Watch*. Indeed, Hellman wrote that Kurt "was, of course, a form of" her vigorously antifascist, heroic friend Julia (*Pen* 187). The "of course" denotes Hellman's assumption of the unproblematic transposing of gender, a move that in reality erases gender as constructed through history. Early on in "Julia," Hellman marks her own awareness of the ideology of gender by noting her uneasiness around a man who made "pretend-good-natured feminine jibes" (*Pen* 102). And later, she marks the suspiciousness and derision of homophobic acquaintances in response to her friendship with Julia, implicating them in a narrow, conventional morality and selfishness that gives them a kind of fascist potential. As a work written in the 1970s, "Julia" is also the post-text to *Watch on the Rhine*; it comments on the play's function as a pro-war text written in the historical moment of the 1940s by narrating a history of intimacy between women in the context of political struggle against fascism. Thus "Julia" serves as the supplement to *Watch on the Rhine*: everything that the "Kurt" version of Julia cannot contain circulates invisibly through the play, creating the "one character too many" Hellman thought was in this play but could not identify.

Instead of enfolding resistance to fascism within the confines of the symbolic ideological units of marriage and family, "Julia" presents an anonymous network of women and men "of Catholic, Communist, many beliefs" (*Pen* 106) that foregrounds politically committed, ordinary women taking grave risks. The notion that the foundation for antifascism is to be found in various specific systems of belief replaces the individual moral dilemmas of *Watch*, which suggests context, even history itself did not change people's values. And if *Watch* posits fascism as an evil based on its opposition to the nuclear family, "Julia" repoliticizes the struggle against fascism by reconfiguring whom fascism most directly threatens and who must be rescued by the underground as "Jews. . . . And political people. Socialists, Communists, plain old Catholic dissenters" (*Pen* 139).

Through Hellman the character, the text charts the uncertainty and disorientation of American intellectuals in the early thirties over the extent of the dangers of fascism, thereby offering both a sense of the historical forces of that time and a response to them by which readers can evaluate and contextualize their own awareness of what contemporary events mean (i.e., a text that positions readers to historicize more than watch). *Watch on the Rhine* and "Julia" are both teaching texts and texts about teaching, but while the education of a family is crucial in the play, in "Julia" it is a woman, a writer and political person, i.e., Hellman herself, whose education and development are central. And this learning begins in a bond between two women in early adolescence. Replacing Babette, the daughter positioned solely by her relationship to her family, is a close friendship between unrelated girls—an intense one, full of questioning and speculation about the world.

Heroism itself is no longer the province of males, of fathers and sons vested with familial authority, when Hellman relocates acts of courage within a matrix of female friendships. The story marks out the way Julia depends on this friendship to seduce Hellman via letters to come to Europe, recognize the gravity of what is happening, and risk carrying money across the border to Germany to secure the release of those interned in concentration camps. Even the props of this resistance work—fur hat and candy box—portray the paraphernalia of femininity as a strategy to defeat fascists instead of as a trivialized comic device. In its focus on female friendship, "Julia" historicizes the role of emotion and personal feeling outside the family and marriage in relation to politics. The text also reconceives women's anger: while Kurt polices Sara if she gets "too angry," Julia tells Hellman that she's "always liked [Hellman's] anger, trusted it" and "not to let people talk you out of it" (*Pen* 140) and, by implication, the insight and power to act that anger gives. The converse of anger in "Julia" is not the comfortably subordinate Sara but "that kind of outward early-learned passive quality that in women so often hides anger" (*Pen* 119), i.e., a concealed and ineffectual rage conditioned by patriarchal norms.

While Hellman thought the film version of "Julia" did a good job of showing "that two women can be totally devoted to one another, and that each will do for the other what each wants" (Adams 228), her own text rarely risks dehistoricizing the two women's political activity by subordinating it to an essentialized narrative of female friendship. When Hellman has accomplished her mission, Julia tells her to "believe that you have been better than a good friend to me, you have done something important" (*Pen* 138–39), implicitly enlarging the territory of friendship and its obligations while refusing to make it a transgressive political action in itself. Still, "Julia" does reconfigure the site of love and intense feeling outside marriage and into female friendship; and unlike the aggressively heterosexual text of *Watch*, "Julia" is grounded in a historically specific, sexual, intellectual, and political rapport between two women. Thus the text and its defamiliarizing configurations depict the conditions in which women become social subjects, rather than, given the gender ideology of *Watch*, subjecting them to a particular position in a social structure. As a text of many overlapping contexts that can't be tracked or sorted out, "Julia" portrays the historical process as both complex and discontinuous—a place of exclusion on the basis of gender, class, sexual orientation, and race instead of a continuing, causal, naturalized chain of events.

The text of "Julia" contains many "illegitimate" aspects. Illegitimate means unlawful, illegal, irregular, or illogical. So established structures of authority are the context for deciding which term of this legitimate/illegitimate opposition applies. The only family in "Julia" is her unpleasant, fragmented upper-class one, which she rejects and which repudiates her once she joins with the working class of Vienna. She uses her money in an illegitimate way—not in accordance with upper-class standards and outside the discourse of consumerism—to bankroll the resistance. If the Muellers are repatriated into America in *Watch*, "Julia" is the unpatriotic text in which a woman must leave America to express her politics. The text itself does not psychoanalyze Julia, as is so often the case with realism; it is precisely her reading of history and her place in it that are confirmed. The depoliticized Kurt is replaced by the socialist Julia, thereby grounding in a politics Julia's early thirties awareness of "the holocaust that was on its way" (*Pen* 121) and her defense of Vienna's Fljoridsdorf district against violent attack by fascist thugs.

Julia has an illegitimate child whom she comfortably describes as "fat and handsome," quickly dismissing the father as "an ordinary social climber." For Julia, the term "bastard" is reserved for Nazis, not children, so, by implication, actions and ideology should determine legitimacy, not legal relations within the structure of the family. While the characterization of Sara relies on the traditional psychology of the maternal, in "Julia" there is no conflict between motherhood and active political struggle. Nor is the matriarchal rendered as threatening in this feminocentric world. Hellman gives her character her own mother's name and Julia gives her daughter the name Lilly after Hellman. Both reflect the way that the boundaries between female identities such as mother and daughter, as well as the borders between the relationships of lover and friend collapse and blur in this gynocentric text. If, using Kurt's profession (of engineer) as a figuration for the play's structure, *Watch* is the engineered, fixed, logical text, "Julia" is its disruptive, repressed counterpart. One definition of legitimate refers to theatre: "the normal or regular type of stage plays." "Julia" is the illegitimate theatre of *Watch on the Rhine*, containing what cannot be placed into the historical perspective of a pro-war 1940s play, and further, what won't fit into the borders of the realistic system of representation in general.

If a text contains the seeds of what it does not say, of its opposite, *Watch on the Rhine* has elements that undermine its critique of fascism. Fascism denies history, replaces it with a myth of itself, constructs rigid oppositions and hierarchies of difference that are both menacingly authoritative and flexible. This process is reflected in the play's reinscribing of the patriarchal narrative of the nuclear family. The strategy of making the dehistoricized nuclear family the bulwark of benign patriarchal opposition to fascism erases the historical reality of the fascist family and the organizing of Nazism (at least on the level of propaganda) around a pro-family, pro-natal ideology. Perhaps fascism, with its severe gender asymmetries, is rendered no longer threatening, is recuperated into dominant ideology via the domestic arena when Hellman insists on a false opposition between a sugary version of patriarchy and fascism.

In response to her own historical dilemma, Hellman tried to explode the insularity of the family by familiarizing what was outside of it, tried to internationalize political concerns and social relations by relocating them all within the United States and American democratic ideology. The result conveyed an aggregate national identity that is based on individual acts and appropriates history and politics as the province of the normal, acceptable, inescapable, and ultimately ahistorical structure of the family. And, as a pro-war play of the forties, *Watch on the Rhine* doesn't explore the question of how we resist fascism if we don't go to war. Not tied to a war ideology, the retrospective presentation of Julia's antifascism may better serve as a model for political action, including the more fully gendered historicizing the text accomplishes. If, in *Watch on the Rhine*, Hellman opposes one set of fixed ideological metaphors to another set implied by fascism, in "Julia" she destabilizes the most traditional tropes of configuration in her network of female resistance to fascism outside of the family structure. This suggests the instability of gender identity, of male and female, as products of culture and subject to redefinition. Transgressive structures operate on both the "personal" and "political" level of "Julia" so that class and gender issues are more fully integrated into this work's antifascist ideology. In *Watch on the Rhine* the dead body of Teck is concealed; the body buried, so to speak, in this realistic American family plot is the body of women, as, for example, political resisters, close companions, and transgressors of the injunction to legitimize children through marriage. In its rejection of hierarchizing, of fixed identities enclosed in a thematics, and of naturalizing myths of origin that erase history, the text of "Julia" (and not just the character Julia) operates as a resistance to fascism, a disruptive expression of female desire not corralled into legitimacy or erased by dominant ideology.

5

THEATRE OF INJURY AND INJUSTICE

Staging the Body in Pain

About Auschwitz, Jean Francois Lyotard writes:

> Suppose that an earthquake destroys not only lives, buildings and objects but also the instruments used to measure earthquakes, directly and indirectly. The impossibility of quantitatively measuring it does not prohibit, but rather inspires in the minds of the survivors the idea of a very great seismic force. . . . [W]ith Auschwitz, something new has happened in history (which can only be a sign and not a fact), which is that the facts, the testimonies which bore the traces of *here's* and *now's*, the documents which indicated the sense or senses of the facts, and the names, finally the possibility of various kinds of phrases whose conjunctions makes reality, all this has been destroyed as much as possible. Is it up to the historian to take into account not only the [injury], but also the [injustice]? Not only the reality, but also the meta-reality that is the destruction of reality? . . . Its name marks the confines wherein historical knowledge sees its competence impugned. (56–58)

Lyotard is asserting that not only has Auschwitz destroyed our competence in knowing *what* we know; it has destroyed our security in the structures of *how* we know. Although he refers most directly to historical knowledge and its modes of representation, by implication Auschwitz—Lyotard's metonymy for the events of the Holocaust—is also the site where theatrical representation sees its competence impugned. As Herbert Blau remarks, "There's little that one sees in postmodern forms—rejecting mimesis, catharsis, and the plot with its bleeding eyeballs—that in any way diminishes, short of forgetting it altogether, the massive overdose of pain we have inherited from the past—and which, in various parts of the world (to which we look now for alternative therapies as well as Alternative Theater), is being miserably exceeded" (170). By which I think he means that not only does our experimentation in the present offer no assurance of better forms to convey this inheritance of pain, but that these forms, in themselves, cannot be cathartic, cannot, even if effective, release us from the historical pain of past events

precisely because we have not (cannot?) gained knowledge from past genocides (which, as Lyotard says, ruin knowledge) to prevent the present ones.

To the extent that contemporary and postmodern theatre engage in creating new strategies for representing this massive overdose of pain, and in
particular the events of the Holocaust, they must take into account not only
the incommensurability of acts of genocide, but Elaine Scarry's assertion of
the unsharability of physical pain and Lyotard's insistence on its historical
erasure. To some degree, Holocaust testimony, the embodied "I" narrating
outside the juridical rules of evidence, is the critical act of resistance—the
attempt to express, against the odds, both a historical and somatic remembrance. But, as I argue below, testimony is not easily translatable into theatre.
Nonetheless, our efforts, in theatre and performance, to trace the dual events
of human suffering and injustice should continue: if Lyotard depicts Auschwitz as the name for destruction, not only of persons, culture, and historical
narrative, but of signification itself, nonetheless *not* to try to represent it
becomes a kind of denial, the move toward "forgetting it altogether" to which
Blau alludes.

In *The Body in Pain*, Elaine Scarry asserts that another person's physical
pain is an invisible geography, especially in extreme cases such as torture,
that not only resists language but actively destroys it. Unlike any other state
of consciousness, physical pain has no referential content. And yet, "What is
remembered in the body is well remembered" (Scarry 152). Both Scarry and
Lyotard posit an unmaking in pain—of "reality," of language, of history, of
referentiality itself—for the individual victim in one case and for us and the
mass of victims in another. Neither is exploring a limit, but asserting, in this
idea of unmaking, a going beyond limits to a place of (absolute) destruction.
Both claim the resistance to representation of this imposition of pain and
terror on bodies. Taken together they outline a complex intersection in genocide between a collective experience and a highly private, subjective one.
This raises the question: how can we portray genocide, the mass noun, and
signify the individual if fragmented subjectivities subjected to these terrible
events? The question is particularly apt for the Nazi genocide because part
of its process was a violent and deliberate shredding of those subjectivities in
order to reinscribe over and over the nonhuman status of the killable Other.

Can we assign a cultural "use value" to the Holocaust? What can we
learn from ruination? Isn't "Never again!" a desperate performative rather
than a prediction? Does this "use value" reside in the necessity to represent
atrocity, in this case in theatre, if the only alternatives are silence and entertainment? I include entertainment, because far from believing that we have
no language for representing the body in pain, I think we have parceled out
pain, humiliation, and atrocity into mass culture forms for spectatorial pleasure. Both horror and forms of violent pornography are modes for repre-

senting the "excesses" of atrocity that, for example, conventional realism excises and conceals.

Parceling Out Pain for Spectatorial Pleasure: Horrality and Atrocity

Horror films are one site of direct representation of graphic physical violence to the body, including elaborate acts of atrocity in which the camera specifically focuses on damage to the revealed insides of the body (often erasing their relation to a recognizable body as such). According to Philip Brophy, the primary aim of this form is:

> to generate suspense, shock and horror. [It is] . . . textual manipulation that has no time for the critical ordinances of social realism, cultural enlightenment or emotional humanism. The gratification of the contemporary Horror film is based upon tension, fear, anxiety, sadism and masochism—a disposition that is overall both tasteless and morbid. . . . "Horrality" involves the construction, deployment and manipulation of horror—in all its various guises—as a textual mode . . . and this mode of *showing* as opposed to *telling* . . . is strongly connected to the destruction of the Body. . . . The horror is conveyed through torture and [the] agony of havoc wrought upon a body devoid of control. (5, 8, 10)

"Horrality," then, is a genre for showing the violated, disintegrating body.[1] But the fascinated voyeurism that horror elicits from the spectator is attached to a saturated form that simultaneously fills you up and leaves you empty, desiring more of the same in a continuing, addictive cycle. This delight (and terror) in the inevitable destruction of the body is opposite to the acknowledgment, credulity, and even understanding of our own complicity that inform Lawrence Langer's call for an "aesthetics of atrocity" in *The Holocaust and the Literary Imagination* (22).

"Horrality" offers the pleasure of suspense predicated on certain formulaic emplotments (however imaginatively negotiated) of who will get killed (and who won't), when, and how. The conventions of "horrality" generate suspense in the spectator by setting up recognizable scenarios, by hinting that their resolution might differ from our expectations, and by confirming our expectations with a formulaic conclusion. Suspense, then, simultaneously confirms our own knowledge of the workings of "horrality" (i.e., "I knew that would happen all along") and distances us from the characters of the story itself (i.e., ultimately we do not care about what is happening in the story as much as we care whether it happens as we expected). Spectators are cued to associate themselves not too deeply with those marked for death but with a character who is just as savvy about the workings of the genre as we are, thereby offering us a narcissistic pleasure. An aesthetics of atrocity would remove this pleasure in seeing our expectations fulfilled by the impending death of another. It would represent horrific, non-formulaic scenarios that challenge our frames of knowing and disallow distance from the persons whose bodies are injured. It would displace suspense and cause spectators to view a historically inevitable outcome with loathing and dread.

But can we read structures set up by certain horror films so that they shed light on genocide and its representation? The Blob, in the 1958 film *The Blob*, may help to expose the othering process by which bodies and peoples become reduced to protoplasmic mass that is genocidally killable in self-defense. The Blob is an alien, purely parasitical, hostile biological life force, whose blind motivation is its sheer survival. If exterminating Jews is simultaneously about violence to individual bodies and to the cultural body, then in the logic of the film, the Blob is conceived as a damaging, alien organism that is both single and able to reconstruct itself from its freestanding pieces—pieces that are both a part of the larger organism and literally the organism itself. Hence, even the smallest piece of alien protoplasm must be destroyed. Of course it is the genocidal logic inscribed in the structure of such films that is truly engulfing and dangerous (and hardly as alien as we'd like to imagine), but my point is that hidden in this film, for our spectatorial pleasure, is the genocidal imagining.

Horrality led me to one of its progenitors, the theatre of the Grand Guignol, in my efforts to conceive a theatrical aesthetics of atrocity. But the effects upon spectators of this mode of staging graphic bodily violence have been described as fascinated revulsion, terror sometimes culminating in faint or flight, or sophisticated amusement. This description suggests a mode of showing that is unhelpful to my project because the aesthetics of atrocity used by the Grand Guignol either creates a cathartic effect based on fear without any pity or facilitates a distance amenable to the connoisseur of simulated pain. More interesting are Charles Noonon's comments in the late fifties on the demise of Grand Guignol: "We could never equal Buchenwald. Before the war, everyone felt that what was happening on stage was impossible. Now we know that these things, and worse, are possible in reality" (qtd. in Gordon 33). Apart from its grotesque lamenting over the inability to equal Buchenwald, the comment implies that it was the impossibility *in* history of what this theatre enacted on the body that gave its spectators pleasure; thus the historical horror of the Holocaust canceled out this "innocent" pleasure.

Rather a pious note to end on, and misleading if we look to a decade earlier. In the late 1940s, Mel Gordon notes, "[the] documentary footage of the Nazi death camps and medical experiments on humans that was shown in neighborhood movie houses became impossible competition" for the

Grand Guignol (31). Clearly the fascination of horrality extended to the form of documentary, at least to raw footage (and its presumption of offering the "Real thing"). Add to this the 1947 comment by Eva Berkson, who, in 1939, before she fled from France to England, had tried unsuccessfully to expand the horror form by mounting a play that dealt with Nazi atrocities in Poland. Before leaving the Grand Guignol a second time (in 1951), she stated, "I've come to the conclusion that the only way to frighten a French audience since the war is to cut up a woman on stage—a live woman, of course—and throw them the pieces!" (qtd. in Gordon 31). Besides confirming the usual gender of the victim of violence in Grand Guignol, Berkson's comment sheds light on the way an addictive form of horrality must continue to escalate the graphic aspects (the simulated "realness") of its violence. But it also marks the way that, after the war, Holocaust film footage and the like became the yardstick against which commodified representations of atrocity could be measured. Perhaps "frighten" had become too tame a concept by mid-century—which points to a second genre for parceling out spectatorial pleasure in atrocity: violent pornography.

Nazi S/M constitutes a central trope in the repertoire of pornography—a trope that sexualizes violations to a gendered female body by confusing damage and pain with the sexual and thereby eroticizing the imposition of violence. Moreover, by positing a contractual relationship between victim and perpetrator, it insists on the victim's collaboration in the process, even in desiring that pain and humiliation. In eroticizing the infliction of pain and humiliation, this pornographic mode of representation displaces the obscenity of violation to the body onto the sexual. In doing so, it reproduces the sexualizing of power constructed by fascist ideology itself. In *Powers of Horror*, Kristeva notes that it is the "economy, one of horror and suffering in their libidinal surplus-value, which has been tapped, rationalized, and made operative by Nazism and Fascism" (155). This economy of bodily injury is positioned as "the truth of the human species" as opposed to "fragile culture," implying that power is derived from violently enacting physical truth on the bodies of others (as well as physically "testing" oneself with pain). Kristeva also describes this seductive economy of horror and suffering as the "'drive foundations'" of fascism: "a drive overload of hatred or death, which prevents images from crystallizing as images of desire and/or nightmare and causes them to break out into sensation (suffering) and denial (horror), into a blasting of sight and sound (fire, uproar)" (154–55). This imposition of suffering, horror, and fire operates to produce sensation, denial, and a blasted relation to the senses, the body's informants of the exterior. This "economy of bodily injury," then, produces a dulling, addictive lust for pain.

But, perhaps, in its emphasis on the sexualized inscription of violence on the body of the victim, the pornography trope of Nazi S/M hides something else. For Foucault, the use of Nazism in pornography poses:

a historical problem: How [he asks] could Nazism, which was represented by lamentable, shabby, puritan young men, by a species of Victorian spinsters, have become everywhere today—in France, in Germany, in the United States—in all the pornographic literature of the whole world, the absolute reference of eroticism? All the shoddiest aspects of the erotic imagination are now put under the sign of Nazism. (written in 1974, qtd. in Friedlander 39)

Perhaps Foucault's notion of eroticism doesn't leave enough space for the fetishistic quality of the trappings of totalitarian regimes, and most particularly the Nazi regime—a part of the erotic charge that even run-of-the-mill pornography draws on. The question may really be "Whose erotic imaginings for whom?" or, in Foucault's terms, "for whom does power carry an erotic charge?" What if the fascist sadomasochistic exchange is not between the masculinized perpetrator of violence and the feminized victim, but between powerful Nazis and their male Nazi followers—men who eroticize a power they both submit to and see themselves reflected in? Perhaps, in spectatorial terms, it is only this male, heterosexual, highly homosocial fascist follower who gets to "play all the parts" of the sadomasochistic exchange.[2]

Even the grotesque intimacy of torture that S/M pornography purposefully distorts into a collaboration hides how genocide functions. Writing of state terrorism in Argentina, Diana Taylor remarks that its scenes of torture and abduction were calculated to be highly theatrical in a deliberately mystifying way (165). But despite the endless sadisms imposed on Holocaust victims, the goal of this genocide was not to intensify relations that acts of torture seek to establish between the perpetrator and the victim, in order to frighten and control other, potential victims as well as to convert "real human pain" "into a regime's fiction of power" (Scarry 18). Lyotard observes that there is only one party in genocide, the perpetrator, for whom victims are under an inescapable sentence already conceptually enacted on them. The goal of The Final Solution was annihilation of any relations at all, even if sadism always gave the obvious and continual lie to the indifferent, impersonal machine of genocide and the "fiction of power" it created.

As an example of how representing atrocity is inscribed within certain conventions of pornography, consider an inheritor of what Eva Berkson marked as the spectatorial desire for a real "cut up woman," i.e., the genre of snuff films, where the "cut up woman" is no longer intended to frighten (as in Guignol) but to please. If most of pornography is all process, the snuff film is not. Snuff borrows the codes of representation in other pornography only, in its acts of violence, pleasurably to disrupt them through horrality. Snuff is about the real spectatorial desire to watch a filmic re-presentation of a "real" woman being really killed.[3] Only the unsuspecting female victim of the snuff film mistakenly thinks a sexual act will occur, that there is some contractual arrangement, some reciprocity between perpetrator and victim. The death sentence is ordained in advance of the film, is in fact the film's precondition, irrespective of what the female victim "did" or "does" either in her private person or as a participant in the film. What does occur can be said to be about the production of relations between men and women, the production, as described in Sarah Daniels's play *Masterpieces*, of power, pleasure, and triumph for one, and pain, terror, and death for the other. But in another sense, within the film's narrative, "she" does not exist at all, and her literal death is proof of this initial assumption. The snuff film can thus be read as the intersection of relations between male makers and male spectators, a demonstration by men for men of the genocidal imagination symbolically enacted upon an individual woman. Snuff also literalizes the way in which fantasy production is social production with material consequences. And snuff clarifies how much of what is read as "about sex"—including acts read as symbolic substitutions for something else, such as the violence of the death spasm for the sexual spasm of orgasm (Williams 194)—is actually not about sex, but the annihilation of a (gendered) body partly in response to a threatening desire the male filmmaker/viewer connects to that body.

Thus, the grotesquely impersonal way snuff films echo genocide's inescapable death sentence enacted in advance is designed to give pleasure to its spectators. Not only is this form in no way commensurate to the Holocaust and its representation; it also is the antithesis of Langer's aesthetics of atrocity. But snuff, with its transmutation of desire into murder, may be a fruitful site for exploring the fascist, genocidal mentality. This is especially evident in Klaus Theweleit's analysis of fascism in *Male Fantasies* (and the woman as "bloody mass" to which I refer below). First, let me note that if Scarry's analysis of the body in pain leaves the body ungendered, Theweleit, in his study of the fantasies that preoccupied the fascist men in the Freikorps, makes a clear link between the gendered body and a fascist ideology of violence. For Theweleit "[the Freikorps'] . . . male identity was shaped by the dread and revulsion that characterized their relations with women—real and imagined—and . . . this dread was, in turn, linked to the aggressive racism and anti-communism at the heart of most fascist movements" (publisher's description). Theweleit speculates that fascism's transmutation of desiring-production into murdering-production is a current reality "whenever we try to establish what kinds of reality present-day male-female relations produce" (221).

Theweleit highlights the Freikorps' obsessed assault on what they called the "Rifle Women" or the "Red Nurses" who fought alongside men on the left against the private army of the Freikorps hired by Germany in 1918 to put down revolutionary opposition. Theweleit analyzes the murders of these women thus:

It's as if two male compulsions are tearing at the women with equal strength. One is trying to push them away, to keep them at arm's length (defense); the other wants to penetrate them to have them very near. Both compulsions seem to find satisfaction in the act of killing, where the man pushes a woman far away (takes her life) and gets very close to her (penetrates her with a bullet, stab wound, club, etc.). The closeness is made possible by robbing the woman of her identity as an object with concrete dimensions and a unique name. Once she has lost all that and is reduced to a pulp, a shapeless, bloody mass, the man can breathe a sigh of relief. The wound in question here goes beyond castration, in which one can at least still identify the body to which the wound belongs. What we are dealing with here is the dissolution of the body itself, and of the woman as bodily entity. (196)

The concrete dimensions and unique name of the threatening women constitute a kind of exterior border to the body; their murder (like the convention of snuff) excessively breaches this border to reduce the women to interior body—fluctuating, perishable, uncontained, and no longer recognizable as human per se. The reduction of the woman's body to shapeless, bloody mass seems retrospectively to prove Lyotard's notion that death "proves [for the killer] that what ought not to live cannot live" (103).

In analyzing the French fascist writer Celine, Kristeva too speaks of "this compound of abomination and fascination, sex and murder, attraction and repulsion," adhering, especially in war, to those conceived as prostitutes and nymphomaniacs and who come to represent "a wild, obscene, and threatening femininity" (167) for the fascist imagination. Theweleit remarks on how, in the representations of the Freikorps, proletarian nurses and female fighters were often to be "discovered" in what the Freikorps referred to as "their true profession" of whorishness just before the Freikorps murdered them (81–83). Part of what is being obliterated in this discovery of a "true profession," part of what is being sexualized, is a denial of another "profession"—that of the leftist, proletarian (female) fighter against fascism. Transgressions of any sort committed by women thus become saturated with gender and sexuality.

Theweleit's work focuses on fascist constructions of the female. He clarifies how the perpetrator's desire to wipe out what has been connected (in his mind) to the body of the opposite sex is not a projecting but a transmutating imposition. And although Theweleit doesn't focus on this transmutation in relation to Jews, parallels can be drawn from the imposition on Jews of a particular set of threatening attributes that makes the Jew, in Kristeva's terms, into "an object of hatred and desire, of threat and aggressivity, of envy and abomination" (178). That this, too, is made into a sexual narrative is readily apparent in some of Celine's passages about Jews to which Kristeva refers:

He's mimetic, he's a whore, he would have dissolved long ago, after assimi-
lating to others so much, if it weren't for his greed, his greed saves him.
(181)
The kikes stick it up your ass and if you want to be corn-holed just let us
know. (183)
Fifteen million Jews will corn-hole five hundred million Aryans. (183)
There's always a little Jew there in the corner, crouching, mocking, thinking
it over . . . watching the goy, who's seething . . . now heartened he comes
closer. . . . Seeing the object so fully aflame . . . runs his hand over that lovely
cunt! (183)

Based on these and other examples, Kristeva asserts that in his own imagining, "the anti-Semite . . . [is] reduced to a feminine and masochistic position,
as a passive object and slave to this jouissance, aggressed, sadisticized" (183).[4]
And the Jew is rendered so threatening (and so threateningly close, similar,
unrecognizable as Other) as to justify homicide.

In both the case of the left and the Jew, the fascist creates himself as the
victim[5] of a sexualized imagining he imposes on the Other: both Theweleit's
Freikorps' representations of the leftist, proletarian "she" and Kristeva's
Celinian representations of the Jewish "he" insist on dangerous sexualities
spanning the heterosexual and the homosexual. In the process, both the leftist, proletarian "he" and the Jewish "she" disappear, circulating invisibly in
this discourse, while receiving internment and death in practice. Thus, neither the construction of the Jew nor the construction of the leftist by the
fascist is gender neutral, contrary to how it is most often viewed. The intersection of *two* gendered areas, then—one related to class and political
orientation and one to ethnicity and/or race—is a place we need to look to
understand the connection between gender and a fascist ideology of violence, and how this connection is inscribed on bodies.

The reconfiguration of the Jew as murderer and the Aryan as victim continues to erupt in our present. Describing the Women's Medical Escorting
Program at Brown University, in which students escort women who seek
abortions at a local clinic past the antiabortion demonstrators (Brown and
Kohn 100–101), Karen Brown reports that the demonstrators hurled frequent references to the Holocaust at them: "The death camps in Nazi Germany were like this—but this is worse, because you are making money off of
it"; or "Everyone talks about the Jewish Holocaust but this is the real holocaust, the American one, and you're all part of it. Hitler would congratulate
you" (101). But their taunts went beyond using the Holocaust as a metaphor
for abortion. Almost without fail, demonstrators would shriek phrases such
as "Jewish doctors killing Christian babies!" (101). Thus once again a fascistic imagination constructs itself as victim (in this case interpreting abortion
as a genocidal plot by Jews against Christians) to justify its own violence
(against the abortion clinics and their patients). Curiously, this example ren-

ders what is often regarded as the struggle of women to control their own bodies and sexuality, as both fascistic and "Jewish."

Another example tellingly enlarges the scope of the perpetrators, echoing the fascist construction of danger and victimization on many fronts. This instance comes from Tom Metzger's White Aryan Resistance "Dial-A-Racist" phone message:

> Almost all abortion doctors are Jews. Abortion makes money for Jews. Almost all abortion nurses are lesbians. Abortion gives thrills to lesbians. Abortion in Orange County is promoted by the corrupt Jewish organization called Planned Parenthood. . . . They can't stop now because when abortion is declared to be murder they would be hung by piano wires for the holocaust of twenty million white children. . . . Jews must be punished for this holocaust and murder of white children along with their perverted lesbian nurses who enjoy their jobs too much. (Ridgeway 172)

The formulation of the male Jewish doctors and the lesbian nurses is a kind of doubling strategy that enacts a conspiracy of Otherness. The equation of the Holocaust with abortion is a strategy of denial, not just of the Jewish genocide, but of any ethical underpinnings potentially generated by such events in relation to anti-Semitism: the "real" holocaust belongs to (white) Christians and is perpetrated by Jews and lesbians. A perfect example of the splitting (Christians and Jews; white and black) and binding (Jews and lesbians), recycling (the abortion debate) and appropriation (the Holocaust) connected to fascist ideology—a process mentioned in chapter 2. There are, of course, historical differences: Nazis rendered lesbianism invisible as a category (and deported real lesbians under the category of "asocial"); contemporary white supremacists in the U.S. give lesbians the same lethal heightened visibility that Nazis extended only to male homosexuals. This increased visibility is no accident if, in the contemporary example, reproduction has become a crisis concerning the scarcity of white babies.

The pleasurable safety of horror, snuff, and Grand Guignol is that the text of our own (feared) physical vulnerability is teased and exploited so as to make it irrelevant to our response to the represented body in pain. In Lyotard's terms, these forms all show the injury to the body *without* showing the injustice to it. Moreover, the "bloody mass" of these forms is divorced not only from the materiality of history and the (gendered) body's historical referents, but from recognizable humanness itself. I realize the word "humanness" implies a biologic essential whereas, as Ann Balsamo states at the outset of *Technologies of the Gendered Body*:

> "the body" is a social, cultural, and historical production: "production" here means both product and process. As a *product*, it is the material embodiment

of ethnic, racial, and gender identities, as well as a staged performance of
personal identity, of beauty, of health (among other things). As a *process*, it is
a way of knowing and marking the world, as well as a way of knowing and
marking a "self." (3)

Certainly, for example, the gendered effects of Holocaust atrocities should
be obvious by now—from the condition of nudity, which even if applied
equally to women and men has a particular humiliating cultural meaning for
the former, to the death sentence for pregnant women. But extreme pain
and dying are also the site of dissolving cultural inscriptions, an undoing of
the body as a process of knowing and marking the world and a self. If the
body is always mediated in representation, is it always mediated in experience, in particular that of genocide? Whenever they opened the door of the
gas chamber (where gas flowed in from the bottom), the pile of bodies was
organized in this way: "Babies children and the sick at the bottom/ Women
above them/ And at the very top the strongest men" (Weiss 297). This may
happen to mimic a social structure that grounds itself in biology, but it is
actually a specific, historical image of violence to bodies that points, horrifically, to the crudity of that mediation. How would we represent this theatrically, and why would we want to? To reclaim what Brophy calls the "agony
of havoc wrought upon a body devoid of control" (10) from the geography
of horror?

And yet, even this representation hides another history: the pile of corpses
that is the signature of this particular genocide, the Holocaust, is in one way
misleading because it always points to the end product of this genocide, never
to the process itself. By process, I do not simply mean the mass production
of death. What the pile of corpses erases, beyond the sense that what is left
was ever human, is the technology of producing docile bodies in slow death
that the Nazis tried to impose on all those who were not killed immediately.
Yes, people were gassed, shot, hanged, tortured, and beaten to death; but
they also died slowly of disease, fatigue, starvation, misery, and shock. It is
hard to imagine what Terrence Des Pres describes as the profound confusion created by a landscape in which live, dying, and dead bodies were cha-
otically mixed. Moreover, Des Pres points out that inmates in the death camps
were subject to what he calls an excremental assault: "Prisoners were *systematically* subjected to filth. . . . Defilement was a constant threat, a condition of
life from day to day, and at any moment it was liable to take abruptly vicious
and sometimes fatal forms. Prisoners in the Nazi camps were virtually drown-
ing in their own waste, and . . . death by excrement was common" (57, 58).
These aren't metaphors. These are means by which, in Susan Bordo's words,
the body becomes a "practical, direct locus of social control" in the crudest
sense (13). Thus, as Des Pres describes it, this excremental assault func-
tioned to induce disgust and self-loathing, to stifle in common loathing the

impulse toward solidarity, and to make mass murder less terrible to the murderers, because the victims appeared less than human (60–61). The process of producing the excremental body erases the body as a bearer of value; it produces, in Judith Butler's terms, an excluded and illegible domain of unthinkable, abject, unlivable bodies that don't "matter," thereby constituting the "proof" of the Aryan ideal, i.e., the bodies that do "matter" (*Bodies That Matter* xi).

This excremental assault has further implications. Kristeva notes that "maternal authority is the trustee of [the] mapping of the self's clean and proper body" and is thereby "distinguished from paternal laws within which, with the phallic phase and acquisition of language, the destiny of man will take shape" (72). Thus the Nazi technology of the body went beyond undoing the paternal laws of the linguistic and the symbolic to unmake the maternal authority inscribed as "a primal mapping of the body" (72). This infantilization marks a radical fissure between social identity and the body. Again, how would we stage this and why would we want to? To show the way the fascist's terror of dissolution of the borders of his body was enacted upon the bodies of his victims in visual form? To get past the task of revealing the constructedness of ideology and representation to illuminate the unmaking of destruction? We might want to examine this slow dying and excremental assault as the site where the crucial drama for the survivor is one of self-reinscribing onto the body whatever shreds of one's culture one could muster.

Is It True That Hell Has No Proscenium? Puppets, Toy Guns, and the Holocaust Body

Of course, the use of the metaphoric term Hell in the subhead above contradicts the absence of a mediating frame. In fact, Hell has no proscenium only for the recipients of violence and murder in the moment of their injury. The first theatrical frame for staging the body in extremity is the actor's (healthy if mortal) body upon which the violence is inscribed. This inscription is further framed, for example, in Liliane Atlan's play *Mister Fugue or Earth Sick* by having adult actors play the children who are being driven in a van from the ghetto to Rotburg, a place of death. This use of adult actors also creates a mediation between violence and children's bodies. Moreover, while the physical suffering of the children is foregrounded, an additional framing device rescues this suffering from the most extreme anonymity of genocide: they are the last four Jews of this ghetto and so have a symbolic significance for the spectator, as well as, in the play itself, for the Nazi commandant. His obsession with killing them creates a personalized relationship, however grotesque, when often there was no recognition of the victims as human at all.

In more general terms, even the notion of violence to the collective, cultural body is a kind of framing and, in one sense, a displacing of violence to the individual body. And what happens when the actor's body is signifying not an individual death, which presumably all of us can conceive of, but a mass death, which basically none of us can conceive of? It may be that representing genocide theatrically means the absence/presence of the body and the ruining of representation that the absent/present body causes. Are live bodies the basis of theatre in a way that we can't get beyond?

One way playwrights respond to this challenge is by replacing actors' bodies with dummies or puppets. Peter Barnes's *Laughter!* uses dummies, for example, to serve as a mediating frame for the recently dead body. During an explosive scene in the play, the file cabinets in an office that both administers death and denies it fly open to reveal a mound of blue dummies among which actors move to pry open their jaws and extract their gold teeth. In fact, seeing isn't believing for the office workers who manage, after the file doors slam shut, to rationalize their way out of what was placed before them. In their anonymity, Barnes's dummies also evoke the dehumanizing perspective of the perpetrators. When the dying body actually is enacted in the short epilogue, Barnes emplots the two men being gassed in a stereotypic Jewish comedy routine ("our final number") that underscores the horrific in its grotesque reversion to a humor that cannot encompass it:

> *Bimko*: According to the latest statistics, one man dies in this camp everytime I breathe.
> *Bieberstein*: Have you tried toothpaste?
>   . . . . (They cough and stagger.)
> *Bieberstein*: I could be wrong but I think this act is dying.
> *Bimko*: The way to beat hydro-cyanide gas is by holding your breath for five minutes. It's just a question of mind over matter. They don't mind and we don't matter.
> (They fall to their knees.)
> *Bieberstein*: Those foul, polluted German bastardized . . .
> *Bimko*: Hymie, Hymie, please; what you want to do—cause trouble?
> (They collapse on the floor, gasping. . . . They die in darkness.) (69–70)

"The Boffo Boys of Birkenau" perform a kind of vaudeville routine. Like puppets, the personae of vaudeville—the straight man and the joker—are just types, repeatable and expendable. If vaudeville performers are types, then anyone could do this routine and once "The Boffo Boys" are dead, Barnes implies that another pair of "hollow eyed" boys in shapeless uniforms will be performing the act of dying. Thus the vaudeville convention itself plays against the repeating murder of the expendable bodies in genocide. When they say "this act is dying," the conventional, comic means of reengaging an audience plays against, and makes even more stark, the literal death enacted by the two characters.

The substitution of the puppet for the actor's body is also a technique in *Replika* by Jozef Szajna; the puppets in the hands of the actors ritually reconnect us with the dead. Unlike Barnes's neutered dummies, these puppets are sexed, including the crippled "Pregnant One" and the "Mother-grandmother" one; so the pathos of this work partly rests on traditional meanings that accrue to particular categories of women. The performance scenario begins with a mound like a huge refuse dump containing objects, actors, and puppets. "The actors . . . [who] are in a way relics of the dead, living reminders of those who managed to survive" excavate the puppets out of the mound and try to bring them back to life. "They appeal to the audience for help," finding it impossible to steady the unstable puppets. They speak familiarly to the puppets as if they "were someone close and dear to them" and "treat them as their partners in the play" (150).

Recognizing "the tragedy of the puppet-creature[s] as if it were [their] own" (150), the actors finally hang the puppet creatures up in an altar-like space. As a mystery, a ritualized mourning, *Replika* uses the bodies of the actor/survivors as a mediation between the living spectators and the dead puppets. But the actors' intimate handling of the puppets, as opposed to the deliberately brutal handling of the crematorium dummies in *Laughter!*, may also create a double seeing for the spectator: unlike a realistic flashback to what once was, which temporarily erases death, this handling allows the dummies ironically to underscore the humanness of the dead, including the anonymous dead of genocide, even as it insists on the finality of that death.

The dance of the coats in Joshua Sobol's play *Ghetto* (1987) is a metaphorical disembodying and reanimating of "nobody." The clothing of past ghetto victims is animated by current characters who are actors in the Wilna ghetto. This gives us a triple vision of the already lost bodies enacted by the invisible but live actors' bodies playing performer-characters whose own loss of bodies will be enacted in the future. At the end of this macabre dance, to which the clothes sing a metaphoric lament of what has been done to them, the actors' heads pop up out of their clothing, to reconstitute and so underscore the vitality of what has been lost.[6]

If, according to Sobol's play, one *can* perform theatre in a graveyard, can one perform a graveyard in the theatre? Exactly what are the "dramatic" or "stageable" actions of genocide? Is genocide an "action" in theatrical terms at all? As noted above, Lyotard proposes that there is only one party in genocide, the perpetrator, for whom the victim is already dead, nonhuman, under an inescapable sentence already conceptually enacted upon him or her (101). "The deportee . . . cannot be the addressee of an order to die, because one would have to be capable of giving one's life in order to carry out the order. But one cannot give a life that one doesn't have the right to have." "It is a 'terror' without a tribunal, and without a pronounced punishment. Death is sufficient, since it proves that what ought not to live cannot live. The solution is final" (103). Only Barnes represents genocide from the perpetrators' point of view and in that play the stageable action is their narrative of denial, not the actual killing. To make genocide a stageable action and to counteract the conceptual nonexistence of the victims of genocide from the point of view of the killers, dramatists often imply some kind of agency on the part of the victims, including resistances of various kinds within the camp setting: choosing to go on living, bonding with other prisoners, refusing an inhumane action at great cost to the self, and so on.

This need for agency also explains the preference for plays set in ghettos where there was a sense, however fictitious, that the death sentence was not so final, and that prisoners could negotiate their own survival, or that of others. This category includes plays that evaluate the decisions and strategies of Jews who administered the ghettos. Sobol's *Ghetto* foregrounds the resistance of Jews who create concerts, theatre, songs, writing—culture of all kinds—in the ghetto out of next to nothing. But, finally, this play is about the obscenity of the so-called choices the Nazis imposed on their victims, including these ghettos' Jewish administrators, and the kind of ruination of larger ethical systems these "choices" produced (this time, should we give up children or old people to death?). The pleasure for the Nazis of this challenge to Jews and their ethical systems is not simply in getting the Jews to do the "dirty work" but in displaying the undoing of a cultural body. The life-sized dummy in this play, attached to the character Srulik, is a comic convention for expressing a wisecracking, bitter hostility that the actual inhabitants of the ghetto must repress.

Several Holocaust plays are emplotted in the frame of a redemptive moral narrative. But sometimes this frame contains more than it intends. The link I suggest above between the gendered body and a fascist ideology of violence leaves unanswered the question of how the relationship between patriarchy and fascism, established through the female body, can be represented on stage without pornographically sexualizing the body in pain in the way that Holocaust scholars have repeatedly deplored. One answer is to keep the female body in pain offstage.

Martin Sherman's *Bent* (1979) and Peter Flannery's *Singer* (1989), though different in their conventions (one is more realistic, one more expressionistic) and their content, both contain a scene in which violence is graphically enacted upon a male. Rudy, Max's lover in *Bent*, is brutally beaten by an SS Officer on a prisoner transport train, and Manik, in *Singer*, is beaten by a Ukrainian camp guard. Both Max, in *Bent*, and Singer, in *Singer*, are threatened into denying any relationship to the beaten man and then forced into beating the victim brutally themselves—in Max's case, to death. So while the beating takes place before our eyes, it is mediated by its effect on the other character and the moral narrative of that character's development that each play enacts. Each of these beating scenes is tied to another, adjacent one that represents the only mention of women in the Holocaust and that is narrated rather than embodied. Max must have intercourse with a dead girl to prove he isn't "bent," i.e., homosexual, in order to receive what he expects will be a more privileged status in the camps. Singer and his nephew Stefan amass coupons so that when it is announced that "Tonight, there will be a fresh consignment of Polish females. Kapos and civilian workers will be allowed to partake, provided they have some coupons" (5), they can trade their coupons to men who want sex and receive food and objects in exchange. Both plays, then, literally represent a traffic in the sexualized bodies of women between male camp inmate and male camp administrator. It could be that both plays seek to avoid a pornographically sexualized representation of women by using verbal description instead. But since the only time women are mentioned is as objects of sex and since this mention is in the service of a male's moral development, it can also be said that in order to implement their narratives both texts themselves traffic in the bodies of women, whose pain remains invisible to us.

If seeing wasn't believing for Barnes's office workers, is seeing believing for us? Paradoxically, on stage, visualizing the injured body in pain is both too real and too artificial—pain is so excessively real as to dissolve the neat border of imitation, and it is necessarily sustained in representation by considerable artifice. As Elin Diamond has pointed out:

> The phenomenal body has an equivocal function when it is called upon to represent pain or to stop "being there." The actor's body is a site of experience that cannot in fact *have* experience; physical death is always a matter of a toy gun while in language the body can be immolated and resurrected. [In *The Theater and Its Double*] Artaud reviled the theater of representation because it cannot "break through language in order to touch life" (Artaud 13). But as Herbert Blau notes [in *Blooded Thought*], language, not body, "has the amplitude we long for, and the indeterminacy in its precisions" (Blau 149). ("(In)Visible Bodies" 263)

Thus words are breathed/voiced by a living body and are theatrical even without the visible enactment by bodies. In *Presence and Desire*, Jill Dolan notes that "in fiction the body can be imagined, trespassed and transgressed, but, ultimately, its corporeality is kept at bay" (185). In their liveness, theatre and performance prevent that corporeality from being "kept at bay," even as the "authentic" body can always only be the actor's. Some of the strategies used by theatre suggest that at least for the body in the extreme pain of genocide, remembering is not re-membering, and enacting isn't embodying. Yet the dangers of the visual in staging the theatre of the Holocaust are double-edged: first, that the anguish of suffering bodies will be conveyed on stage as "real" and somehow comprehensible, manageable, able to convey what is actually an immeasurable absence; or second, conversely, that the suffering, mediated by "the toy gun," will have the seduction of the unreal.

The preference for language, embodied in the human voice—that is, the preference for telling rather than showing horror and pornography—reflects the importance granted to Holocaust survivor testimony. Yet, a wholesale appropriation of testimony is not the best strategy. Peter Weiss's *The Investigation* (1986) presents the testimony of Holocaust survivors and others at the Auschwitz trials in the 1960s as numbered witnesses in opposition to the responses of the numbered accused. Weiss describes this testimony as a "condensation of the evidence" that "should contain nothing but facts" (5). Further, "inasmuch as the witnesses in the play lose their names, they become mere speaking tubes" (5). This is a curious detail since the accused, according to Weiss's description, do not become mere speaking tubes, mere disembodied voices, in the same way. By disembodying these voices, Weiss makes the living body of testimony by the survivor, as well as the living body of the survivor itself, stand in for the dead. In one sense, then, his conception annihilates the survivors of genocide. Moreover, the embodying of the voices of the accused (who are not speaking tubes but "themselves") suggests that the narrative underlying this seemingly unmediated presentation of "the facts" is actually a narrative of Germany's past and present guilt for the events of fascism and the Holocaust, a narrative paradoxically staged at the expense of survivors and their experience of atrocity.

The second major production of this piece in 1980 further imposed on the experience of survivors in an attempt to historicize and force reaction to what the revisionist director Thomas Schulte-Michels refers to as "the reception of Auschwitz" (qtd. in Zielinski 81). He emphasized the pornographic underside of this reception—"obscene, frivolous, dishonest" (80)—hidden by sanctimoniousness. The text constructed by the performance of actors' bodies, then, became opposite to the content of the testimony, a mirror to the (German) audience's own private reception: this Auschwitz trial takes place, according to Siegried Zielinski, "in the repugnant . . . superficiality of a sleazy night club atmosphere" and "the actors [sport garish make-up and wear gaudy, tawdry evening dress]." Predictably, this tawdry sluttishness is especially pronounced in the bodies and gestures of the actresses. The actors "sip champagne and eat candy . . . and the spectators have the opportunity to do likewise" (80). Such a performance may well impugn the genre of survivor testimony itself, implying that suffering is a pornography beyond the particular reception to which this performance refers. Indeed, this version of the work seems further to cannibalize the body of the past for a political exploration of the present. Thus, even the historicizing of our reception of these events, normally construed as an automatic good, can be dangerous. Brechtian alienation effects were cited in defense of this production, but it is useful to remember that Brecht used parable, not testimony, and avoided the danger of literalism in his work altogether. As Loren Kruger points out, the use of "formal" Brecht as a sign of political effectiveness in theatre is a way of appropriating Brechtian strategies without grounding them in his larger social goals.

Three texts—Delbo's *Who Will Carry the Word?* (French 1972; English 1982), Sack's *The Survivor and the Translator* (1980), and Deb Margolin's "O Wholly Night and Other Jewish Solecisms" (1996)—use disjunctions between seeing and hearing not only to render testimony more effectively but to heighten, in Lyotard's terms, both the injury and the injustice enacted on the body. In each text the body on stage and its function are produced by the playwright or performance artist's own relation to the historical events of the Holocaust. Charlotte Delbo was a survivor of a death camp; her play is autobiographical. The subjectivity of all her characters is contained within the contours of these events. Leeny Sack is a child of survivors who is presenting her grandmother's testimony about her experience. She performs a split subject—the grandmother and the granddaughter, the survivor and the translator, the voiced telling and the bodily showing—to enact her simultaneous "I/Not I" relation to the Holocaust. Deb Margolin, an American whose parents are Jews but not Holocaust survivors, but whose childhood was mapped by film images of atrocity, portrays the live Jewish body in the present as it grapples with the history of slaughtered Jewish bodies from the past. What has been enacted on her body and psyche—the unmaking, in pain, of Jews—is located and refracted through a performance of making, of creating her body and its relation to the world in the present.

Delbo's *Who Will Carry the Word?* concerns the determination of French women political prisoners in a death camp that "There . . . be one who comes back, one who will tell. Would you want millions of people to have been destroyed here and all those cadavers to remain mute for all eternity?" (278). Through monologue, dialogue, and choral form, the actors inhabit the cadavers to make them speak the recollections of the one who survives to tell their story. Delbo's narrative is not enacted visually; the actor's body remains the actor's body even as the actor as character responds to the narrated events. Her play stages the excremental body of the Holocaust through voice:

> When I joined my resistance group, I thought of torture; I thought of it a lot, so as not to be caught unaware, to get used to resisting it, and I acquired a certain strength, the certainty of resisting torture. Before, I was afraid. I was especially afraid of myself, afraid of weakness. That's why until we came here, I believed that nothing could divest a human being of his pride. Nothing except dysentery. You can no longer look at yourself when you gradually

dissolve, turning into dirty water, when diarrhea is dripping from you night and day without being able to do anything to stop it, to hide yourself, to wash. I am turning into dirty water. My strength is ebbing, stinking, it flows, right here, right now, while I stand still because if I move it will be worse. My strength and my will are going. I am emptying. It is normal for life to expire through the lips. When it goes through the intestines—that's complete humiliation. (279–80)

Without enacting this humiliation and degradation on the bodies of the women on stage, Delbo nonetheless creates for her spectators a radical paradigm shift in relation to the nature of the body, the relationship between self and body, and the concept of agency in relation to physical pain enacted on the body. The material body here exists in a space beyond visual representation. Delbo disrupts the relation between what we see (the actor's body) and what we hear (the character's "testimony" of suffering, disintegration, and humiliation) in order to mark the limits of any representational frame in relation to the injury and injustice of genocide. Seeing can never be believing, because the stories that the cadavers have to tell are too horrific, too seemingly unreal, to escape the "toy gun" illusion of theatre. But hearing these stories as they emerge from the healthy body of the actor exposes the constructedness of any representation of genocide and engages the audience in an active process of imagining the material human consequences to which "the toy gun" refers.

Delbo's evocation of cold in this play amounts to a "poetics of atrocity"—one that renders through metaphor, works through, tries to measure, however incompletely, the shift in a fundamental understanding of the body, i.e., what cold means in the "other universe" of the concentration camp:

We are in the cold, we are cold, blocks of cold. Before we didn't know what cold was. Yet in the freight cars it was cold. The bread froze; we couldn't eat. Here, blades, needles of cold pierce you straight though. Jaws of cold crush you. Cold contracts the fibers of your flesh, even those on the tongue, even those of the heart. Cold feet is nothing. Cold in the heart, cold veins, cold drafts in the lungs, as though they were hanging in the wind naked. A thorn of cold stuck into every vertebra. It's as though the cold peels you and strips you inside of you. (283)

For the characters, "cold" becomes a place where even language breaks down, where cold becomes a state of being, a state not only *of* the body but the material conditions *in which* that body exists. Because the characters exist not only "in the cold" but also as the cold, they remain static in language, as this one term comes to define their bodies, their worlds, and their lives. As such, they must thus be rendered presentationally, not mimetically. But "cold" (or "hunger" or "fatigue") is not static for Delbo, who carefully deploys the term in different ways to describe the levels of intensity as well as the sites targeted for pain. Language, then, represents for Delbo the one means of revealing the conflation of pains in genocide under a single rubric as well as exposing how even one term can convey both so much and so little.

Leeny Sack's performance piece *The Survivor and the Translator* also makes effective use of disjunction between showing and telling. Sack describes the piece as "A solo theatre work about not having experienced the Holocaust, by a daughter of concentration camp survivors" (123). In the opening stage directions she notes:

> As the spectators enter I sit on the battered leather suitcase near the foot of the bed and whisper just audibly parts of the text I am afraid I have forgotten. But I have never forgotten. The story I tell was slipped under my skin before I could say yes or no or Mama. I sit inside the memory of where I was not. (124)

For Sack, the experience of the Holocaust is beyond her language, her lived experience, and her body, yet she also cannot forget it precisely because the memory of that event is a legacy passed to her and inscribed on her body by her grandmother, the survivor. By merging the body (of Sack) and the voice (of her grandmother) on her own body in performance, Sack demonstrates the urgent necessity to represent the Holocaust, even when words and representational frames are inadequate, even when, as persons who are not survivors, we can only ever sit inside someone else's memory of the events. The act of translation that frames the piece attempts to connect the experiences of the grandmother and the granddaughter, but this act is always partial, because Sack and her grandmother speak two entirely different languages (both literally and symbolically).

At various moments in the piece, Sack alternates words with active physicalizing. She runs frantically on a bed; she recites through clenched teeth; she hits the back of a rocking chair; she screams. These physical activities, located before the testimony narrative begins, enact, if abstractly, the violence done to the body that her grandmother's voice will describe. Unhooked from the telling, the non-narrative showing gives us a chance to contemplate the body in pain outside of spectacle. Also, the voice of the translator in the first section is flat, monotonous, devoid of any feeling but fear. But the performer's body insists on reacting to what it has taken in, on physicalizing its pain in response to the experience and the struggle to translate. This piece, then, is about the process of translation not just through words, but also through the body of the translator.

In the second half of the piece, Sack, speaking in her grandmother's voice, describes the torture inflicted upon Jewish bodies during the Holocaust:

"They had whips. The whip was so long and so over everyone they gave it with the whip on all sides. You understand what they did? Such sadism you can't imagine" (144). The "you" here is directed not only at the spectators, but also at Sack. The translation fails (and we "can't imagine") precisely because what the grandmother's words (made audible in the voice of Sack) describe is what Scarry terms the "invisible geography" of torture. In this piece, then, we cannot see the acts of genocide, the material consequences of genocide, nor the process by which genocide annihilates an entire group of people. Yet Sack insists that we sit inside our memories of the Holocaust, however untranslatable or incomprehensible those memories may be, in order to better understand how that history has shaped us in the current historical moment.

Margolin's "O Wholly Night and Other Jewish Solecisms" (1996) begins with narratives about a dress used in the performance and about being labeled a "Christ-Killer" in school. It also speaks about her delighted anticipation, as a child, of fully embracing her concept of a Jewish identity. She moves to a performance of that identity in relation to the Holocaust:

> My love of my [Jewish] identity was tested on a deeper level by the Yiddish sunday school my parents sent me to, the Sholem Alechem School. . . . I was 4, or 5, or 6 but no more, and they used to show us two films over and over again. They were both those kinds of films that are scratchy, full of black blobs and white flashes which themselves bespeak the apocalypse, and they were hard to hear and see. One of them was called "The Dead Sea Scrolls." . . . The other film they showed us at the Yiddish school was a holocaust film, and it was never boring. In contrast to "The Dead Sea Scrolls," it was striking and clean. This film also suffered from age spots and other technical problems, but it was arresting, like a high-pitched sound, or like that noise your phone makes when it's off the hook. I believe the film itself was silent. I have no memory of any voice. It was visual: naked bodies thrown together like crumpled kleenexes or other soft garbage . . . desiccated babies . . . people falling down and being shot, or being shot and falling down . . . impossible to tell the order of the events, to determine any causality . . . the feeling that maybe the film was going backwards . . . comical . . . Charlie Chaplinesque. Then children of my age, kind of like me, only their faces full of some dark music . . . trees that looked burnt and embarrassed . . . big holes in the ground with very skinny people lined up around them, swaying like reeds . . . always people in lines, waiting . . . waiting. Everything seemed italicized: tilted, leaning, thin and heightened in importance, the way letters in italics seem heightened in importance.
>
> After the holocaust movie . . . , there was a great deal of talk about how lucky we were, and about how if we're not careful these things could happen to us. That seemed both believable and ridiculous. I think I remember a baby being thrown up in the air and shot. . . . This was fine fare for a preschooler, just fine! . . .

This passage describes Jewish children receiving knowledge about the Holocaust in the 1950s, before skillful technologies and pedagogies of the Holocaust museums had evolved. For the child Margolin, the film immersed her in a sea of images, devoid of any linearity, which were shocking, disturbing, but "never boring." Moreover, by describing the images of the film as "tilted," Margolin evokes for me the image of one of the sculptures located outside of the U.S. Holocaust Museum—a house tilted at an unnatural angle, as if broken. The "heightened" importance of these film images suggests a need to remember similar to that in Sack's piece. Born in America, Margolin, like the sculpture, is broken, fragmented from a history that she carries on her body but is only partly her own. She must remember, even if her memories are at once "believable and ridiculous." But she also has a less predictable response to this narrative:

> So, I'm here before you, trembling, and I love being a Jew, in this body, wondering, shuddering, trembling with a nearly sexual suspense over what force is going to have the power to separate this body from this soul, my weightless, immortal *neshumah* from its coveted resting place between my two mortal, falling breasts; and I'm allowing myself the many distractions from that question that a full, rich Jewish life offers.

Margolin includes the experience of the Holocaust in the piece without letting it annul her own experiences in her body in the present moment. She refracts her vision of her own "Jewishness" through the Holocaust, thereby marking her commitment to memorialize these events, without allowing the death and pain of a destroyed Jewish cultural body to separate her from Jewish life in the everyday. There is a powerful sense of both resistance to genocide and affirmation of vitality when Margolin asserts, "I love being a Jew, in this body." She honors and respects the events of the Holocaust but, in Jenny Bourne's terms, does not allow that history to haunt her "feminist Jewish psyche like a spectre" (16). The question of the force that will destroy her is still present, but she *allows* herself to be "distracted" from that question by "a full, rich Jewish life," and the rest of the piece works through her unique, iconoclastic vision of what that life is.

It is, I think, a legacy of genocide for those of the group who survive it—or some of them—to be surrounded by death and, in some profound sense, to live there in mind and, even, body. Another damaging legacy from the perpetrators. But Margolin, using her complex, original take on "Jewishness," performs her own body and its relation to history with a special kind of fluidity that gestures toward the future.

It would be a mistake to insist on a narrative based on the dates when each of these three pieces was written and/or performed—Delbo's in 1972, Sack's in 1980, and Margolin's in 1996. Yet, taken together, they do outline a trajectory of potential responses to these events written out of different historical moments and different struggles with representing and not knowing, each conditioned by the labor of those who wrote and thought before them about the Holocaust.

On August 2, 1990, William H. Honan reported in *The New York Times* that "On Monday, John E. Frohnmayer, the chairman of the arts endowment, told an independent commission reviewing the grant-making procedures of the endowment that in the future, before approving grants, he would have to consider 'how it's going to play with the audience' [since all the meetings would now be open to the public.]" He then proceeded to give the commission his version of that public's spectatorial taste. Testifying before the independent commission that was reviewing the grant-making procedures of the endowment, "Mr. Frohnmayer disturbed a number of his listeners when he responded to a question about what he had meant when he referred to certain art [as] 'not appropriate' for public financing. He said a photograph of 'Holocaust victims might be inappropriate for display in the entrance of a museum where all would have to confront it, whether they chose to or not'" (C19).

Despite the centrality of the historical referent of the Holocaust, Frohnmayer asserted *not* having to see it as the crucial example of our rights as individuals and as "audience." By implication, given this example, the most inappropriate art would seem to be art that represents atrocity unmediated by the pleasurable codes of representation of, for example, horror or pornography. But after all the grotesque pictures of supposedly aborted fetuses that the right has displayed, it is clear that atrocity and human suffering are obscene *only when* they don't support a dominant ideological function: the Holocaust victim, as a horrific example of what happens when difference is rejected, evidently did not.

But, of course, it turned out differently. As one gets off the elevator leading to the main exhibits of the U.S. Holocaust Memorial Museum in Washington, D.C., the first images encountered are enlarged photographs of Nazi atrocities in the camps. And people flooded the museum to see them. And they stayed there so long to see and read three floors of exhibits that guards had to hurry them along. This incident attests to how the events of the Holocaust insist on being spoken, even when the words escape us; how we continue to negotiate our identities in the present against our memories of the Holocaust; how we struggle to see what can never fully be seen; and how liberating and limiting our words, our bodies, and our memories really are.

6

SPECTACULAR SUFFERING

Performing Presence, Absence, and Witness
at U.S. Holocaust Museums

No historical referent is stable, transparent in its meaning, agreed upon in its usage, or even engaged with in the same way by any large group of people.[1] One way of contextualizing the current movement of the term Holocaust to which I referred in the introduction is by invoking Michel de Certeau's distinction between a place and a space in his application of spatial terms to narrative. For de Certeau, the opposition between "place" and "space" refers to "two sorts of stories" or narratives about how meaning is made. Place refers to those operations that make its object ultimately reducible to a fixed location, "to the *being there* of something dead, [and to] the law of a place" where the stable and "the law of the 'proper'" rules. Place "excludes the possibility of two things being in the same location. . . . Space occurs as the effect produced by the operations that orient it, situate it, temporalize it, and make it function in a polyvalent way." Thus space is created "by the actions of historical *subjects*." These actions multiply spaces and what can be positioned within them. Finally, as noted in the train-car example later in this chapter, the relation between place and space is a process whereby "stories thus carry out a labor that constantly transforms places into spaces or spaces into places" (117–18). De Certeau's distinction between a place and a space is crucial to my argument in the way it clarifies the differing strategies of attempting to move people through a landscape whose meanings are uniquely determined in contrast to providing an opportunity for contestation and multiplicity of association.

I want to employ this distinction between place and space in considering how the referent of the Holocaust is configured by contemporary American Jews.[2] Indeed, for generations of American Jews born in the 1940s and after, it can be said that the Holocaust is constitutive of our "Jewishness" itself, sometimes operating at the expense of other Jewish traditions and histories. So despite the very palpable differences among us, both culturally and politically, it is still the case that many of our responses to the images, objects, and words connected to the Holocaust are "hardwired," provoking automatic emotional meanings and an attitude of reverence. This widespread response makes it hard to get beyond a consensus on the agony, the loss, and the mindful viciousness that produced them so we can discern the actual discourse generated about the Holocaust and how it functions. Some of the strategies of this discourse are manipulative; they solicit our anguish, horror, and fear as the grounds for asserting larger meanings to which we may not wish to assent. But neither avoidance of the places in which these "fixed" narratives reside nor simple dismissal is, I think, useful. For this would risk separating us from our own emotions about the Holocaust, entombing them in these monumental stories so that they are no longer available for either examination or change. Instead, we have to create spaces for critique within and among those seemingly inevitable emotional hardwirings and the places to which they get connected.

The following discussion is a step in that direction. I explore how the referent of the Holocaust is configured at sites in the United States where a cultural performance of Holocaust history is being staged for public consumption—the U.S. Holocaust Memorial Museum in Washington, D.C., and the Beit Hashoah Museum of Tolerance in L.A. My purpose in doing so is to honor this history, but also to renegotiate its effects by rethinking the set of practices set up by these two important museums for the sake of both the present and the future. I also want to view each of the museums against the background of their mass-mailed fund-raising letters to explore some of their ideological underpinnings. Finally, my intent in the discussion that follows is to enact a performative, de Certeauian space by not fixing the museums in advance within particular Holocaust narratives, so I can continue a process of discovery for both myself and my readers.

The fund-raising letters of both museums claim the term Holocaust in its Jewish specificity by enlarging its applications to include or relate to other oppressed groups. Both articulate the United States to genocide, but in contrasting ways: the D.C. letters locate the United States as a site of release from genocide;[3] the L.A. letters configure the U.S. as a potential site for genocide. Finally, the announcements of both museums reveal how each museum, perhaps inevitably given the desire to memorialize, oscillates between space and place—between the desire to provide spaces where museum-goers can perform acts of reinterpretation as historical subjects and the need to insist on the more public modality of inscribing over and over on a more passive audience the logic of a place conveying the monumental meaning of the Holocaust.

The U.S. Holocaust Memorial Museum: Narratives of Liberation and Democracy

We had downstairs [in the museum] waiting in line a lady being asked by a little child, what is the difference between freedom and liberated? And the mother, I couldn't butt into the middle, couldn't give that child the difference. But when you

say liberated, you have to be enslaved first in order to be liberated, but freedom
doesn't matter, wherever you are you can be free.
    —Mr. Harold Zissman, member of the Jewish resistance and survivor of the Holocaust,
    spoken to the author at the United States Holocaust Memorial Museum, 1993

In order to elicit donations, the fund-raising materials for the United States
Holocaust Memorial Museum in Washington, D.C. indicate what the museum promises to accomplish—a self-presentation that represents the main
thrust of this institution (Bal 558) and prefigures many of the strategies designed for the museum itself. I believe the target audience for these fund-
raising letters is, primarily, the American Jewish community, while the letters identify the target spectatorship for the museum as the public at large. A
captioned photograph locates the museum by its proximity to the Washington Monument as a means of validating it spatially as a national project.
Quotations by Presidents Carter, Reagan, and Bush about the Holocaust
further authenticate this undertaking, along with a 1945 statement by
Eisenhower—not as President, but as General and liberator—asserting that
he could give "firsthand evidence" of the horrors he saw "if ever there develops a tendency to charge these allegations merely to 'propaganda.'" Also
included on the flyer is an official-looking image of the 1980 Public Law to
create an independent federal establishment that will house "a permanent
living memorial museum to the victims of the Holocaust" (only "a short
walk from our great national memorials" and hence, implicitly, connected to
them). The effect of this link is deliberately to blur the boundaries between
the privately sponsored and the governmentally mandated as a way to inscribe the museum as much as possible within the legitimizing discourse of
its host country.[4]

Of course, any Holocaust Museum must enter into a dialogue with the
country in which it is located and with the positioning of that country in
Holocaust events, but the D.C. museum's emphasis on its geographies of
announcement is insistent. A clear anxiety about denials of both the events
of the Holocaust and its moral significance for Americans is embedded in
these recurrent claims for legitimacy, even if some of the hyperbolic language can be chalked up to the discourse of fund-raising, which in itself
constitutes a kind of melodrama of persuasion. Inevitably, an American Holocaust museum is caught on the cusp of happened here/happened there, a
conundrum, as James Young formulated it ("America's Holocaust"), over
whether American history means events happening here or the histories
Americans carry with them. But given the large proportion of Jews living in
America compared to Europe, this museum has a context of survival, of a
"living memorial" *by* the living (as framers, funders, visitors) that those in
the devastated landscape of Europe can never possess. This, too, is part of
American history.

Presumably, then, learning about the events of the Holocaust, *precisely* because they didn't happen here, creates what one newsletter calls a "meaningful testament" to the values and ideals of democracy, thereby inscribing the museum within the history of American democracy and our rituals of consensus about what that democracy means, if not within American history per se. It could be argued, then, that in this museum the Constitution is to be viewed through the prism of Jewish history as much as Jewish history is to be viewed through the prism of the Constitution. Thus one of the central strategies of the museum is to assert the way in which American mechanisms of liberal democratic government would prevent such a genocidal action from occurring in the United States, as well as partially to overlap, for the U.S. viewer, the perspective of the victims of genocide with that of the victors of World War II. This latter aspect would enhance what Philip Gourevitch describes as the museum's project to reinforce "the ethical ideals of American political culture by presenting the negation of those ideals" as well as our historical response to them (55). In fact, images of American troops liberating the concentration camps constitute part of the final exhibit of the museum as well as the opening tactic of the Holocaust exhibit proper, where all that is seen and heard is presented through the eyes and ears of the liberating soldiers. Even the survivor testimony played for us in an amphitheater at the end of the exhibit prominently includes one narrative by a Holocaust survivor who eventually married the soldier who liberated her. Indeed, this marriage emplotment seems to embody a crucial strategy of the whole museum, with Jews and Jewish history (the feminized victim) married to American democracy (the masculinized liberator). Recalling that the American liberator in this survivor testimony is Jewish as well, I must note another, more implicit enactment in the museum, that of consolidating an American Jewish identity by marrying the positions of liberator and victim.

If what is critical for the museum's project is to extend our fictions of nationhood by the premise that a democratic state comes to the aid of those peoples outside its borders subjected to genocide, then the conferring of liberation becomes the story of American democracy. To assert this story entails backgrounding the masses of people who died before liberation (as opposed to the pitiful remnant left). It entails foregrounding the assumption that waging war can actually accomplish something and, more precisely, that saving Jews, Gypsies, leftists, Catholic dissenters, homosexuals, and Polish forced labor from the Nazis was one of the goals of WWII, rather than a by-product of winning the war by invading the enemies' territory. I could dismiss the museum's overall strategy as a simplistic appeal to hegemonic structures of governance. But to do so would be to deny that the museum *must engage* United States viewers with an ethical narrative of national identity in direct relation to the Holocaust. The alternative is to risk becoming a site for viewing the travails of the exoticized Other from elsewhere ("once upon a time"), or, even worse, "a museum of natural history for an endangered species" (Bal 560).

Moreover, the museum itself does not produce this idea of liberation from genocide as a completely unproblematic and unquestioned historical reality. Within the physical and conceptual envelope of its democratic discourse, the museum offers viewers a display of documents that echo and summarize parts of David Wyman's examination of "The Abandonment of the Jews" by the United States government. The museum displays the actual telegrams that communicate how, as late as February of 1943, with the Final Solution fully operational in European death camps, the State Department tried to shut down the channel for receiving information about what was happening to European Jews (information also designated for delivery via the State Department to the Jewish American community). The rationale was that such information would compromise our relations with the neutral countries from which these secret communications were emanating (Berenbaum, *The World Must Know* 161–62). This policy of suppression of information about and denial of aid to European Jews was challenged only by the intense labor of several men in the Treasury Department who had secretly learned of the State Department's policy. Their efforts finally culminated in Randolph Paul's January 1944 "Report to the Secretary [of the Treasury] on the Acquiescence of This Government in the Murder of the Jews." To make a long, painful story short, in January 1944, Secretary of the Treasury Morgenthau took this information to FDR, persuading him to establish the War Refugee Board by threatening (in a presidential election year) to release documents pertaining to the government's suppression of information and assistance (163–64).

This display of information within the museum operates in an interesting way with both the museum's architecture and locale. Despite the references to its proximity to national memorials in the fund-raising materials, the museum is actually closest physically to four mundane-looking government buildings, including the Treasury Building diagonally across the street. Much has been made of the way the museum copies the blocky functionality of these buildings in its initial entranceway, because this entrance is a false one, without a roof, while the actual doors to the museum are located several feet behind it. Thus the facade of the building recreates the solemn, neoclassical, and universalizing style of the government buildings around it, but marks its relationship to them as architecturally false. However, the documents issuing from the Treasury Building during the forties manifest another relationship, one based in precise historical detail, previously suppressed. This creates a chronotopic connection—i.e., a scene of interaction produced simultaneously out of temporal and spatial relations—between the two buildings and the histories they contain. In offering this information, the museum constructs a localized historical contradiction to its own ideological claims about how democracies respond to genocides, thereby complicating the narrative of our national identity and, in so doing, turning an ostensible narrative place into a space for negotiating meanings. Ideally, this contradiction opens a space of possibility for the spectator to consider how representative democracy operates in the present with regard to genocides elsewhere, rather than entirely soliciting a sense of disillusion, betrayal, and despair about the past.

Conversely, the fund-raising materials promise us another narrative context for making meaning out of the exhibits—one which is less palpable in the actual museum. They describe the museum's Identity Card Project, a kind of interactive theatre of identification. Each museum visitor is to receive a passport-sized ID card similar to the one a victim of the Holocaust was "forced to carry in Nazi Germany." At first the card is only to show the photograph of an actual person, with a brief background; then the card can be "updated" at "regular computer stations" for a fuller account. Most interesting is the actual list of victims from which these identity cards are drawn: they include Jews, Gypsies, homosexuals, Jehovah's Witnesses, and the handicapped, as well as others the Nazis labeled "undesirables." Thus, while still emphasizing the specific reference to Jews, the canon of the Holocaust victims has been reinterpreted and expanded, most pertinently to include homosexuals, whose desire for institutionalized recognition in the past had often been met with silence or resistance. This could offer us one means of considering the relationship of Jews to Other(ed) differences.[5] Moreover, if the actual colored badges of these groups were to become part of the representation, they could convey the way the Nazis visually constructed categories of color upon religious, ethnic, sexual, political, and physical differences, thereby creating a racialized spectacle of visible difference where none existed. Such color coding could also complicate the monolith of European "whiteness" by exemplifying the ease with which that racial strategy was and continues to be manipulated for ideological and economic gain. The goal would be not to instill a passive "white terror" in white spectators, but to demonstrate the constructedness of "whiteness," its instability as a category, and the undesirability of relying on it for either self-knowledge or protection.

In the actual museum, the number of computers is inadequate to allow the enormous number of museum-goers to update their identity cards periodically, so we are simply given an identity card printed with the full individual narrative as we wait on line for the elevators to go up to the main exhibit.[6] And while the museum does exhibit multimedia materials on the persecution of Gypsies, homosexuals, and the handicapped, its documentation on the treatment of the German left by the Nazis turns out to be most critical to complicating its narrative of the Holocaust for the following reason: most conventional "how did it happen" histories of the Holocaust portray an escalating narrative of obsession with, and restrictions and violence against, Jews that culminates in the Final Solution. By contrast, the D.C. museum fills in some of the vacuum surrounding that history by documenting the ruthless suppression (including incarceration and murder) of Socialists and Communists from the start of the Nazi Era (and early on in the exhibit, while museum-goers are still trying to read everything). This inclusion creates a fuller sense of Nazi ideology by offering the additional insight that this violence was constituative of Nazism itself: Nazism, then, both founds itself in violence and escalates its violence in order to perpetuate itself. Including the left in this configuration also challenges the simple binary emplotment of democracy versus fascism.

However, while my readings of the actual museum emphasize sites for constructing multiple meanings and relationships, the fund-raising materials recall the larger ways in which the exhibits are to function. One flyer promises the museum will orchestrate our emotions in the mode of a spectacle designed to command attention, transfix spectators, and narrativize in advance the experience of those who approach it: "You will watch, horrified" and "you will weep" over this "heroic and tragic story." But there is also an overpowering sense of desire in all these descriptions, a need to create an utterly convincing spectacle that will say it all, stop time and space, prevent denial, and make the suffering known. Of course, no representation can do that even if we hear the "actual voices of death camp survivors tell of unspeakable horror and pain." How could the unspeakable of genocide be spoken? How could the interiority of individual suffering on a massive scale be turned inside out into an exterior, if respectful, spectacle? Perhaps this consuming desire for the real in representation, for the convincing spectacular, is inversely proportionate to the process of genocide itself, which includes the production of silence, disappearance, dispersal, and concealment as the underside of its fascistic public spectacles. Perhaps this desire responds to the fear that whatever little is left to mark it afterwards will be forgotten. Or responds to the intense anxiety created by the growing trend Deborah Lipstadt documents in *Denying the Holocaust: The Growing Assault on Truth and Memory*, operating in tandem with the temporal reality that many Holocaust survivors are very old or have died, so that the live, embodied narrative that functions as a bulwark against denial is being extinguished. But the personal artifacts that the letters claim will be collected in one of the museum's rooms—the suitcases, hairbrushes, razors, photographs, diaries, dolls, toys, shoes, eyeglasses, and wedding rings—despite their vivid materiality, are finally only the small detritus of annihilation that point to the inevitable absence of complete representation.

Even the sites of artifacts whose meaning is intended to be self-evident can become spaces, instead of places, changed by the paths visitors themselves create as historical subjects. The museum went to great pains, including revising its architectural plans, to exhibit a fifteen-ton freight car used to deport Jews. Walking through it offers us a physical trace of the frightening darkness and claustrophobic agony of the one hundred people crushed into this and other such cars. But as I moved toward this train-car on the second day of my visit to the museum, I was approached by a married couple, Mrs. Sonya Zissman and Mr. Harold Zissman, who noticed I was speaking into a tape recorder and came to talk to me. Both had been involved in resistance in rural Poland and were eager to speak about this experience. They also criticized the museum for overemphasizing victimization in its portrayal of the Holocaust, while not including enough material on Jewish acts of resistance in its exhibit. I reproduce part of our conversation at the site of this freight car:

VP: You're survivors?

SZ: I can't look at it [the freight car], I'm sick already. My husband, he was the head of a ghetto uprising . . . it's sickening to look at. You live day and night with that, day and night, as a matter of fact we were in the underground, we [both] escaped to the underground.

VP: Were you in a particular organization, is that what made you join the underground?

SZ: Organization? Nah. We were in the ghettos. . . . We were in the Eastern part of Poland and we knew what was going on. . . . Small towns, they had wooded areas, thousands and thousands of miles with wooded areas. We ran to these areas when the killing [of Jews in the ghettos] started and this was how we survived.

HZ: I escaped the ghetto. She ran away after the massacre was taking place in her town while she was in hiding. I escaped before it started in our ghetto—and I have very bad emotions between my family who dared why I should escape [and felt betrayed and who were subsequently killed]. [He weeps.]

SZ: And then the men were forming a fighting squadron . . . and the young ones were fighting.

VP: Did you get to be part of the fighting squad?

SZ: I was. My husband was. Down there in the underground.

VP: What's it like to be in the museum today?

SZ: Horrible. I got a headache already. . . . *But we gave them hell too*, don't worry.

VP: What does that mean?

SZ: Hell. The Germans.

VP: You gave them hell? How?

SZ: We used to mine the trains that were going to the front . . . so the soldiers were going on ten, twenty—that's how long the cars, you know, and they had ammunition going there with the train and [we would] tear them apart [by planting bombs under them]. We had the Russians [helping us], in the later years, '43, I think. They used to send us down sugar and salt and what we needed for [the fighting squadron] to live on. . . . My [previous]

husband, my two brothers, my mother, got killed in the ghetto. [She weeps.]
VP: How many years were you in the underground?
SZ: For three years, because as soon as the ghetto started we had an underground.
VP: You mean you two were invisible and in hiding for three years?
SZ: Of course. We had to. You had no choice.

The live performance of survivor testimony by the Zissmans, "unmanaged" as it was by the museum proper, powerfully produced me as an engaged witness to their history, forcing me to negotiate their "unofficial" story with the "official" one surrounding it. More particularly, what this conversation marked for me was how the museum's larger project of locating itself within a narrative of U.S. democracy displaced representations of acts of resistance by Jews in order to embed its narrative in the frame of American liberation (and appeal more directly to U.S. consumers of museum information). Mr. Harold Zissman put it more trenchantly when I asked him what he thought about the exhibits:

HZ: It's not so much important what I think because we have [lived] through that [history]. . . . We've [gone] through the ghetto part [of the museum]. Only very few stories of our part [in this history] is being told. I wrote a scholar of the Holocaust . . . because very little is shown about our part [i.e., the Jewish resistance] for reasons beyond my understanding in forty some years. . . . My own feeling is too much commercializing became the Holocaust here, the telling about the resistance and the participation of the Jews throughout Europe in resisting the enemy does not bring money, evidently.
VP: Victims do?
HZ: Exactly. Victims do.

Ideologically speaking, then, liberation requires a victim; there don't have to be resisters, and it is American liberators not Jewish resisters that "sell" the museum to the larger public in this American locale.

The Beit Hashoah Museum of Tolerance: Narratives of Prejudice and Democracy

In the process of evaluating aspects of the U.S. Holocaust Memorial Museum, I've asked myself "Just what would *you* have such a museum do? Position spectators as complicitous bystanders? As potential perpetrators of genocide? Who would come to such a museum?" The answers to these questions are not self-evident. Locale and funding sources play a part in shaping what a Holocaust museum shows and who sees it. That the U.S. Holocaust

Memorial Museum identifies itself as a national project imbricates the Holocaust into our national narratives, and keeps a tight focus on the history of the Holocaust, suits its Washington, D.C. locale and its federal grant of extremely scarce land. Although the museum is privately funded, its quasi-governmental status helps produce what is and is not displayed within its walls.

The Beit Hashoah Museum of Tolerance is located in Los Angeles, California, adjacent to the Simon Wiesenthal Center (to which it is organizationally connected). It was built on private land, but received considerable funding from the State of California. As a result, this museum has a more insistent emphasis on pedagogy and is more explicitly targeted for school children and adolescents (i.e., an involuntary audience), although claims for current technologies of representation are clearly intended to lure the public at large and attract funding from private donors. Under the rubric of teaching tolerance by providing examples of intolerance, it can display injustice in the United States and include a multiracial awareness of past and current American events. It also responds to its more immediate locale, L.A., as a site of racial and ethnic tensions, and includes those tensions (witness its speedy creation of an exhibit on the L.A. Uprising) in its exhibits. While responding to the local, the museum also locates itself as an international project that globally documents past and present violations to human rights.[7]

In accordance with these projects, the fund-raising letters sent to private donors prior to the museum's opening employ a primary strategy opposite to that of the U.S. Holocaust Memorial Museum: The Beit Hashoah Museum of Tolerance would represent the United States as a site of "bigotry and intolerance," that is, as a potential place of genocide, with the Holocaust as the most horrific illustration of where intolerance could lead. While the D.C. museum quoted U.S. presidents to authenticate its project, the Beit Hashoah's Charter Member fund-raising flyer quotes Martin Luther King, Jr.: "Like life, racial understanding is not something that we find, but something that we must create." Thus the Beit Hashoah articulates the history of the Holocaust to an American landscape of prejudice and racism, a more liberal narrative that, to some degree, troubles our sense of national identity if not, ultimately, our fundamental fictions of nationhood. Moreover, given the Beit Hashoah's claim to respond to and represent the international, the national, and the local, the focus of the museum is as diffuse (despite the presence of Holocaust exhibits that take up a fair share, but by no means most, of the museum's space and much, but not all, of the fund-raising descriptions) as the U.S. Holocaust Memorial Museum's focus is specific. This diverse range of arenas configured under the rubric of intolerance is represented in the materials that describe the path of this museum as follows:

First, visitors are confronted by ethnic and minority stereotypes as a means to challenge their current attitudes and perceptions. Second, they enter a

Tolerance Workshop where they are given an "authentic social dilemma" and asked to choose and motivate others to moral action (actually a large area resembling a video arcade where multiple interactive "games" about prejudice can be played). Third, visitors view "stereotypical ethnic and racial depictions from early movies," hear demagogues vilifying minorities, and "meet" via video "individuals who have made a difference," including Martin Luther King, Jr., Robert Kennedy, and Raoul Wallenberg. Fourth, "in a series of illuminated computer-synchronized tableaux" that are "amazingly lifelike," visitors "go back in time" to experience "the events of the Holocaust" (and Nazism). Fifth, and finally, visitors stand before a replica of the Gates of Auschwitz and hear the voices of Holocaust victims speak of "suffering and heroism."

While I can appreciate the goals of a Holocaust museum that seeks to serve not only as a place to memorialize victims of persecution, but also as a laboratory for devising strategies to combat hate, violence, and prejudice in the present, I note several problems in the strategies proposed to achieve this. The continued insistence that the museum presents "real life" to viewers obscures the way it is adjusting the parameters of a discourse. Moreover, while "persecution and devastation" have been the results of both anti-Semitism and racism, the museum risks creating an abstract equivalence between the two by configuring both as "an internalized matter of prejudice" (Bourne 14). When tolerance becomes a personal matter, it cannot, for example, take into account the way racism functions as "a structural and institutional issue" within a system of power "hierarchically structured to get the maximum benefit from differentiation" (14). Showing this system of exploitative differentiation and the kinds of subject positions it produces is especially critical for a museum about genocide: it helps bridge the gap between genocide as unthinkable (when linked to the behavior of individuals per se) and its pervasive historical reality. Moreover, discourses of various genocides themselves can be positioned as competing narratives of suffering within a system of differentiated hierarchy, resulting in what Michael Berenbaum calls "a calculus of calamity" ("Uniqueness" 34). I recognize that this competitive differentiation is exactly what the Beit Hashoah Museum of Tolerance is trying to avoid, but I don't think it takes its goals far enough. And missing from the museum's landscape of intolerance are contemporary, violent outbreaks of homophobia occurring in the United States,[8] as well as much mention of sexism: in practice the museum privileges racism as the site of intolerance, which is not surprising if its purpose is to forge links with other genocidal situations using the more traditional notions of "group" that govern definitions of genocide. Finally, the threat of genocide and even actions deemed potentially genocidal may not be the best measure for evaluating the everyday oppressions to which people and groups are subject, and such a treatment may even serve to minimize the importance of daily oppressions, especially when they are not in line with a teleological narrative of escalating violence.

And, despite its emphasis on the interactive, by ending with the gates of Auschwitz the museum takes the space it tries to open up for a consideration of the interconnections among oppressions and recontains it into a (computer-synchronized) place. Auschwitz becomes a monumental metonymy for the Holocaust, for all anti-Semitism(s), and for the consequences of intolerance. Using Auschwitz as an emblem for all anti-Semitism(s) may actually obscure the current mechanisms by which they function. Using Auschwitz as a metonymy for the consequences of intolerance facilitates the museum's Eurocentric gesture of locating its history of genocide only in the twentieth century. In so doing, the museum erases the historical reality that not only could genocide happen here, it *has* happened here, if not with the same obsessive deliberations associated with the Final Solution. A museum with the goals of this one must take into account the massive genocidal annihilations in the Americas, and in particular, the United States, committed against indigenous peoples and against Africans during slavery.

Why doesn't it? Is showing genocide within our borders "going too far" for such a museum (while including visible timelines of other injustices to these groups is not)? More generally, should we assume that if the Jewish genocide in Europe were minimized in a site dedicated to showing intolerance, other genocides, indigenous to the United States, would inevitably become historically more visible? There are African American and Native American museums slated for the Smithsonian Mall but, as Philip Gourevitch has noted (62), no "Museum of Slavery" or "Trail of Tears" museum. Perhaps recognizing the contributions of specific ethnicities, emphasizing what their continuing presence and vitality offers us as a nation, constitutes a celebratory means of covering over what was done to them and who and what has been permanently lost. Our democratic discourse must repress highly visible representations of any genocide that occurred within our own national borders. Thus, in order to sustain its fictions of nationhood and its imagined community, it must produce yet another set of highly visible representations of what it marks as a genocide occurring "elsewhere." Indeed, the genocide film shown at the Beit Hashoah pertains to South American indigenous peoples, to Armenians, and to Cambodians. Curiously, then, at the Beit Hashoah, the perspective of the global with which it enhances its scope is in itself a tactful drawing of attention away from the full excess of "intolerance" in this country. From this perspective, it is the very performance of hegemonic democratic discourse, more pertinently our own "hardwired" fictions of nationhood, that we would need to interrogate and revise in order to make genocide "at home" visible.[9]

But that still doesn't fully account for what *is* shown at the Beit Hashoah as the last big exhibit before the Holocaust wing and how it is situated: the multiscreen feature on the Civil Rights Movement struggle, "Ain't You Gotta Right?," directed by Orlando Bagwell, who also directed the series "Eyes on the Prize." Between the Civil Rights film viewing area and the Holocaust wing, is a peculiar little film displaying the lives of the rich in the 1920s. It's like a sorbet, a palate cleanser between two gourmet courses. Why this rupture? Perhaps because historically, the directional signals are different: the call for African American civil rights is the call for removing the last vestiges of genocidal slavery; although a grotesque and disorienting action in itself, the elimination of civil rights for Jews in Germany is the beginning of the escalation toward genocide (a teleological narrative that would not suit the African American example). The call for extending democracy to everyone, based on a model of civil rights, fits with our "imagined communities of nationalism" even if this assimilative model, drawing as it does on the experience of white ethnic immigrants to the U.S., fails to describe the circumstances of those brought here forcibly *to* genocidal conditions or those here before us submitted to them. That even U.S. progressives have a deep ideological and political investment in the arguments of legal personhood is clarified in *Nationalisms and Sexualities*,which notes a convergence between the "persistence of nationalism explained as a passionate 'need,'" and "the rights of sexual minorities legitimated through a discourse of civil liberties" (Parker 2). Yet, the historical reality of slavery existing legally within democracy does not fit our national ideological fictions and is therefore always already in danger of being suppressed.

To some degree, then, the model of civil rights and tolerance used by the museum, though certainly useful, glosses over very different histories and obscures the ideological interconnections of genocidal events that "happened here" and "happened there." In other words it is problematic to assume that because of the history of the Holocaust, Jews can function as the best guides to the larger landscape of intolerance in this country; such an assumption imparts an overarching symbolic significance to the events of the Holocaust. And yet, to the degree that this museum and this ethnicity assume the responsibilities of representing oppressions beyond their own, they make a gesture unparalleled in the U.S., a fact that dismissals of this museum as a Disneyesque theme park do not acknowledge. This museum, though flawed, is at least an ambitious first step toward putting the mechanisms of oppression (and not simply diversity) into public discourse.

Holocaust Museum as Performance Site

It is the museum-goers (along with the guards) who constitute the live, performing bodies in museums. They are the focus of a variety of performance strategies deployed by museums for the sake of "the production of knowledge taken in and taken home" (Bal 560). Some of these strategies produce the passivity and fascination of "gawking;" some induce a confirming sense of "seeing" by covering over what cannot be "seen" in the very act of offering us valuable information; and some position us to struggle *to see* at the same time we are conscious of our own difficult engagement in "seeing."

If the above applies generally to museums, it has special significance for museums that represent the Holocaust. In a museum of the dead, the critical actors are gone, and it is up to us to perform acts of reinterpretation to make meaning and memory. To some degree, then, the usual museum situation (in which we look at objects) is exploited to underscore the absence to be read in the presence of objects that stand for the violent loss of which they are only the remains. To the degree that this historical, material, human loss is allowed to remain a tangible "presence," a Holocaust museum can constitute a particular metonymic situation: inanimate material objects document and mark the loss instead of simply substituting for them through representation. In this case, the enormity of the absent referent is neither contained nor scaled down through a representation that claims its presence over the terrible absence produced by genocide.

Along with the notion of a moving spectatorship, the idea of performance relates to these Holocaust museums in the sense that they are so site specific. The museum is also a performance site in the sense that its architect, designers, and management produce representations through objects and so produce a space, a subjectivity for the spectator. In terms of the notion of the museum as performance site, the individual performance strategies are not so much at issue; rather, the museum is a complicated, crowded stage that solicits a certain spectatorial gaze through skilled presentations. Everything one sees in a museum is a production by somebody. A Holocaust museum, in particular, can be a performance environment where we are asked to change from spectator/bystander to witness, where we are asked to make our specific memory into historical memory. In a Holocaust museum, when we are really solicited to change, we are asked to become performers in the event of understanding and remembering the Holocaust. If the self-depiction of the D.C. museum as *"living* memorial" is to be accurate, it is precisely because of this spectatorial performance.

In order to explore Holocaust museums as performance sites, I need to create a working model that intersects reading strategies from cultural and performance studies. Such a model requires adding performance dimensions to de Certeau's notions of "place" and "space." It also implies expanding the concept of performance beyond the prescript of the "live" in the sense of "I'm standing up and you're watching me," however important to performance that prescript continues to be. For my purposes, place means a prescripted performance of interpretation, and space produces sites for multiple performances of interpretation that situate/produce the spectator as historical subject.

How is the concept of de Certeauian place related to specific performance sites that produce subjects in particular ways? Place is a site that produces and manages a delimited interpretation. Performance place, then, is narrativized in advance and we are solicited to perform the narrative that is organized for and given to us. A clear example of such a place occurs as spectators enter the tolerance section of the Beit Hashoah: We seemingly are faced with two sets of doors by which to enter—one set, outlined in bright red light, is marked "Prejudiced" and one set, outlined in green light, is marked "Unprejudiced." In actuality, the museum makes the decision for us: the "unprejudiced" doors are just a prop, unusable; everyone is herded through the "prejudiced" doors when the computer-synchronized exhibit mechanism opens them. Although linked to a single narrative, place is more than that; it is a single performance of interpretation elicited by that narrative, in this case a forced acknowledgment of our own inevitable status as prejudiced. Moreover, our bodies are implicated in the task by performing the required movement.

How is the concept of de Certeauian space related to performance in material spaces and not simply to kinds of stories identified as space? De Certeau maintains that we all live in places but should think of them as spaces. Thus the liberating countermove that allows us to understand the experience of everyday life is a move from place to space. When linked to performance, de Certeauian space must be a site for multiple performances, multiple and so not delimited by place. And if space is a site for multiple performances by spectators, it is not just a question of interpreting. Interpretation itself becomes a kind of multiple performance: performance doesn't contain the idea of space until space is connected to multiple performances—which is to say that this kind of performance is predicated on provisional subjectivity. The environment of the museum becomes performative: not only are there multiple performances of interpretation, but the museum design provides multiple scenarios for these performances—scenarios whose relationship to each other are not narrativized in advance.

Throughout the D.C. museum, architectural detail creates a performance environment for multiple, overlapping spaces of interpretation. This especially pertains to the Hall of Witness, a huge, skewed, multistoried, glass-topped courtyard at the center of the museum to which museum-goers have free access (and which contains the museum information desk, some spaces to rest, and so on). In this Hall, repeating architectural detail reverberates associatively: the curved archways in this large sculpted space of brick and metal suggest a train station for deportation; windowlike structures with geometric plates of metal covering them suggest the small spaces of restricted visibility to the outside world left after the ghettos were closed up; metal-barred windows and protruding one-bulb lights suggest the outside of a concentration camp (and structures resembling guard towers surround the glass-topped courtyard ceiling); metal doors shaped like ovens (repeated in the doors to the archive downstairs) along with metal-slatted niches, whose slats open inward, suggest the crematorium itself. These associative details resonate with the literal images documenting these historical events, but provide a greater sense of surprise and discovery, however ominous, for the spectator.

Another provisional and multiple performance of subjectivity at the D.C. museum is elicited when spectators cross metal bridges enclosed in glass. These bridges, which we cross from one part of the exhibit to another, span the Hall of Witness (i.e., the large, open courtyard below). The glass walls of the bridges have writing etched into them: on one bridge a listing of the names of predominantly Jewish towns or communities destroyed during the Holocaust, on another a listing of the first names of people killed in the Holocaust, as if to underscore the impossibility of ever listing the massive number of people killed. So, unlike the Vietnam Memorial, which used the names of specific individuals for its powerful effect, this generic death list emphasizes the destruction of a culture and a cultural body. Moreover, unlike the Vietnam Memorial, the transparent glass walls allow us to view past the inscriptions to the courtyard below.

The bridges are structured to allow us to see people moving about the courtyard, but because of its height, enclosure, and inscriptions, we cannot communicate with the people below or even be seen by them except in a shadowy way. Thus, the bridges are architecturally structured to resonate with the experience of victims – distanced from, isolated from, and ignored by an everyday world of bystanders. Moreover, the bridges become even more suggestive if we notice a photograph of the Lodz Ghetto included in the Holocaust exhibit. As Berenbaum notes, "When the Lodz ghetto was established, the trolley car system could not be rerouted around the ghetto. Three bridges were built [so] Jews could walk over the bridges that divided the ghetto" (*The World Must Know* 82). With "90 per cent of its starving residents working," Lodz Ghetto was akin to a slave-labor camp located in the heart of a city, its laboring Jews undeniably visible. In no way does our walk across the bridges suggest a simpleminded "you are there" reproduction. But it does put the bystander/spectator into a process of discovery and potential transformation into witness, even into a chilling resonance with ghetto inhabitants.

My assumption here, then, is that witnessing is an active process of spectatorship rather than a passive consumption of a pre-narrated spectacle. Another possible performance of interpretation at the same site might focus more on the inscriptions than the bridges. Etched on glass, these inscriptions surround spectators, almost hovering in the air. Our perception is colored by them and the absences they gesture toward, because they are in front of everything we see. Thus names of towns and people destroyed get in the way of seeing the everyday in the courtyard. This also could serve as a larger comment on the experience of the museum itself and the way what it inscribes in individual memory filters how we see the world.

In one sense, we can understand representation in general as about place, while performance is about space. But in another sense, both place and space construct the subject as a performer. If both are performances, the *place* of performance is much more rigid, more likely to be about the spectacular or the quest for the Real. It is the possibility of multiple performances by spectators that might crisscross each other, the possibility of multiple interpretations as historical subjects, that creates a different kind of performance. The critical word is multiple, whatever the particular strategies used to achieve this. But if we think of space in relation to performance, we must think of multiple performances. It is then that the performance interpretation becomes performative.

Walking through the museum can be performative in the sense of discovering it. There has to be a cognitive moment when the spectator realizes she is doing it (spectating), when the spectator realizes she is *in* a doing. (She can also be in a very fixed kind of doing that is unconscious precisely because it is so fixed and pre-narrativized.) One cognitive moment at the D.C. museum hinges on how its designers located some of the video monitors showing archival film footage: they are often located at floor level in such a way that spectator crowding is required even to see what is on the screen. An extreme example occurs on the middle floor, which includes the most elaborate depictions of atrocity: in a kind of raised well are located several monitors (all showing the same thing). Spectators are already clustered tightly around the well, so later spectators must crowd in aggressively to see what the monitors depict. Once there, one views videos of grotesque medical experiments forced by Nazi doctors upon concentration camp inmates. Physical agony and humiliation. And our awareness of pushing to see is foregrounded in the process. What a performance environment like this can do, then, is allow us to experience our subjectivity in unusual ways: When we crowd around the monitors, we are turning ourselves into voyeurs (and not a community of witness). Our curiosity, even our curiosity *to see* itself is thrown back at us. We are challenged, I think, to create a more self-conscious relationship to viewing materials about atrocity and take more responsibility for what we've seen.

Close by this video well, in a glass enclosed space with benches where we hear Auschwitz survivor testimony (no visuals), the museum exploits spatial possibilities differently. Here, in order to make out the words, we must share loose-leaf notebooks containing xeroxed testimony with other museum-goers. The only other thing to look at in this space are the responses of other spectators to the painful material on atrocity. The potential for physical intimacy in the design of this exhibit space creates a site for a community of witness amongst strangers because we are confronted with the presence of other spectators, other bodies, with whom we must cooperate.

Thus, a Holocaust museum becomes a performance space when different activities are performed simultaneously, producing different subjectivities and different goals and aims within the incoherence of that space. It is not analogous to representational theatre because no one perspective can manage it. Due to its more explicit pedagogical purpose, the Beit Hashoah does create something analogous to representational theatre in some parts of its Holocaust exhibit. In the first half of this exhibit, what is presented is enclosed in raised dioramas, suggesting information that can be managed by a single representational frame. Each diorama includes the same three figures—a historian, a researcher, and an exhibit designer—cast out of plaster, three-quarter sized (scale as a way of manipulating performance space), and unmoving. They could function in a self-referential way to make viewers aware of the constructedness of the narrative being presented, but they actually constitute another fixed frame for making meaning within the diorama proscenium frame. Although the three "characters" can't "perform" physically on stage, media technologies such as voice-overs represent them, and films and videos that relate Holocaust history do the performing. Moreover, each diorama exhibit is computer synchronized; each lights up and, after the timed presentation is finished, blacks out. Just like a little theatre. Groups of spectators led by a volunteer walk from the now darkened site to the next one lighting up (against the darkness of the larger space for spectator movement) in the prescribed path. This mode of framed display means spectators have more equal access to the Holocaust information, since, like much theatre, it is arranged to be visible and audible from as many positions as possible. But the guarantee to each viewer of an equal place comes at the price of restricted movement, passivity in response to "the show," and a place everyone engages in and moves through in a standardized way.

Holocaust History and "Manageability"

The exhibition was designed, in a number of places, to make you feel confused, disoriented, closed in. The same way that the people who lived during the Holocaust felt. It's narrow in more than one place during the exhibition. You think everything is going all right, you've come into a lot of space, and then all of a sudden it gets narrow again. It creates a mood. The whole exhibition.
    —Museum guard at the United States Memorial Holocaust Museum, spoken to the author

You have to personalize the story. We are using technology to that end.
    —Rabbi Marvin Hier, founder and dean of the Simon Wiesenthal Center, about the Beit Hashoah (Anderson 1993)

In answer to the problematic question of "How can we know the Holocaust?" both museums try to impart knowledge, not only about the history of these events, but about how to remember the Holocaust, how to make memory and experience performatively. Ostensibly, then, the project of both museums is to make the unmanageable history of the Holocaust manageable. This effort to make accessible to us what cannot be absorbed into anything other than itself is both highly ambitious and impossible.

Much of the U.S. Holocaust Memorial Museum presents the history of the Holocaust as an accretion of detail. The irony is that in an effort to make the unmanageable manageable through this accretion of detail (place), the D.C. museum produces a sense of unmanageability (space). The use of artifacts and dense documentation to produce knowledge and historical presence, and to shape memory, also convey the incommeasurability of the loss by making this density unmanageable for the viewer. What is critical about the D.C. museum, then, in its use of small bits of everything—shoes, documents, photographs, artifacts—is the sheer, unbearable magnitude of detail. An example of the way we are made to enact this unmanageability of detail occurs at what I refer to as the tower of pictures. During the exhibit, we must cross via walkways through a tower of pictures that is taller than the exhibit's three stories. The enlarged photographs, taken between 1890 and 1941, convey the quality of Jewish life and culture that was extinguished in the Polish town of Ejszyszki where almost no one Jewish survived. One virtue of these pictures is that they represent how these people wanted to be seen, rather than how the Nazis made them look or how they looked when the liberators found them. But while the photographs' arrangement in the structure of a tower keeps directing us to look up, the top photos are so high they recede into invisibility. So we rehearse with our bodies not only the immeasurability of the loss, but the imperfect structure of memory itself. This is one of many spaces in the museum that call for physical activity in combination with our hermeneutic and emotional activity.

Insofar as history also is an accretion of human detail, of lists, of too much, the museum offers the unmanageability of history itself. Moreover, these details represent only fragments of the people and the genocidal event that killed them. Thus the museum conveys the unmanageability of this particular genocidal history, and the unmanageability of the detail of that history. Accretion of detail, then, makes the Holocaust not just a fearful absence, but totally unmanageable in a cognitive sense. In doing so it points to the terrifying abyss, the horrific rupture, that is the history of the Holocaust. The shoes are a case in point.

The museum's choice to include a roomful of nothing but piles of shoes is effective, in part because shoes are malleable enough to retain the shape of their individual owners and, even, here and there, an impractical bow or a tassel. So each shoe provides a small, intimate remnant of survival in the loss; collected in piles, the shoes convey the magnitude of that loss without becoming abstracted or aestheticized. The piles of shoes metonymically represent the huge body of shoes collected by the Nazis, which, in turn, meto-

nymically represent the murdered people who wore them, and in so doing
convey the unmanageability of the history to which they point. In their very
materiality the shoes represent at once absence and presence. Moreover,
despite constantly blowing fans, the shoes smell (from their own disintegration) and thus involve our bodies in making memory. The smell of the shoes
is organic, like a live body, and in that way they become performers, standing in for the live bodies that are absent. Thus the shoes, as objects made to
perform an absent subjectivity, are performative. Their accumulated detail
buttresses the specificity of who has been lost, while we performatively enact
the trajectory of memory in relation to them. To borrow Peggy Phelan's
words in *Unmarked*, the shoes, as objects made to perform, do "not reproduce" what is lost, but "rather help us to restage and restate the effort to
remember what is lost." The performativity of the shoes "rehearses and repeats the disappearance of the subject who longs always to be remembered"
(147).

In fact, the D.C. museum seems to acknowledge in its very architecture
that such a modernist project of accretion is only a rearguard effort to produce manageability. The sense of this history as absence and as loss echoes
through the great empty Halls that alternate with the densely detailed exhibits. These large spaces of absence become part of the performance space:
the horrific notion of absence, which is all one can really experience of the
slaughter, is built into the museum architecture itself. Edifice produces
edification. Inviting us into emptiness allows us an awareness of the unseeable
of genocide. And, by creating subtle links among objects, repeating structures and movement elicited from spectators, the D.C. museum provides
resonances that are not limited to one narrative performance but position
spectators to perform in spaces that are, ultimately, unmanageable.

Even the seeming obviousness of the ideological envelope of democracy
and liberation that encases the museum is overlapped with a subtler narrative that could render the ideological narrative unmanageable. There are
repeating metal gates throughout the inside and surrounding the outside of
the museum (including the loading dock). They look, at first glance, like
prison doors and so seem to fit in with the resonating architectural details I
mentioned earlier. But, unobtrusively located among other exhibits is the
artifact that inspired this repeating design: the double gates of a Jewish cemetery, brought here, to North America. They signify the desecrated realm of
the Jewish dead. But the echoes of the cemetery gates encircling the museum also suggest another enveloping structure for the museum itself: we
move in the topography of the desecrated dead of Jewish genocide whenever
we enter this museum. The gates of the cemetery and the gates of the museum make it clear that the whole museum is a graveyard. Notably, even the
presidential inscriptions on the outside of the museum that confirm the
"Americanness" of this project also look like inscriptions on giant tomb-

stones, so that not even the most obvious ideological narrative is wholly manageable. The gates, in relation to the cemetery, lend the museum a sense of unreality; it bursts out of the boxes, the containment, of the usual museum exhibit.

While the D.C. museum acknowledges that it can never manage, the Beit Hashoah museum in L.A. primarily asserts, however reverentially, the manageability of Holocaust history and of its relation to our experience and worldview. In this it foregrounds its use of postmodern technologies, its applications of what Constance Penley and Andrew Ross term "technoculture," with its "postmodernist celebrations of the technological" and its employment of "new information and media technologies" (xii). It relies much more on computer-synchronized and computer-created exhibits, which, in a way, reduce history to information that then can be simulated and re-simulated through various performance technologies. Unlike the D.C. museum, then, which presents its spectators with an accretion of detail, the Beit Hashoah museum provides its spectators with an accretion of information, thereby suggesting that technologies in the current historical moment can reenact the events of the Holocaust in a coherent, complete narrative of memory.

That these media technologies are performance technologies is made especially clear when, as in this museum, they are used to simulate and invoke live presence. The "Agent Provocateur," as the museum calls him in its publicity—the white male middle-class guide to the tolerance exhibit who is designed to express "polite" or unthinking intolerance—repeatedly turns up. He appears as/on a pile of video monitors, each one a screen for a different part of his body. Since he only simulates tolerance in the first place, simulating him on multiple screens (like a creature with multiple media parts threatening to impinge on our frames of reference) is an effective visual deconstruction, as well as a comment on his cultural ubiquity.

The techniques of simulation (combined with the 1960s-era exhibit technologies of the three-quarter sized plaster cast figures in the dioramas) employed to perform live presence are more problematic as used in the Holocaust section. In general at the Beit Hashoah, what is heard by visitors is privileged over what is read. Here music is used to narrativize our emotions in advance throughout the exhibit. Actor voice-overs, most often performing survivor testimony, are heard throughout as well. We are offered a kind of "you are there" melodrama of plaster figures seated at tables in a cafe (not in a diorama, but at our level) with voices of actors representing the figures' conversations about whether they should flee 1930s Germany. We are then given a narrative of what happened to each of them; it turns out these were "real" people whose situations are simulated to create a theatre of identification for us. .

Finally, one diorama contains a holographic image of the table at Wannsee at which the Final Solution was planned. The table is littered with glasses, filled ashtrays, and so on (while voice-overs convey the Nazi presence). I know this "scene" ought to induce horror, but when I saw it, I was fascinated by the simulation itself and how it was made, as well as faintly embarrassed that I was peering at it as I would into a department-store window. What I'm suggesting is that, because of what it seeks to depict, in this part of the museum simulation as a performance technology actually incorporates fairly traditional modes of representation in its simulations of live presence. Moreover, because in simulation there is no link to the referent anymore, the copy passes itself off as the real, thereby covering over the historical trauma of the incommensurable absence of the genocidal referent. More successful is another section of the museum, called the Other America. It includes a large wooden colored map of the U.S. that charts the locations, state by state, of 250 hate groups. By touching a computer screen, visitors can choose to learn more about each group, but the entire body of information would be unmanageable for a viewer. The map, itself frighteningly effective, is made more so by the use of computers, thereby combining low and high tech to create an unmanageable space.

In general, the Beit Hashoah stages a postmodern project of presenting history as a flow of information. Sometimes it is a "one way flow" of information (places for single performances of interpretation); sometimes there is a "multidirectional distribution of cultural and data flows" (spaces for multiple performances of interpretation) (Penley x–xi). Interestingly, one of the most extensive sites for multiple performances at the Beit Hashoah occurs in hyperspace. When visitors come in, they are directed to the top floor of the museum first. This floor contains an archival collection room; the rest of the floor is devoted to computer stations. Volunteer greeters of various ages and genders welcome us to these computers, urging us to play with them, and giving us any information we might need to operate them. We need very little. At the D.C. museum, the computers seem only to point users to well-presented films of survivor testimony or to sounds of Jewish music; however, any other information is hard to access. This creates a de Certeauian place in hyperspace. But at the Beit Hashoah, we need only touch the screen with one finger and more information is provided. Everything seems connected to everything else, so each visitor can create multiple paths for information and multiple relationships among the Holocaust information offered.

If the D.C. museum alternates between intensity of detail and spaces of absence, neither of which is manageable, the Beit Hashoah creates manageability through simulation and a scaled-down narrative of Holocaust history. Moreover, in its focus on tolerance, the Beit Hashoah simulates social problems and prejudices in a way that asserts their manageability (i.e., places masquerading as interactive spaces) even if they exist on sixteen different television screens at the same time. In a structure like a video arcade, multiple "tolerance" games can be played in any order. It is frenetic and noisy there. But the games are all abstracted encounters with difference that ultimately lead to the same one narrative about tolerance. In general, however, the way the L.A museum's presentations are configured under the rubric of information makes them more available for contemporary linkages among differing cultural concepts and historical events related to the theme of intolerance. Nonetheless, because of its urgent desire for narrative connections to the present, it is less available than the D.C. museum for the project of making memory and witness in response to the historical events of the Holocaust, except in a space of absence called the Hall of Testimony. This hall is at the end of the Holocaust section, and made of concrete, with concrete benches and raised video monitors encased in concrete. It is a big, cold, windowless room, suggestive of a bunker or a crematorium. Holocaust survivor testimony and the words of those who did not survive play on the monitors. Between showings of individual narratives, cantorial voices sing. The voices are full of sorrow that cannot be managed, full of the weight of a history that cannot be absorbed, absences that can never be filled, contradictions that can never be resolved.

NOTES

Introduction

1. Beginning in the Middle Ages, Stannard creates a network of relations and meanings among internal Others—i.e., Jews and Moors who are literally within national boundaries—and external others who are being colonized beyond these boundaries. He accomplishes this through interweavings of precise historical detail and without analogizing or promoting a kind of pluralistic equality among all participants. Here are some examples of how Stannard accomplishes this in his text:

> Throughout the Middle Ages, then, war against the infidel in the holy land was a virtual perpetual Christian endeavor, while within Europe tens of thousands of captured Muslim men, women, and children were held as chattel—and Jews lived in a near-permanent state of crisis. (181)

> This, then, was the Old World on the eve of Columbus's departure in 1492. For almost half a millennium Christians had been launching hideously destructive holy wars and massive enslavement campaigns against external enemies they viewed as carnal demons and described as infidels—all in an effort to recapture the Holy Land, and all of which, it now seemed to many, effectively had come to naught. During those same long centuries they had further expressed their ruthless intolerance of all persons and things that were non-Christian by conducting pogroms against the Jews who lived among them and whom they regarded as the embodiment of Antichrist—imposing torture, exile, and mass destruction on those who refused to succumb to evangelical persuasion. (190)

Throughout the book Stannard interweaves actions against internal and external enemies—e.g., "the 'memorable victory' over the infidel Moors in Granada, the expulsion of the Jews from Spain, and the exploration of lands inhabited by 'very dark and grim-visaged' cannibals and other uncivilized brutes"(206)—perpetrated to fulfill "the prophecies ordering them to convert or destroy the ungodly, be they Moors, Jews, or the beastly denizens of 'the shores of the Orient'" (206).

2. The 1997 Women and Theatre Program conference included a discussion of the proliferation of genres and categories for all acts of testimony and witness.

3. This early portion of volume 2, while portraying the author as a mouse (because he is Jewish), and thereby visibly connecting him to this history in an intimate way, is one of the times in *Maus* when the mouse head has strings and functions as a mask. This image not only marks the machinery of constructing the character Spiegelman within the comic book, but points to the way he is not seamlessly in that history; however deeply he relates to it, he puts it on consciously and with the self-questioning that comes with accountability.

4. The Museum of African American History, in Detroit, Michigan, exemplifies a museum that does devote space to genocide in U.S. history. It contains a large section on the history of slavery. Moreover, a key feature of the museum is a reconstruction of a slave ship at its center: viewers use a ramp to move through the museum on both sides of which are replicas of the galleys of a slave ship and the people who suffered in them. Thus the literal space of the museum is configured to repre-

sent slavery as central to African American experience. I also have been told that there exists a plan to create a Museum of Slavery in Cincinnati, Ohio, including information about the city's own role in the Underground Railroad. Cities, perhaps, reflecting their own histories and populations in relation to these events along with national ones, will be the places from which other such museums will emerge.

1. Shattered Cartographies

1. Bertolt Brecht, "Jottings" 458. In "Interview with an Exile," Brecht commented further on the place of Hitler: "In modern society the motions of the individual psyche are utterly uninteresting; it was only in feudal times that a king's or a leader's passions meant anything. Today they don't. Not even Hitler's personal passions; that's not what has brought Germany to her present condition, worse luck. Far more than he himself imagines he is the tool and not the guiding hand" (*Brecht on Theatre* 66–67). This point of view represents one pole in a continuing debate: the other represents Hitler as a diabolically powerful figure. For example, when Hitler speaks at the end of Christopher Hampton's adaptation of *George Steiner's The Portage to San Cristobal of A. H.*, his "hell language" is particularly diabolic because it contains not only a violent rejection of Jewish culture and theology but a grotesque and distorted appropriation of that culture and theology in order to transform himself into a German messiah. Hampton's play doesn't necessarily challenge an economic analysis of Nazism, but it does convey better than Brecht's play that more than economic analysis is necessary to comprehend the murderous Jew-hating of the Third Reich. In *Imagining Hitler* (100–101), Alvin H. Rosenfeld criticizes the Steiner novel and the Hampton adaptation of it for, among other things, giving Hitler the power of the last speech of the work, his uncontested performance of "Nazi apologetics" creating fascination in the viewer. Rosenfeld also points out that works that construct Hitler as a mesmerizer and enchanter are in danger of assenting to the myths that Hitler himself sought to create about his power.

2. By contrast to this depiction of female fascists (as well as to the recurrent idea of fascists having an irresistible sexual appeal for women), David Edgar's *Destiny* clarifies the operations of fascist ideology on ordinary white women by showing its manipulation of the fears of widows alone in racially changing neighborhoods, of elderly women on fixed incomes who are unprotected by unions, and of lower-middle-class women afraid of their husbands losing their jobs and of the coupling of unaffordable mortgages with red-lined real estate.

2. Reproduction, Appropriation, and Binary Machinery

1. Kaplan goes on to ask:

Is fascism modern or antimodern? Is it revolutionary or conservative, left or right ? [Or is this an] attempt to reduce fascism's power by intellectually stopping its binding mechanism [?] . . . [And] splitting, after all, is really much the same activity as binding done in reverse. . . . [T]he fascist anti-Semite was also a 'splitter,' separating what he feared from what he desired by projecting all he didn't understand in modern life onto the Jews, and all that he wished to recuperate in modern life onto the fascist state (24).

2. Kaplan's and Friedlander's theorizing of aestheticization and its effects, with its contemporary emphasis on obscuring binaries, builds on the earlier theorizing of fascist aestheticization by Walter Benjamin:

> The growing proletarianization of modern man and the increasing formation of masses are two aspects of the same process. Fascism attempts to organize the newly created proletarian masses without affecting the property structure which the masses strive to eliminate. Fascism sees its salvation in giving these masses not their right, but instead a chance to express themselves. The masses have a right to change property relations; Fascism seeks to give them an expression while preserving property. The logical result of fascism is the introduction of aesthetics into political life. . . . All efforts to render politics aesthetic culminate in one thing: war. War and war only can set a goal for mass movements on the largest scale while respecting the traditional property system. This is the political formula for the situation. ("Work of Art" 241)

3. In "The Author as Producer," Benjamin states:

> This [mainstream, illusionist] theatre, with its complicated machinery, its gigantic supporting staff, its sophisticated effects, has become a "means against the producers" not least in seeking to enlist them in the hopeless competitive struggle in which film and radio have enmeshed it. This theatre—whether in its educating or its entertaining role; the two are complementary—is that of a sated class for which everything it touches becomes a stimulant. Its position is lost. Not so that of a theatre that, instead of competing with newer instruments of publication, seeks to use and learn from them, in short, to enter into debate with them. This debate the epic theatre has made its own affair. (306)

4. In "'A Culture That Isn't Just Sexual': Dramatizing Gay Male History," John M. Clum identifies this historical impulse as a central genre of gay male drama: "Oppression and resistance and survival and heroic making are the stuff of gay history, much of what can be called gay drama is an expression of what might be called 'historical impulse' in gay literature—depicting and defining the collective past of gay men to affirm a sense of identity and solidarity, and to educate the dominant culture about the brutality of its homophobia" (169).

5. For a discussion of the relation of realism to lesbian representation in theatre, see Jill Dolan's "'Lesbian' Subjectivity in Realism: Dragging at the Margins of Structure and Ideology."

6. Richard Plant does note, however, that "the mortality rate for homosexuals incarcerated by the Nazis was, it appears, relatively higher, in the camps and after their release, than that of other persecuted groups. Researchers learned that the gays, marked by pink triangles, were a relatively small minority in the camps but had

a proportionately higher mortality rate than, for example, the more numerous political prisoners, who wore red patches" (14).

7. "Whether heroes or chief opponents, fathers are categorically denied a voice. . . . To a remarkable extent, they are simply dispensed with. Even the generals whose reports appear here . . . write as *sons*. . . . They write as the sons who have survived the disgraceful abdication of their father, Wilhelm II, and who now intend to make up for his errors. . . . Patriarchy secures its dominance under fascism in the form of a 'filiarchy'—that much is clear. Nothing but sons as far as the eye can see—Hitler too is one of their number" (Theweleit 108).

8. In fact, the historical event of AIDS, twinned with the denial of funds to art affirming homosexuality in the Thatcher period, affected the site and circumstance of production when *Bent* was repeated in 1990 at the National Theatre. As Gerard Raymond notes in "Ch-Ch-Ch-Changing at the National," "This current production began its life as a single benefit performance on June 25, 1989 celebrating the tenth anniversary of the play. It was held at the Adelphi Theatre, in the West End, to fund-raise for The Stonewall Group, which lobbies for gay rights. Leading actors were cast in every role, including the late Iaan Charleson (who died from AIDS this year)" (21).

3. Feminism and the Jewish Subject

1. In addition to Joan Ringelheim's article, "Women and the Holocaust: A Reconsideration of Research," see also Sybil Milton, "Women and the Holocaust: The Case of German and German-Jewish Women."

2. For an extended discussion of these categories of writing about the Holocaust, see Ezrahi's chapter "Documentation as Art," 24–48.

3. For a selection in English of Sachs's poetry see Nelly Sachs, *O The Chimneys: Selected Poems, Including the Verse Play, Eli.*

4. This was the subject of a grant she directed for a conference in 1983 entitled "Women Surviving the Holocaust." See *Proceedings of the Conference on Women Surviving the Holocaust*, ed. Esther Katz and Joan Miriam Ringelheim (New York: Institute for Research in History, 1983). In later work, Ringelheim would replace "survival," given its celebratory connotations, with "maintenance," thereby distinguishing the support systems women constructed to endure deprivation from the omnipresent threat of death in the camps that made survival a matter of luck.

5. Taken from the *Newsletter* for *The Holocaust Project* 2 (October 1988). Judy Chicago's desire to create a "gender-balanced" (8) work on the history of the Holocaust in her Holocaust Project resulted in the work "Double Jeopardy," which she used "to reflect the ways in which women were victimized in terms of both race and gender" (124). "Double Jeopardy" combines sprayed acrylic, oil paint and photography on photolinen, silkscreen, and embroidery on linen to form a 43–1/4" by 22' 5–3/4" collection of six panels. These six panels intersperse photographic images of men's experiences during the Holocaust with those (painted by Chicago) of women's experience. For example, an image of men in concentration camps who are building a wall is combined with two painted images of women cooking and speaking about food. An image of a line of nude men is juxtaposed with one of nude women who are trying to take care of each other in a barracks-like structure. A photograph of hol-

low-eyed men staring out of slatted wooden shelves in a barracks is intersected with interred women who are being raped by inmates, by Nazis, and by liberating soldiers. For me, Chicago's means of bringing a "gender balance" to our understanding of the Holocaust is shockingly literal. I do recognize, however, that her gesture of overlapping more recognizable, documentary images of the Holocaust with ones of women she painted herself represents an uncomfortable challenge to the kinds of images we have come to associate with the Holocaust and so revere. In challenging our investments in these images, Chicago is trying to dislodge them from their generic positioning so that the absence of images of women becomes visible to us.

4. Realism, Gender, and Historical Crisis

1. For a groundbreaking exploration of the potentiality of Brecht's theory for feminism and a re-radicalization of his theory through feminist theory, see Elin Diamond's "Brechtian Theory/Feminist Theory: Toward a Gestic Feminist Criticism."

2. Herman Shumlin directed the 1943 screen version of *Watch on the Rhine* with a screenplay by Dashiell Hammett and additional passages by Lillian Hellman.

3. See, for example, William Wright's *Lillian Hellman: The Image, The Woman*, where he continues to speculate that "So great were the advantages of secrecy to both Hellman and the Party, she may well have been encouraged in her few well-aired deviations from Party policy—primarily her writing *Watch on the Rhine* when she did" (365). Carl Rollyson's newer biography *Lillian Hellman, Her Legend and Her Legacy* (1988) is a less gossip-laden, more reverential treatment of Hellman by an author more sympathetic to Hellman's politics and how she was treated because of them. By contrast, Wright goes so far as to accuse Hellman of "intellectual totalitarianism" (133) as well as obsessively returning to the subject of her "Communist affiliations."

4. See, for example, Samuel McCracken's "Julia and Other Fictions by Lillian Hellman," *Commentary* June 1984.

5. In her discussion of melodrama in America, Christine Gledhill notes how "The country [in contrast to the Europeanized city] was invested with America's founding ideology, egalitarianism, and regeneration was found in its rural past"; Hellman's use of the country home, including references to the cleanness and openness of the house and the Edenic beauty of its garden, suggests these values. Fighting fascism then becomes a necessary "getting dirty," as in the violent response to the dirty business Teck brings into the house with him (24).

6. In a 1964 interview with John Phillips and Anne Hollander, Hellman stated that she had "felt very strongly that people had . . . gotten us into a war that could have been avoided if Fascism had been recognized early enough." So the historical crisis is not recognizing the dangers of fascism in time to prevent war. In this sense, foregrounding Kurt's early recognition of and struggle against fascism's dangers gives *Watch on the Rhine* an antiwar subtext, an emphasis on how things should have been instead of how they ought to be (Phillips 66).

7. In *The Twentieth Century, a People's History*, Howard Zinn maintains that the perceived crisis that determined our entry into World War II occurred "when Japan threatened potential U.S. markets by its attempted takeover of China, but especially

as it moved toward the tin, rubber, and oil of Southeast Asia" and threatened our supply of raw materials (112).

8. In his biography of Hellman, William Wright reveals that in response to the 1943 film version of *Watch*, the Hays Office "balked at the unpunished killing at the play's conclusion. They insisted that the script include some sort of 'punishment' for the killer, Kurt Mueller." In response, "in a scathing letter to Joseph Breen [Hellman] asked if he was aware that killing Nazis was at the moment the national policy of the United States?" and chastised the Hays Office for the incongruity of its response (*Wright* 182). This incident outlines the contrast between the official code of morality for domestic melodrama and the wartime code Hellman imported into the home once she metaphorically relocated the invasion of fascism to the American living room. In her use of the metaphor of invasion, Hellman was creating dramatically what had not happened historically.

9. What may be repressed but traceable in the text's focus on familial crisis and its choice of a European family to convey it is Hellman's awareness of the historically specific threat to the Jewish family by the Nazis, who pursued the destruction of the Jewish family unit to fulfill their fascist biological determinisms of "racial hygiene." It is also possible to trace in the metaphor of the international marriage between American and European a desire for a marriage of Christian with Jew that would lead to protest and struggle against the events of the Holocaust.

10. In *Pentimento*, Hellman relates how the representation of the heroic character Kurt differed from the behavior of the actor who played him. The Hungarian born Paul Lukas had been "a trusted follower of the Hungarian Communist Bela Kun, but the week before Kun fell he had joined Kun's enemies. He saw nothing contradictory in now playing a self-sacrificing anti-Fascist." More of a Teck than a Kurt in real life, Lukas also cheated at tennis, and "Eric Roberts, who played [Bodo], disliked him so much that some nights he ate garlic before he climbed into Paul's lap and other nights he rubbed his hair with foul-smelling whale oil"(*Pen* 190). The angry comedy arising from the gap between what Hellman erected on stage and what actually was never permeates the religiosity of the text itself.

5. Theatre of Injury and Injustice

1. The scopophilic gaze that traditional horror films invite is self-consciously reiterated in Wes Craven's 1997 film *Scream*. The film calls our attention to how the formulaic structure of the horror film can render the violated, disintegrated body as just another convention of horrality. At the beginning of *Scream*, an ingenue asks a menacing anonymous caller "What do you want?" His answer: "To see what your insides look like." When this fate is fulfilled, the other characters describe what happened in terms of the conventional gestures associated with horrality: "her insides on the outside," "cut open from end to end," "completely hollowed out [and gutted]." While this particular film plays with our spectatorial relations to horror, in doing so it marks what is addictive in the genre as a whole.

2. David Savran's "The Sadomasochist in the Closet: White Masculinity and the Culture of Victimization" theorizes a contemporary revision of white masculinist hegemony expressed by the "so-called Patriot movement" and its close relatives among extreme Christian evangelical right-wingers and avowed white supremacist

groups (127). Savran links the most ominous mutation of this "newly hegemonic masculinity" to a particularly "enterprising, malignant" version connected to events such as the Oklahoma City bombing (146). While what Savran theorizes is historically specific to the present-day United States, it resonates powerfully with certain aspects of an earlier fascistic psychic economy. Savran quotes Robert Stolorow, who "argues that both masochism and sadism often function 'to repair . . . damaged self-representation.' Rather than endangering the coherence of the subject, they prove particularly useful in times of [not only] psychic [but also] social and economic crisis because they can operate 'to restore and maintain the structural cohesiveness' of the male psyche that images itself as under siege" (144).

3. In reference to the 1976 film *Snuff*, Linda Williams states that it "seemed an utterly sadistic perversion of the pornographic genre's original desire for visual knowledge of pleasure—the desire of the male performer and viewer to probe the wonders of the unseen world of the female body" (192). In actuality, for Williams, it is a generic "mistake that reads *Snuff*'s violent horror as pornography" (194). Thus Williams's excellent chapter on sadomasochistic film pornography takes as its starting point a film that represents the snuff genre rather than beginning with an actual snuff film. Then, as a generic mistake, *Snuff* gets discussed and put aside early in the chapter.

My discussion assumes the possible existence of snuff films in which an actual murder occurs. Likewise, Richard Schechner assumes an extant genre of "pornographic 'snuff films' . . . where people are actually murdered," while still noting that these actions "are as symbolic and make-believe as anything else on stage" because "living beings are reified into symbolic agents" (170). He also notes that the mode of distribution for such films is "exhibit[ion] for high admissions at private parties" (185, n.10). Curiously, although he describes snuff films as "pornographic," he consistently refers to the one killed as the person or the victim, keeping the usual (female) gender of the victim offstage.

4. In a contemporary example, this sexualized imagining of the Jewish man was enacted in reverse when, in May of 1990 in the southern French town of Carpentras, anti-Semitic vandals desecrated thirty-four graves, dragging the corpse of an eighty-one-year-old man buried two weeks earlier out of his grave, mutilating it, and impaling the corpse through the rectum with a parasol. In response to the event, Jean-Marie Le Pen, head of the extreme-right National Front, availed himself of a theatrical metaphor to reinstate himself as victim. He was quoted as saying: "Given the circumstances, and the reactions of the anti-racism professionals, [the incident] seems to be . . . a macabre stage-managed scene [performed] by professionals of provocation." Ruth Marshall, "Ugly Acts of Desecration: Anti-Semitism in France," *Newsweek* May 21, 1990: 40. Le Pen's version would turn us into the naive realists who have been manipulated by a hidden performance on corpses.

5. David Savran's analysis of what he calls "the new white male fantasmatic" (135) is also configured around the construction of the white male as victim, thereby justifying the instigation of an "alternate authority" with potentially murderous consequences. His article especially investigates how "reflexive sadomasochism has become the primary libidinal logic of the white male as victim" (146).

6. This "dance of the coats," referring to victims of the Holocaust, appears in the American version of *Ghetto* adapted by Jack Viertel. In the British version, adapted

by David Lan (1989), there is an equally effective but different "dance": "Empty Nazi Uniforms" rise out of the clothes to "assemble as though at a Nazi mass meeting to listen to the Fuhrer who is represented by a uniform of the kind Hitler wore when addressing a military parade" (62). This version is a grotesque celebration of being "finally free of the Jew!" who "boiled us in boric and chloric . . . and wrung . . . and ironed us" (64–65). At the same time, the ventriloquial dummy is slashed, whipped, and poisoned. It is a dance of death, an anti-Semitic, genocidal cabaret number performed by the sightless Nazi uniforms, and thereby visually embodying the erasure of the wearers' subjectivity and ethical responsibility.

6. Spectacular Suffering

1. For example, on April 19, 1993, three days before the United States Holocaust Memorial Museum actually opened, front-page news for the Bowling Green *Sentinel-Tribune* (and I'm sure many other local newspapers) included an article entitled "Survey: One in 5 doubt Holocaust happened." A Holocaust survey (referred to as "the first systematic study of Americans' knowledge of the Nazi's extermination of six million Jews before and during World War II") done by the Roper Organization in the United States in November of 1992 and provided by the American Jewish Committee, sampled 992 adults. To the question "Does it seem possible or does it seem impossible to you that the Nazi extermination of the Jews never happened?" twenty-two percent said "It seems possible" it never happened, sixty-five percent said "It seems impossible" it never happened, and twelve percent replied with "Don't know/ No answer." These statistics were framed in a box next to the article.

Furthermore, the Roper Survey found "that thirty-eight percent of adults and fifty-three percent of high school students did not know the meaning of the term the Holocaust." The information presented here, as well as its placement in time, constitutes a kind of self-evident rationale for an American Holocaust museum (though the museum is never directly mentioned) or for a Holocaust pedagogy in U.S. public schools, potentially increasing a favorable reception among the four out of five who believe it is impossible that the Nazi extermination never happened.

2. As Jim Young notes in *The Texture of Memory*, "Over time, the only 'common' experience uniting an otherwise diverse, often fractious, community of Jewish Americans has been the vicarious memory of the Holocaust. Left-wing and right-wing Jewish groups, religious and secular, Zionist and non-Zionist may all draw different conclusions from the Holocaust. But all agree that it must be remembered, if to entirely disparate ideological ends" (348).

3. On the April 18, 1993, op-ed page of the *New York Times*, Jonathan Rosen, editor of *The Forward*, quotes Michael Berenbaum, who was the director of the projected museum, as saying "What we are about is the Americanization of the Holocaust." In response, Rosen critiqued the soon-to-open museum as "building a shrine to Jewish victimization" and so inscribing this (Christian created) role of suffering onto Jews within an American context. What interests me is the underlying debate this exchange represents: Will publicizing and creating a pedagogy for conveying the historical sufferings and injustices imposed upon a particular group result in

better treatment for that group in the present? Or will it reinscribe their position as sufferers, possibly rationalizing or setting a precedent for further suffering? Neither assumption per se suggests fitting the historical events of the Holocaust into a discourse emphasizing the larger structures that produce atrocity and oppression, although Holocaust educational groups like The Facing History Project do try to include this in their pedagogy. Nor does either of the two link this "Americanized" Jewish narrative of suffering and oppression to the production of other discourses of historical suffering and oppression currently circulating: "founding" narratives crucial (however "essentialized") to the struggle against injustice, especially when configured under the rubric of identity politics. It is at the Beit Hashoah Museum of Tolerance, in L.A., that museum designers have tried to place, however imperfectly, this history of Jewish suffering in relation to that of other groups, most notably African Americans.

4. Actually, the Washington Monument, by means of which the museum locates itself within a national landscape, was also privately sponsored on government land. For an analysis of the political and funding history of the Washington Monument, see Savage.

5. Over the years the museum has increased its efforts to depict the histories of Gypsies, homosexuals, Jehovah's Witnesses and the handicapped. For example, the spring 1997 special issue of "Update: United States Holocaust Memorial Museum" contains the article "Gay and Lesbian Campaign Passes $1 Million Mark." These funds are to go to two activities: "an endowment for the study of homosexuals in the Holocaust" and "the further documentation of gay oral histories, location of artifacts for the permanent collection, lectures and special programs" (Update, supplement 2). The museum also coordinated an exhibit of artifacts related to the "experiences of homosexuals living under Nazism" during the time the NAMES Project Memorial Quilt was on display in Washington.

6. More interesting in terms of the use of computers in relation to the Holocaust is the display, within the exhibit, of the Hollerith, a very early data-processing device. This device enabled the Nazis to assert in 1934, "We are recording the individual characteristics of every single member of the nation onto a little card," thus using technology as a means to impose and process the essentialized "characteristics" used to constitute people into groups. While these data were used to persecute Jews and other groups, the reference to "every single member of the nation" recollects the way in which persecution is interrelated with the regulation and containment of the population as a whole. Such reduction of the population to life-affirming or life-denying data ought to clarify the stakes for "normative" groups in resisting genocidal actions.

7. The Global Documentation Room is made to resemble a newsroom in order to give viewers a sense of both immediacy and objectivity. However, as Barbara Harlow states, human rights reporting is both a genre and a mode of intervention, and not only documentation:

Human rights reporting, itself a genre in the contemporary world of writing and rights, entails both documentation and intervention. A recording of facts and events, of abuses of individual lives and national histories, as well as an effort to correct an official record that has systematically obscured those abuses, the writing of human rights draws of necessity on conventions of narrative and auto/biography, of dramatic representation, and of discursive practice. (38)

Some of the museum's educational events and talks are about a wide variety of both internally and internationally persecuted groups; these represent an attempt to take its mission beyond documentation.

8. For example, in 1992, *Connection Journal*, a newsletter for gay Seventh-Day Adventists, reproduced a letter it clearly does not support by a group called The Oregon Citizens Alliance, which calls for "God's solutions," namely the "Execution, Castration, and Imprisonment" of homosexuals (1). In a distinct echo of Nazism (or is it McCarthyism?), the Alliance solicits "the names of suspected or self admitted homosexuals" for its "Homosexual Names-Collection Division" (1). Having buttressed my argument with this horrific example, it's worth noting in general that ejaculations of hate from the far right may exert their own spectacular lure for us as a way of quickly validating whatever operates against it. "Oregon Citizens Alliance." *Connection Journal: A Community Newsletter for Seventh-day Adventist Kinship International* 16.8 (October 1992).

9. For such an exploration and reconfiguring of American democracy, see Brian Wallis's *Democracy: A Project by Group Material*, and Chantal Mouffe's "Radical Democracy: Modern or Postmodern?"

REFERENCES

Adams, Peter. "Unfinished Woman." Interview with Lillian Hellman. *Conversations with Lillian Hellman.* Ed. Jackson R. Bryer. Jackson: UP of Mississippi, 1986. 218–31.

Allardyce, Gilbert, ed. *The Place of Fascism in European History.* Englewood Cliffs: Prentice-Hall, 1971.

Anderson, James. "A high-tech tour through hate." *Orange County Register* Jan. 31, 1993.

Antrobus, John. *Hitler in Liverpool and Other Plays.* London: John Calder, 1983: 11–44.

Arendt, Hannah. *The Origins of Totalitarianism.* New York: Harcourt, Brace, 1966.

Atkinson, Brooks. *New York Times* Apr. 13, 1941: 9:1.

Atlan, Liliane. *The Carriage of the Flames and Voices.* Trans. Marguerite Feitlowitz. Atlan, *Theatre Pieces* 168–229.

———. *Mister Fugue or Earth Sick.* Trans. Marguerite Feitlowitz. *Anthology.* Fuchs 53–104.

———. *Theatre Pieces: An Anthology by Liliane Atlan.* Trans. Marguerite Feitlowitz. Greenwood, FL: Penkevill Publishing, 1985.

Bal, Mieke. "Telling, Showing, Showing Off." *Critical Inquiry* 18 (Spring 1992): 556–94.

Balsamo, Anne. *Technologies of the Gendered Body: Reading Cyborg Women.* Durham: Duke UP, 1996.

Barker, Howard. *Two Plays for the Right: The Loud Boys' Life and Birth on a Hard Shoulder.* London: John Calder, 1982.

Barnes, Peter. "Auschwitz." Barnes, *Laughter!* 27–70.

———. *Laughter!* London: Heinemann, 1978.

———. *The Ruling Class. Landmarks of Modern British Drama: The Plays of the Sixties.* Ed. Roger Cornish and Violet Ketels. London: Methuen, 1985. 619–732.

Baudrillard, Jean. "The Precession of Simulacra." *Art After Modernism: Rethinking Representation.* Ed. Brian Wallis. New York: The New Museum of Contemporary Art, 1984. 253–81.

Bauer, Yehuda. *The Holocaust in Historical Perspective.* Seattle: U of Washington P, 1978.

———. "The Place of the Holocaust in Contemporary History." *Holocaust: Religious and Philosophical Implications.* Ed. John Roth and Michael Berenbaum. New York: Paragon House, 1989. 16–42.

Beit Hashoah Museum of Tolerance. Fund-raising letters to author, especially from 1991 and 1992. Arts and Lectures Program flyers, 1993 and 1994.

Benjamin, Walter. "The Author as Producer." *Art after Modernism: Rethinking Representation.* Ed. Brian Wallis. New York: The New Museum of Contemporary Art, 1984. 296–309.

———. "The Work of Art in the Age of Mechanical Reproduction." *Illuminations.* 1955. Trans. Harry Zohn. Ed. Hannah Arendt. 1968. New York: Schocken Books, 1969. 217–51.

Berenbaum, Michael. "The Uniqueness and Universality of the Holocaust." *A Mosaic of Victims: Non-Jews Persecuted and Murdered By the Nazis*. Ed. Michael Berenbaum. New York: New York UP, 1990.

———. *The World Must Know: The History of the Holocaust as Told in the United States Holocaust Memorial Museum*. Boston: Little, 1993.

Berger, Zdnea. *Tell Me Another Morning*. New York: Harper, 1961.

Bernhard, Thomas. *The President and Eve of Retirement*. Trans. Gitta Honegger. New York: Performing Art Journal Publications, 1982.

Betsko, Kathleen, and Rachel Koenig. "Liliane Atlan." *Interviews with Contemporary Women Playwrights*. Ed. Kathleen Betsko and Raechel Koenig. New York: Beech Tree Books, 1987. 15–30.

Blau, Herbert. *The Audience*. Baltimore: The Johns Hopkins UP, 1990.

The Blob. United States. Dir. Irvin S. Yeaworth. Tonylyn Productions Inc., 1958.

Bloom, Harold. *A Map of Misreading*. New York: Oxford UP, 1975.

Bly, Mark, and Doug Wager. "Theater of the Extreme: An Interview with Peter Barnes." *Theater* 12.2 (1981): 43–48.

Bock, Gisela. "Racism and Sexism in Nazi Germany: Motherhood, Compulsory Sterilization and the State." Bridenthal 271–96.

Bond, Edward. *Summer*. Chicago: The Dramatic Publishing Co., 1982.

Bordo, Susan R. "The Body and the Reproduction of Femininity: A Feminist Appropriation of Foucault." *Gender/Body/Knowledge: Feminist Reconstructions of Being and Knowing*. Ed. Alison M. Jaggar and Susan R. Bordo. New Brunswick: Rutgers UP, 1989. 13–33.

Bosmajian, Hamida. "German Literature About the Holocaust—A Literature of Limitations." *Modern Language Studies* 16.1 (Winter 1986): 51–61.

Bourne, Jenny. "Homelands of the Mind: Jewish Feminism and Identity Politics." *Race and Class: A Journal for Black and Third World Liberation* 29.1 (Summer 1987): 1–24.

Boyarin, Jonathan. *Storm from Paradise: The Politics of Jewish Memory*. Minneapolis: U of Minnesota P, 1992.

Boyarin, Jonathan, and Daniel Boyarin, eds. *Jews and Other Differences: The New Jewish Cultural Studies*. Minneapolis: U of Minnesota P, 1997.

Brecht, Bertolt. *Brecht on Theatre*. Trans. John Willett. New York: Hill and Wang, 1964.

———. *Galileo*. Trans. Charles Laughton. *The Bedford Introduction to Drama*. Ed. Lee A. Jacobus. 2nd ed. Boston: Bedford Books-St. Martin's Press, 1993: 878–904.

———. "Jottings." *Bertolt Brecht: Collected Plays*. Vol. 6. Ed. Ralph Manheim and John Willett. New York: Vintage Books, 1976. 458–59.

———. *Mother Courage and Her Children*. Trans. Ralph Manheim. *Bertolt Brecht: Collected Plays*. Vol. 5. Ed. Ralph Manheim and John Willett. New York: Vintage Books, 1972. 133–210.

———. *The Resistable Rise of Arturo Ui: A Parable Play*. Trans. Ralph Manheim, in collaboration with M. Steffin. *Bertolt Brecht: Collected Plays*. Vol. 6. Ed. Ralph Manheim and John Willet. New York: Vintage Books, 1976. 195–303.

Bridenthal, Renate, Atina Grossman, and Marion Kaplan, eds. *When Biology Became*

Destiny: Women in Weimar and Nazi Germany. New York: New Feminist Library/ Monthly Review Press, 1985.

Brophy, Philip. "Horrality—The Textuality of Contemporary Films." *Screen: Incorporating Screen Education* 27 (Jan./Feb. 1986): 2–13.

Brown, Karen, and Jennifer Kohn. "Reports from Two Campuses." *Bridges, A Journal for Jewish Feminists and Our Friends* 1.2 (Fall 1990): 100–101.

Bryer, Jackson R., ed. *Conversations with Lillian Hellman.* Jackson: UP of Mississippi, 1986.

Burrel, Michael. *Hess.* Oxford: Cotswold Press, 1980.

Butler, Judith. *Bodies That Matter: On the Discursive Limits of "Sex".* New York: Routledge, 1993.

———. "Performative Acts and Gender Constitution: An Essay in Phenomenology and Feminist Theory." Case 270–82.

Calandra, Denis. *New German Dramatists: A Study of Peter Handke, Franz Xaver Kroetz, Rainer Werner Fassbinder, Heiner Muller, Thomas Brasch, Thomas Bernhard and Botho Strauss.* New York: Grove Press, 1983.

Calder, Angus. *The People's War in Britain: 1939–45.* New York: Pantheon, 1969.

Case, Sue-Ellen, ed. *Performing Feminisms: Feminist Critical Theory and Theatre.* Baltimore: Johns Hopkins UP, 1990.

Cassels, Alan. *Fascism.* New York: Thomas Y. Crowell, 1975.

Certeau, Michel de. *The Practice of Everyday Life.* Trans. Steven Rendall. Berkeley: U of California P, 1984.

Chicago, Judy. *Holocaust Project: From Darkness Into Light.* New York: Penguin, 1993.

———. *Newsletter for the Holocaust Project* 2 (Oct. 1988).

Clum, John M. "'A Culture That Isn't Just Sexual': Dramatizing Gay Male History." *Theatre Journal* 41.2 (May 1989): 169–89.

Cockburn, Alexander. "Buckley, Decter and Sobran." *The Nation* 5 (July 1986): 7.

Daniels, Sarah. *Masterpieces.* London: Methuen, 1984.

Delbo, Charlotte. *Who Will Carry the Word?.* Trans. Cynthia Haft. Skloot, *The Theatre of the Holocaust: Four Plays* 267–325.

Des Pres, Terrence. *The Survivor: An Anatomy of Life in the Death Camps.* New York: Oxford UP, 1976.

Diamond, Elin. "Brechtian Theory/Feminist Theory: Toward a Gestic Feminist Criticism." *The Drama Review* 32.1 (T117) (Spring 1988): 82–93.

———. Introduction. *Performance and Cultural Politics.* Ed. Elin Diamond. New York: Routledge, 1996. 1–12.

———. "(In)Visible Bodies in Churchill's Theater." *Making a Spectacle: Feminist Essays on Contemporary Women's Theatre.* Ed. Lynda Hart. Ann Arbor: U of Michigan P, 1989. 259–81.

———. "Refusing the Romanticism of Identity: Narrative Interventions in Churchill, Benmussa, Duras." Case 92–105.

Doane, Janice, and Devon Hodges. *Nostalgia and Sexual Difference: The Resistance to Contemporary Feminism.* New York: Methuen, 1987.

Dolan, Jill. "'Lesbian' Subjectivity in Realism: Dragging at the Margins of Structure and Ideology." Case 40–53.

———. "Practicing Cultural Disruptions: Gay and Lesbian Representation and Sexuality." *Critical Theory and Performance*. Ed. Janelle G. Reinelt and Joseph R. Roach. Ann Arbor: U of Michigan P, 1992. 263–75.

———. *Presence and Desire: Essays on Gender, Sexuality, Performance*. Ann Arbor: U of Michigan P, 1993.

Edgar, David. *Destiny*. London: Methuen, 1976.

Ezrahi, Sidra DeKoven. *By Words Alone: The Holocaust in Literature*. London: U of Chicago P, 1980.

Fein, Helen. "Teaching About Genocide in an Age of Genocides." *Teaching About Genocide: A Guide Book for College and University Teachers: Critical Essays, Syllabi and Assignments*. Ed. Joyce Freedman-Apsel, Ph.D., and Helen Fein, Ph.D. Ottawa: Human Rights Internet, 1992.

Flannery, Peter. *Singer*. London: Nick Hern Books, 1989.

Friedlander, Saul. *Reflections of Nazism: An Essay on Kitsch and Death*. Trans. Thomas Weyr. New York: Avon Books, 1984.

Fuchs, Elinor. Introduction. Fuchs, *Plays of the Holocaust* xi–xxii.

Fuchs, Elinor, ed. *Plays of the Holocaust: An International Anthology*. New York: Theatre Communications Group, 1987.

Fuss, Diana. *Essentially Speaking: Feminism, Nature and Difference*. New York: Routledge, 1989.

Germani, Gino. *Authoritarianism, Fascism, and National Populism*. New Brunswick, NJ: Transaction Books, 1978.

Gledhill, Christine, ed. *Home Is Where The Heart Is: Studies in Melodrama and the Woman's Film*. London: British Film Institute, 1987.

Goekjian, Gregory F. "Genocide and Historical Desire." *Semiotica: Journal of the International Association for Semiotic Studies* 83.3/4 (1991): 211–25.

Gordon, Mel. *The Grand Guignol: Theatre of Fear and Terror*. New York: Amok Press, 1988.

Gourevitch, Philip. "Behold Now Behemoth: The Holocaust Memorial Museum: One More American Theme Park." *Harpers* 287.1718 (July 1993): 55–62.

Graebner, Norman A. *The Age of Global Power: The United States Since 1939*. New York: John Wiley, 1979.

Greenberg, Julie. "Seeking a Feminist Judaism." Kaye/Kantrowitz, *The Tribe of Dina* 180–88.

Griffin, Roger. *The Nature of Fascism*. London: Routledge, 1993.

Hampton, Christopher. *George Steiner's The Portage to San Cristobal of A.H.* London: Faber and Faber, 1983.

Haraway, Donna. "A Manifesto for Cyborgs: Science, Technology, and Socialist Feminism in the 1980s." *Socialist Review* 15 (1985): 65–107.

Hare, David. *Licking Hitler*. London: Faber and Faber, 1978.

Harlow, Barbara. "From the 'Civilizing Mission' to 'Humanitarian Interventionism': Postmodernism, Writing, and Human Rights." *Text and Nation*. Ed. Peter C. Pfeiffer and Laura Garcia-Moreno. Columbia, SC: Camden House, 1996. 31–47.

Hellman, Lillian. "Julia." *Pentimento*. New York: Little, 1973. 101–47.

———. *The North Star: A Motion Picture About Some Russian People*. New York: Viking, 1943.

———. *Pentimento*. New York: Little, 1973.

———. *Scoundrel Time*. Boston: Little, 1976.

———. *Watch on the Rhine. Six Plays By Lillian Hellman*. New York: Random House, 1979. 227–301.

Heschel, Susannah, ed. *On Being a Jewish Feminist: A Reader*. New York: Schocken Books, 1983.

Honan, William H. "Two Who Lost Arts Grants Are Up For New Ones." *New York Times* Aug. 2, 1990: C19.

Huyssen, Andreas. *After the Great Divide: Modernism, Mass Culture, Postmodernism*. Bloomington: Indiana UP, 1986.

Itzin, Catherine. "Theater, Politics, and the Working Class." Interview with David Edgar. *Tribune* Apr. 22, 1977.

Kaplan, Alice Yaeger. *Reproductions of Banality: Fascism, Literature, and French Intellectual Life*. Minneapolis: U of Minnesota P, 1986.

Kaplan, E. Ann. "Mothering, Feminism and Representation: The Maternal in Melodrama and the Woman's Film 1910–1940." Gledhill 113–37.

Karmel, Ilona. *An Estate of Memory*. New York: The Feminist Press at the City University of New York, 1986.

Kaye/Kantrowitz, Melanie. "Class, Women, and 'The Black-Jewish Question.'" *Tikkun: A Bimonthly Jewish Critique of Politics, Culture and Society* 4 (July/Aug. 1989): 97–101.

———. "To Be a Radical Jew in the Late 20ᵗʰ Century." Kaye/Kantrowitz, *The Tribe of Dina* 264–287.

Kaye/Kantrowitz, Melanie, and Irena Klepfisz, eds. *The Tribe of Dina: A Jewish Women's Anthology*. Montpelier, VT: Sinister Wisdom Books, 1986.

Kihss, Peter. "Its Cast Rescues 'Rhine.'" *New York Times* Jan. 7, 1980: C15.

King, Katie. *Theory in Its Feminist Travels: Conversations in U.S. Women's Movements*. Bloomington: Indiana UP, 1994.

Klepfisz, Irena. "Bread and Candy: Songs of the Holocaust." *Bridges: A Journal for Jewish Feminists and Our Friends* 2.2 (Fall 1991): 13–43.

Knapp, Bettina L. "Interview with Liliane Atlan." *Off-Stage Voices*. New York: The Whitson Publishing Co., 1977. 197–204.

Kristeva, Julia. *Powers of Horror: An Essay on Abjection*. Trans. Leon S. Rouding. New York: Columbia UP, 1982.

Kruger, Loren. "The Dis-Play's The Thing: Gender and Public Sphere in Contemporary British Theatre." *Theatre Journal* 42.1 (Mar. 1990): 27–47.

Langer, Lawrence L. *The Holocaust and the Literary Imagination*. New Haven: Yale UP, 1975.

Lanzmann, Claude. *Shoah, An Oral History of the Holocaust: The Complete Text of the Film*. New York: Pantheon, 1985.

LaPlace, Maria. "Producing and Consuming the Woman's Film: Discursive Struggle in *Now Voyager*." Gledhill 138–166.

Lemkin, Raphael. *Axis Rule in Occupied Europe: Laws of Occupation, Analysis of Government, Proposals for Redress*. Washington: Carnegie Endowment for International Peace, Division of International Law, 1944.

Lipstadt, Deborah. *Denying the Holocaust: The Growing Assault on Truth and Memory*. New York: The Free Press, 1993.

Lowe, Stephen. *Touched*. London: Methuen, 1979.

Lyotard, Jean-Francois. *The Differend: Phrases in Dispute.* Trans. Georges Van Den Abbeele. Minneapolis: U of Minnesota P, 1988.

MacDonald, Robert. *Summit Conference.* New York: Broadway Play Publishing, Inc., 1983.

Malkin, Jeanette R. "Pulling the Pants Off History: Politics and Postmodernism in Thomas Bernhard's *Eve of Retirement.*" *Theatre Journal* 47.1 (1995): 105–19.

Mantle, Burns. "'Watch on the Rhine' Stirring Drama of a Family of Refugees." *New York Daily News* Apr. 2, 1941.

Margolin, Deb. "O Wholly Night and Other Jewish Solecisms." Unpublished manuscript. 1996.

Margulies, Donald. *The Model Apartment.* New York: Dramatists Play Service Inc., 1990.

Marrus, Michael R. *The Holocaust in History.* Hanover: New England UP, 1987.

Milton, Sybil. "Women and the Holocaust: The Case of German and German-Jewish Women." Bridenthal 297–333.

Modleski, Tania. *Loving with a Vengeance: Mass-Produced Fantasies for Women.* New York: Methuen, 1982.

Moody, Richard. *Lillian Hellman: Playwright.* New York: Pegasus, 1972.

Mosse, George L.. *Masses and Man: Nationalist and Fascist Perceptions of Reality.* New York: Howard Fertig, 1980.

———. *Nazi Culture: Intellectual, Cultural and Social Life in the Third Reich.* New York: Grosset and Dunlap, 1966.

Mouffe, Chantal. "Radical Democracy: Modern or Postmodern?" Trans. Paul Holdengraber. *Universal Abandon? The Politics of Postmodernism.* Ed. Andrew Ross. Minneapolis: U of Minnesota P, 1988. 31–45.

Mueller, Heiner. *The Slaughter. Theatre* 17.2 (1986): 23–29.

Mulvey, Laura. "Visual Pleasure and Narrative Cinema." *Art After Modernism: Rethinking Representation.* Ed. Brian Wallis. New York: The New Museum of Contemporary Art/David R. Godine, 1984. 361–74.

"Museum of Tolerance Rises From Ashes." *The New York Times* Feb. 10, 1993: B1.

Nolte, Ernst. *Three Faces of Fascism: Action Francaise, Italian Fascism, National Socialism.* Trans. L. Vennewitz. New York: Holt, Rinehart and Winston, 1966.

Novick, Julius. "Pentimentality." *Village Voice* Jan. 14, 1980: 84.

Ozick, Cynthia. "Notes Toward Finding the Right Question." Heschel 120–51.

Parker, Andrew, et al., eds. *Nationalisms and Sexualities.* New York: Routledge, 1992.

Penley, Constance, and Andrew Ross, eds. *Technoculture.* Cultural Politics 3. Minneapolis: U of Minnesota P, 1991.

Phelan, Peggy. *Unmarked: The Politics of Performance.* New York: Routledge, 1993.

Phillips, John, and Anne Hollander. "The Art of the Theater I: Lillian Hellman—An Interview." *Paris Review.* Rpt. in *Conversations with Lillian Hellman.* Ed. Jackson R. Bryer, Jackson: UP of Mississippi, 1986. 53–72.

Plant, Richard. *The Pink Triangle: The Nazi War Against Homosexuals.* New York: Henry Holt and Co., 1986.

Plaskow, Judith. "Jewish Feminism: About Men." *Tikkun: A Bimonthly Jewish Critique of Politics, Culture and Society* 7.4 (July/Aug. 1992): 51, 76.

———. "The Right Question Is Theological." Heschel 223–33.

Porter, Dennis. "Soap Time: Thoughts on a Commodity Art Form." *College English* 38 (1977): 782–88.

Rabinbach, Anson G. "Toward a Marxist Theory of Fascism and National Socialism: A Report on Developments in West Germany." *New German Critique* 1.3 (Fall 1974).

Raymond, Gerard. "Ch-Ch-Ch-Changing at the National." *Theatre Week* Apr. 30, 1990: 20–22.

Ridgeway, James. *Blood in the Face: The Ku Klux Klan, Aryan Nations, Nazi Skinheads, and the Rise of a New White Culture*. New York: Thunder's Mouth Press, 1990.

Ringelheim, Joan. "Women and the Holocaust: A Reconsideration of Research." *Signs: A Journal of Women in Culture and Society* 10.4 (Summer 1985): 741–61.

Roberts, Philip. "Edward Bond's *Summer*: 'a voice from the working class.'" *Modern Drama* 26.2 (June 1983): 127–38.

Rodowick, David N. "Madness, Authority, and Ideology: The Domestic Melodrama of the 1950s." Gledhill 268–80.

Rollyson, Carl. *Lillian Hellman, Her Legend and Her Legacy*. New York: St. Martin's, 1988.

Rosen, Jonathan. "The Misguided Holocaust Museum." Op-ed section, *The New York Times* April 18, 1993.

Rosenfeld, Alvin H. *Imagining Hitler*. Bloomington: Indiana UP, 1985.

Rousset, David. *The Other Kingdom*. French version 1947. Trans. Ramon Guthrie. New York: Fertig, 1982.

Ryan, Desmond. "The Day the Nazis Plotted Genocide." *Philadelphia (Pennsylvania) Inquirer* Dec. 6, 1987: 16:A13.

Sachs, Nelly. *Eli: A Mystery Play of the Sufferings of Israel*. Trans. Christopher Holme. Fuchs 1–52.

———. *O The Chimneys: Selected Poems, Including the Verse Play, Eli*. Trans. Michael Hamburger et al. New York: Farrar, 1967.

Sack, Leeny. *The Survivor and the Translator. Out From Under: Texts by Women Performance Artists*. Ed. Lenora Champagne. New York: Theatre Communications Group, 1990. 119–51.

Savage, Kirk. "The Self-made Monument: George Washington and the Fight to Erect a National Memorial." *Critical Issues in Public Art: Content, Context, and Controversy*. Eds. Harriet F. Senie and Sally Webster. New York: Harper Collins Publishers, 1992. 5–32.

Savran, David. "The Sadomasochist in the Closet: White Masculinity and the Culture of Victimization." *Differences* 8.2 (1996): 127–52.

Scarry, Elaine. *The Body in Pain: The Making and Unmaking of the World*. New York: Oxford UP, 1985.

Schechner, Richard. *Performance Theory*. Rev. ed. New York: Routledge, 1988.

Schenkar, Joan. "The Last of Hitler." Unpublished manuscript. 1982.

———. *The Last of Hitler. Signs of Life: Six Comedies of Menace*. Ed. Vivian Patraka. Hanover: Wesleyan UP, 1998. 131–202.

———. *Signs of Life. The Women's Project: Seven New Plays By Women*. Ed. Julia Miles. New York: Performing Arts Publications and American Place Theatre, 1980. 307–62.

Schevill, James. *Cathedral of Ice*. Fuchs 231–301.

Schindler's List. United States. Dir. Steven Spielberg. Universal Pictures, 1993.

Scream. United States. Dir. Wes Craven. Dimension Films, 1996.

Sedgwick, Eve Kosofsky. "Privilege of Unknowing: Lesbianism and Epistemology in Diderot." *Genders* 1 (Spring 1988): 102–24.

Shawn, Wallace. *Aunt Dan and Lemon*. New York: Grove Press, 1985.

Sherman, Martin. *Bent*. New York: Avon Books, 1979.

Sherwood, Robert. *There Shall Be No Night*. New York: Scribner's, 1940.

Shoah. France. Dir. Claude Lanzmann. Les Films Aleph and Historia Films, 1985.

Skloot, Robert. *The Darkness We Carry: The Drama of the Holocaust*. Madison: U of Wisconsin P, 1988.

———., ed. *The Theatre of the Holocaust: Four Plays*. Madison: U of Wisconsin P, 1982.

Smith, Anna Deavere. *Fires in the Mirror: Crown Heights Brooklyn and Other Identities*. New York: Anchor Books, 1993.

Sobol, Joshua. *Ghetto*. Adapted by Jack Viertel. Fuchs 153–230.

———. *Ghetto: In a version by David Lan*. London: Nick Hern Books, 1989.

Solomon, Alisa. "Building a Movement: Jewish Feminists Speak Out on Israel." *Bridges, the Feminist Newsletter of New Jewish Agenda* 1 (Spring 1990): 41–56.

———. "Special Section: Jewish Feminists Organize to End the Occupation." *Bridges: The Feminist Newsletter of New Jewish Agenda* 3.2 (July 1989): 10–19.

Sontag, Susan. *Under the Sign of Saturn*. New York: Farrar, 1980.

Spiegelman, Art. *Maus: A Survivor's Tale*. New York: Pantheon, 1986.

———. *Maus: A Survivor's Tale, II: And Here My Troubles Began*. New York: Pantheon, 1991.

Stannard, David E. *American Holocaust: Columbus and the Conquest of the New World*. New York: Oxford UP, 1992.

Szajna, Jozef. *Replika*. Trans. E. J. Czerwinski. Fuchs. 147–52.

Tabori, George. *The Cannibals*. Skloot, *The Theatre of the Holocaust* 197–266.

Taylor, C. P. *Good, A Tragedy*. London: Methuen, 1982.

Taylor, Diana. "Theatre and Terrorism: Griselda Gambaro's Information for Foreigners." *Theatre Journal* 42 (May 1990): 165–82.

Theweleit, Klaus. *Male Fantasies—Volume 1: Women, Floods, Bodies, History*. Trans. Stephen Conway, in collaboration with Erica Carter and Chris Turner. Minneapolis: U of Minnesota P, 1987.

Triumph of the Will. Germany. Dir. Leni Riefenstahl. 1935.

Turner, Henry, ed. *Reappraisals of Fascism*. New York: New Viewpoints, 1975.

United States Holocaust Memorial Museum. Fund-raising letters to author, especially from 1991 through 1992, including its "Charter Supporter Acceptance Form."

Wade, Brian. *Blitzkrieg. Blitzkrieg and Other Plays*. Ed. Brian Wade. Toronto: Playwrights Press, 1979. 41–76.

Wallis, Brian, ed. *Democracy: A Project by Group Material*. Discussions in Contemporary Culture 5, sponsored by the Dia Art Foundation. Seattle: Bay Press, 1990.

The Wansee Conference. Germany. Dir. Heinz Schirk. Rearguard Pictures/Films Inc., 1984.

Watch on the Rhine. United States. Dir. Herman Shumlin. Warner Brothers, 1943.

Weber, Eugen. *Varieties of Fascism: Doctrines of Revolution in the Twentieth Century.* Melbourne, FL: Robert E. Krieger, 1982.

Weiss, Peter. *The Investigation.* Trans. Jon Swan and Ulu Grosbard. Chicago: The Dramatic Publishing Co., 1966.

White, Hayden. *Tropics of Discourse: Essays in Cultural Criticism.* Baltimore: The Johns Hopkins UP, 1978.

White, Michael. "Auschwitz Victim Counters Student's Hitler Speech." *Bowling Green Sentinal Tribune* March 5, 1992.

Williams, Linda. *Hard Core: Power, Pleasure, and the Frenzy of the Visible.* Berkeley: U of California P, 1989.

Woolf, S. J. [Stuart Joseph], ed. *Fascism in Europe.* New York: Methuen, 1981.

Wright, William. *Lillian Hellman: The Image, The Woman.* New York: Simon, 1986.

Wyman, David S. *The Abandonment of the Jews: America and the Holocaust 1941–1945.* New York: Pantheon, 1984.

Young, James E. "America's Holocaust: Memory and the Politics of Identity." Paper presented for "The Holocaust and the American Jewish Imagination: Memory, Text, and Myth" panel. Modern Language Association Conference. December 1992.

———. *The Texture of Memory: Holocaust Memorials and Meaning.* New Haven: Yale UP, 1993.

———*Writing and Rewriting the Holocaust: Narrative and the Consequences of Interpretation.* Bloomington: Indiana UP, 1988.

Young, Stark. *New Republic* Apr. 14, 1941: 498.

Zielinski, Siegfried. "The New Weiss *Investigation.*" *Theater* 12.1 (Fall/Winter 1980): 81.

Zinn, Howard. *The Twentieth Century, a People's History.* New York: Harper Colophon, 1984.

Zizek, Slavoj. *The Sublime Object of Ideology.* London: Verso, 1994.

INDEX

Abbreviations:
BHMT = Beit Hashoah Museum of
Tolerance
USHMM = United States Holocaust
Memorial Museum
WR = *Watch on the Rhine*

absence, and representation, 7, 63–64
accountability: defined, 7–8; and goneness,
7, 12; and Holocaust museums, 11; for
injury and injustice to bodies, 10–11;
and public schools, 11–12; and unac-
countable language, 32–33; and
voyeurism, 125
"aesthetics of atrocity," and Lawrence
Langer, 20, 88
African-American slavery: and Jewish
genocide, 121; and critique of BHMT,
120–121
After the Great Divide (Huyssen), 45–46
American democracy: and American
liberator, 69, 112; and legal personhood,
121; as potential site for genocide, 118–
121; as wedded to Jewish history, 112
American Holocaust (Stannard), 1, 3, 133n.1
anti-fascism: and gender in *WR*, 70–71; and
"Julia," 82–83, 85
anti-Semitism: as core of Nazism, 17–19;
and Othering, 36, 95
Antrobus, John, 21
architecture: and manageability of history,
128; in narratives of national identity,
113–114; and USHMM, 113–114,
123–125
Atlan, Liliane, 51–53, 60–65, 97
audience: and body in pain in mass culture,
88–89, 95; and fascist ideology, 44; and
identification, 45–46; and manipulation
in *WR*, 73; and responsibility, 65
The Audience (Blau), 86–87
Aunt Dan and Lemon (Shawn), 28
Auschwitz: and Jean-François Lyotard,
86–87; and replica gates at BHMT,
119–121; as signifier of destruction, 87
"Auschwitz" (Barnes). See *Laughter!*
Axis Rule in Occupied Europe (Lemkin), 2

Balsamo, Ann, 95–96
Barker, Howard, 22
Barnes, Peter, 5, 8, 23, 28–30, 49; and
anti-Semitic machinery, 19; compared to
Joan Schenkar, 44; critique of capitalism,

43; and fascist ideology, 35, 42–44; and
humor, 98–99; and reductive literalizing,
42–43; and staging genocide, 100; and
Wannsee Conference, 44. See also
Laughter!
Baudrillard, Jean, 29
Bauer, Yehuda, 1
Beit Hashoah Museum of Tolerance
(BHMT): and "Agent Provocateur," 129;
and America as potential site for
genocide, 118–121; and doors of
prejudice, 123; and exclusion of Native
Americans and slavery, 120–121; and
location, 118; and managing history,
129–131; and postmodern technology,
129–131; and representational theatre,
126; and USHMM, 118–121, 130–131
Benjamin, Walter, 45, 135nn.2,3
Bent (Sherman), 10, 45–49, 100–101; appeal
to spectators, 48; and fascist ideology,
35; and performance issues, 136n.8; and
realism for marginal group, 46
Berenbaum, Michael, 119, 124
Berman, Russell, 40–41
Bernhard, Thomas, 35, 48; compared to
Heiner Muller, 38; and fascist ideology,
37–39; and Klaus Theweleit, 37–38
Blau, Herbert, 86–87
Blitzkrieg (Wade), 21
Bloom, Harold, 20
Bodies That Matter (Butler), 5–6, 36, 97
body: and audience complicity, 88–89; and
history, 103–108; as locus for social
control, 96; in pain, 88–89, 100–101;
and pornography, 87–97; and puppets/
dummies, 98–100
The Body in Pain (Scarry), 87
Bond, Edward, 19, 30–32
Bordo, Susan, 96
Bosmajian, Hamida, 21
Bourne, Jenny, 56–57; critique of tolerance,
119; and Diana Fuss, 57; and Jewish
Feminism, 13; and Deb Margolin, 107
Brecht, Bertolt, 8, 13, 22, 45, 77–78; and
feminism, 137n.1; and historicization,,
69–70; and place of Hitler, 134n.1; and
testimony vs. parable, 103
Brecht on Theatre (Brecht), 134n.1
Bridenthal, Renate, 136n.1
Brophy, Philip, 88, 96
Brown, Karen, and Jennifer Kohn, 94
Burrell, Michael, 21

VIVIAN M. PATRAKA is Professor of English and Theatre and Director of the Institute for the Study of Culture and Society at Bowling Green State University. She has written numerous essays about Holocaust theatre, performance, and museums.